LESBIAN
ADVENTURE
STORIES

Book design by Mara Wild and Mikaya Heart
Computer work (typesetting, formatting and layout) by Mikaya Heart, with help from Pat at the Ukiah Library. Support your local library, it is an invaluable resource!

Cover design concept by Barbara Taylor
Front cover photo of Tonya Lieberknecht on Spirit
Back cover photo by Falling Star
Cover production by Marilyn Chuck, Printing Depot, Santa Rosa, California.

European agent: Ruth Nichol.

First Edition

We believe all of these stories are previously unpublished.

Printed on recycled paper.

ISBN 0-9615129-3-8
Library of Congress Catalog Card Number: 94-60743

Tough Dove Books, PO Box 1152, Laytonville, CA 95454

LESBIAN
ADVENTURE
STORIES

Gathered and edited by
Mara Wild and Mikaya Heart

Tough Dove Books, PO Box 1152, Laytonville, CA 95454

Introduction

An adventure is a heroic act, an achievement in the face of danger, an unusual and exciting experience. In this sense all lesbians lead lives of adventure, taking risks simply by the bold choice they make to be truly who they are in the face of society's disapproval. Lesbians are adventuresses, trailblazers who dare to venture into the unknown.

When we set out to collect these stories we threw the traditional, limiting concept of adventure to the four winds, and invited submissions that reflect the diversity of our daily lives, our desires and our fantasies. We were thrilled to receive stories as delightfully varied and dynamic as their authors. It quickly became apparent that lesbian adventure is sex and romance every bit as much as it is surviving accidents, taking on nature's challenges or standing up to male violence. Emotional and spiritual crises are as vital as physical ones.

We are proud to offer you the originality you will find in these pages. We have chosen to represent a variety of different values and lifestyles. We gave preference to stories where the heroines triumph, since we want this to be a book that will empower women. However, life is life, and some of those with less than happy endings were too good to omit.

Most of these stories are written by North American women but several are from British authors. We haven't changed the spelling or punctuation since we hope the book will be read here AND there ... and everywhere.

We're extremely pleased with the quality of the anthology we have been able to put together. Many many thanks go to the millions of lesbians out there who helped with the coming together of this collection by writing, supporting writers, buying books, reading books and simply by being powerful, bold, visible dykes.

Special thanks go to Kreja, Jesse, Barbara, Sally, Falling Star, Lisa, Robin, Devorah, Kay, Pamela, Sandy, Ruanne, Elayne and Tracey, and to all our authors for their patience, cooperation, and hard work.

To encourage, to empower, to embolden!

Mara Wild and Mikaya Heart

Table of Contents

Julia E. Watts grew up in the tiny town of Jellico, Tennessee, where she was the town freak. She is the proud owner of two cats, Idgie Threadgoode and Margaret Catwood; three tattoos; and more fashion accessories than she can count. Her writing career began at the age of seven with Tales of the Clark Family, a collection of short stories chronicling the adventures of a group of spunky orphans. Since then she has won numerous awards and had several short pieces published. She identifies strongly with her southern roots and tries to bring her experiences as a young queer and a freak in the Bible Belt into her writing. She is currently working on an M.A. at the University of Louisville, where she is a graduate teaching assistant.

MY BAPTISM

First of all, I guess you have to understand that, to my knowledge, my parents haven't so much as slept in the same bed since I was conceived. Despite the fact that they're college educated, they still come from the old Southern Protestant school that says that if men have sex, they turn into testosterone-driven demons, and that women are too innately pure to have any real sexual feelings in the first place. The former I have thought to be true at times, the latter I knew to be bogus as soon as I played my first game of spin-the-bottle at an all-girl slumber party.

The slumber party took place on a Saturday night when I was in fifth grade. It started fairly unremarkably. We listened to some Bee Gees albums, ate some Cheetos, and played the always-shocking Truth or Dare, during which I had to stick my foot in the toilet because I wouldn't say the name of the boy I liked. Truth was, I didn't like a boy. I liked Angel Dixon, who was sitting across from me, so I thought I would die when young hostess Sherry Jo Benton, who would later go on to be a Chi Omega at the University of Kentucky, suggested that we play spin-the-bottle "just for practice." Sure enough, when I sent one of Sherry Jo's dad's many empty beer bottles spinning, it pointed right to Angel. I was terrified. She brushed her stunning red hair away from her face and leaned toward me. I brushed my lips against hers. She kissed back, then drew away, giggling.

"Everybody ought to kiss Connie," she said. "She kisses better'n any old boy."

I looked down at the green shag carpet, blushing. That was my first kiss.The slumber party pretty much degenerated after that episode. Of course, no one got any sleep to speak of, slumber parties being among the least aptly named cultural institutions, and Sherry Jo's mom made us get up early in the morning so our parents could pick us up in time for church. You have to understand that in a town the size of McMillan, Kentucky, just about everybody who isn't practically already in hell goes to church. What else is there to do? McMillan was definitely more "down on the farm" than it was "Paree." We didn't even have a movie theater or a shopping mall, let alone any salons where people gathered for witty conversation. There were the old guys who sat and drank coffee all the time at Louise's Kountry Kafe, but the expatriate Lost Generation literati they were not.

So you went to Sunday school, you went to church, to prayer meetings, to choir practice, to Girls in Action (trust me--it wasn't nearly as much fun as it sounded), to the damned covered-dish suppers where everybody brought a casserole made with Campbell's cream-of-god-knows-what soup. And since all Sundays were exactly alike (and I still think they are even now that I have forsaken organized religion), on this particular one, I found myself in church with my parents as usual, coloring in all the o's in the church program with the little pencils they keep in the pews. I half-heartedly moved my lips along with "Nothing But the Blood of Jesus", put a quarter in the collection plate, and had settled back down to my coloring my o's when the preacher said something that made me scrawl erratically through the words in the church bulletin. "Today, our sermon will be preached by the man who will soon relieve me of my duties, Brother David Dixon." There, standing in the pulpit, with hair the color of hellfire and eyes the color of brimstone, was Angel's father. I had kissed and yes, lusted in my heart for a preacher's (soon to be the preacher's) daughter! No doubt about it, I was going straight to hell.

I couldn't begin to tell you what Brother Dixon's sermon was on that Sunday. Whatever it was, he might as well have been talking about the evil of my Sapphic ways. The next day at school I made a point of avoiding Angel. I skulked around the building, still consumed by guilt and trying desperately to convince myself that I, like everyone else, had only been kissing her as a sort of dress rehearsal for Mr. Right. But

2   *My Baptism - Julia E. Watts*

it was no use. Angel--a vision of paramilitary beauty in her Girl Scout uniform--caught up with me during recess.

"What is it with you? You've not said a word to me all day."

"Oh, it's..." Should I say anything? I was swaying back and forth dejectedly in my swing, dragging my Keds in the dirt. "Angel, why didn't you tell me you were the preacher's girl?"

"I don't know. Maybe it's because I don't want to be the preacher's girl." Her face flushed pink behind her field of freckles, and she whispered, "Maybe I want to be your girl."

I was flattered and flustered and positively terrified. "But...but ...you can't. I mean, boys and girls are supposed...and your dad's the...Oh, Angel, we just can't."

"Let's go for a walk, Connieee," she drawled invitingly.

"Huh?" But I was already being dragged out of the swing, toward the edge of the playground, watching Angel's Girl Scout jumper billow in the breeze. Before I knew what hit me, we were hidden by the trees that outlined the school playground.

"Come here, Connie," she said. "You be John Travolta, and I'll be Olivia Newton-John." She wrapped her arms around me and pressed her parted lips to mine. Oh, Angeloliviaangelolivia....Angel. The chasm of puberty gaped only a few feet before me, and I couldn't wait to jump right in.

From that day on, Angel and I were inseparable. Neither her parents nor mine suspected a thing. Wasn't it sweet how we were always together? Wasn't it sweet how we always did our homework together? Yes, but not as sweet as the hours we'd spend alone together under the covers during sleepovers. Brother Dixon's only complaint about Angel and me was that we giggled too much during church. He credited it to "female silliness"; only we knew that it came from knowledge of our sheer wickedness.

About the time I turned thirteen, my parents started pestering me to get baptized and officially join the church. And they weren't the only ones. One day when I was having supper at Angel's, Brother Dixon looked up from his country fried steak and said, "Now, Connie, I've been thinking that it's high time you give your life to the Lord."

My throat clenched around the clump of biscuit it was trying to swallow. I had always been bad at religious talk. "Well, sir..." I paused. "I've already let Jesus into my heart." Truth was, I always thought that idea was kind of creepy but I had heard it enough to be able to spout it back fairly convincingly.

"Well, honey, that's the hardest step. If you've done that already it seem like all you lack is getting baptized."

"I guess so." I was terrified of putting my face under water and had never done more than cautiously doggie paddle in my life, so the idea of being fully submerged Baptist style by my girlfriend's father in front of the entire congregation of the McMillan Main Street Baptist Church didn't exactly fill me with spiritual ardor.

"Well, I've already talked to your parents about this, and they say that you should go ahead and do it as soon as you're ready."

I was being conspired against and I resented it deeply. But I went ahead and agreed to be baptized as soon as possible. Despite my relative innocence I saw the importance of keeping the elders pacified and, above all, in the dark about my sinning ways.

I opted to spend the night before my baptism with Angel. I wasn't planning on reforming myself after I had been washed in the proverbial blood, but just in case the baptism did hold the power to cleanse me of my shameful desires, I wanted to have one last night of pleasure. As we were snuggled down under the covers that night, pajamaed pubescent bodies entwined, Angel asked, "Connie, do you think you'll ever have a boyfriend?"

"I don't know...What would I want with one?"

"Well, my mamaw says that when a girl gets to be our age she ought to start thinking about...well, she calls it 'courtin'.'"

I pounced on top of her and attacked her with tickles and kisses. "Well, ma'am," I said, thickening my accent, "Ain't this courting?" The tickling and kisses continued until we rolled around in fits of giggles and sighs. At one point Angel interrupted our fun to put her hand over my mouth.

"Not so loud," she said. "He'll hear."

As our hormones had kicked in more thoroughly, my encounters with Angel began to transcend the bounds of the mere kissing games in which we were Travolta and Newton-John, Rhett and Scarlett, and Superman and Lois Lane. We were just Connie and Angel, and for two girls who had never even heard the word "lesbian," we were doing a pretty good job of figuring it out.

I guess we did a particularly good job of it on Baptismal Eve because the first thing I remember that Sunday morning is the good

4   *My Baptism - Julia E. Watts*

Reverend swinging the bedroom door open and saying, "Now, girls, hurry up, you'll be late for chur--!" He never finished the word "church" because what he saw in the bed probably sent his mind reeling back to the land of Sodom and Gomorra. The hours of petting and pawing must have really tired Angel and me out. As I looked up at Reverend Dixon, I realized that his daughter's pajama top was lying at his feet which must mean that it was...not on her body. Angel, groggy from sleep, must have realized this at the same moment I did because she let out a little squeak just before her father grabbed up her top and threw it at her. The brimstone in his eyes was white-hot. He pointed a shaking finger at me. "You...you...SINNER! You whore...you're not even as good as a whore, for what whore would lay down with her own kind?" He dragged me out of bed by the collar of my pajamas. "Oh, yes, you'll be baptized. You'll be washed in the blood of Christ to rid you of your filthy perversion!"

Before I knew what hit me, I had been flung out the door and was lying in a heap in the hallway. Angel's bedroom door slammed shut behind me.

"Now what did I tell you about hanging around with that girl?"

"Daddy, no!" I heard the unmistakable sound of flesh smacking flesh.

"I told you her people was too big for their britches--goin'over to the college, acting like they know everything--" Smack!

"Daddy, please!"

"I'm only doing this for your own good, honey. Our Lord said, "Spare the rod and spoil the child'!"

I couldn't stand it. I flung myself against the door, ready to break it down if I had to, ready to use all the strength in my thirteen-year-old body to save the girl I loved from that Bible-banging psychopath. Suddenly, my arms were being yanked behind me. I whirled around to see Mrs. Dixon, her eyes welled with tears.

"Now, Connie, you go on and get cleaned up." Her voice was chilly. She wasn't sure what was going on, but she knew it was no good. I could still hear Angel's cries from the bedroom.

"Mrs. Dixon, please," I begged. "Everything that happened is my fault. Can't...can't you do something? How can you let him hit her like that?"

"He's the man, Connie. You're young yet, but some day when you're older, you'll understand. Now go on and get cleaned up."

I walked to the bathroom in a daze and splashed cold water on my splotchy, tear-stained face.

* * * *

I glanced nervously around the corner of the baptistry, the front side of which was clear glass so everyone could see you take that big plunge for Jesus. I saw Mom in her ivory dress and Dad in his good blue suit, sharing a hymnal and moving their lips to "Are You Washed in the Blood." They both looked so proud, and so utterly clueless that their devoted daughter was in fact a sinning sister of Sappho.

Angel, of course, was sitting in the front pew with her mother, looking like the perfect preacher's daughter. If her cheeks were a little red from her father's slaps, I'm sure that most people attributed it to the healthy flush of youth. I wondered if her undoubtedly sore bottom hurt from sitting on that hard pew. I looked away from her, but not without thinking what a fine job Brother Dixon did of hiding his sins where people couldn't see them.

I wasn't feeling too well myself, standing on the edge of a pool of freezing cold water next to old Mrs. Hatcher, who had helped me into my baptismal robe. She kept telling me that now that I was giving my life to Jesus, I would be a true woman. On the other side of the pool standing there with Deacon McNabb was Brother Dixon himself. In his starched white robe, he looked for all the world like Lucifer just before he was expelled from heaven. I felt like I was being asked to join hands with the Grim Reaper, and sure enough, as soon as Mrs. Hatcher shoved me toward him, Brother Dixon's bony fingers clenched around mine, his nails digging into my soft, sweaty palm.

He began. "We have before us today a sinner in the eyes of God, a sinner in the eyes of this entire church." I heard a slight murmur arise from the congregation; Brother Dixon didn't usually lay it on this thick for baptisms. "This young woman has sinned against nature, has turned away from the one true Lord, and has chosen instead to serve the Lord of Darkness!" A full-fledged gasp arose from the audience. What could I have done? I was only thirteen years old, for crying out loud.

"But today," he continued, "Today she will be cleansed in the life-giving blood of Jesus Christ Almighty, who has the power--Yes, the Power!--to save this, the lowest of all sinners, and make her turn from her wicked ways." The veins in his neck bulged, and spittle was

6   *My Baptism - Julia E. Watts*

forming in the corners of his mouth. He looked me in the eye. "Connie Marie Harper, I baptize you in the name of the Father, the Son, and the Holy Ghost!"

He didn't dip me so much as tackle me. His hands were on my shoulders and he held me underwater for what seemed like hours. My eyes wide open in terror, I could see through the clear water the picture on the wall above me. Through the distorting lens of the water, the image rippled and swayed, but I could still make out Jesus, his arms outstretched, his eyes averted. "Don't look up there," I felt like screaming. "I'm drowning down here! Do something!" But Jesus couldn't help me; he was just a figure in a cheap painting.

I finally managed to twist my head around and bite Brother Dixon's hand as hard as I could. He jerked away for a second, and I managed to get a quick breath of air before he grabbed me again. He shook me and dunked me, shook me and dunked me, all the time yelling "Slut! Slut! Slut!" at the top of his lungs. Through my water-clogged ears, I heard one old man in the congregation shout, "Praise Jesus! The demon's done left her body and gone into his'n!"

Brother Dixon didn't hold onto me for much longer. Deacon McNabb, who had apparently been in the sidelines all along, leapt into the water and slugged the good reverend so hard that he fell sprawling into the picture of Jesus. Mrs. Hatcher daintily stepped into the pool and tried to lead me to safety, but the allegedly cleansing baptismal waters filled my nose and ears and stomach, and I was too dizzy to walk. I grabbed the top of the glass partition, leaned my head over its edge, and vomited.

Mom and Dad withdrew their membership from the church that day, so I never had to go back. Brother Dixon tried to tell my parents about the "unnatural acts" I had committed with his daughter, but being the largely asexual folk that they are, they refused to believe that what he said was even possible. "Bless his heart," my ever-forgiving mother said. "That man's just as crazy as a bessbug." My father's words for him were somewhat less kind.

Angel and I kind of grew apart after that episode; or rather,she grew apart from me. I never blamed her for it. I guess our involvement was just too dangerous a proposition for her.

She didn't grow up into being the perfect preacher's daughter, though. By our sophomore year, Angel had reached professional bad-girl status. Her father often used her as a bad example in the sermons at the small, off-brand Holy Roller church where he ended up preaching.

Occasionally, when I went into the girls' bathroom, Angel would be there sitting on the counter smoking a cigarette, and we'd exchange a secret grin. Maybe, like the girls kissing each other at the fifth-grade slumber party, Angel was 'just practicing" with me all those nights we spent in each other's arms. But I knew I hadn't been.

Mary Sepulveda *makes her living running machines at a manu-*
facturing plant in Milwaukie, Oregon; she makes her life writing short
stories. She has been creating adventures on paper for as long as she
can remember. Her real life adventures began when she learned to
walk. Her work has appeared in regional newspapers as well as
several literary magazines. She feels her best when she is running in
the woods.

CHOICES

"You go in and ask her for a box. She'll take you into the back
room, then I'll go in and get into the cash register." Rhonda whispered
this to me while we stood outside Inez's store.

"What if she hears you open the cash register?" I asked.

"She's not going to hear me," Rhonda said. "She's old. Just talk
real loud while you're getting a box. And keep her back there for a few
minutes."

"I don't think this is such a good idea. Couldn't we just babysit or
something for the money?" I couldn't get the picture out of my head. I
kept seeing Inez opening the cash register and finding all the money
gone. God, she must be at least eighty years old. It just seemed so
cruel. All the kids around here stole from her, but not like this, not all
her money. Mostly it was packs of gum or a bottle of pop, and
sometimes, the really brave kids would swipe a can or two of beer. But
Rhonda wasn't satisfied with that kind of stuff. "Only babies would
steal gum," she said. She wanted money, and what Rhonda wanted I
went along with.

Rhonda was the mastermind behind a million evil schemes. Her
face was like that of an angel. Blond hair, blue eyes, she always wore
neatly pressed outfits with matching socks. Rhonda could steal you
blind and you'd never notice a thing, so charmed you'd be by her sweet
smile and baby eyes. I knew all this but it didn't matter. When Rhonda
held my hand or whispered secrets to me in the dark I, too, believed
she was an angel.

I didn't look like Rhonda. I seemed to have a hard time staying
clean, no matter how hard I tried. I never combed my hair, wore my
brother's baggy Levi's', had bitten my fingernails to the quick. I had

that sneaky Italian kid look and I was terrified, absolutely terrified, of old lady Inez.

"God, you're such a baby," Rhonda said. "If it makes you feel any better I'll only take fifty dollars. She'll never know. Go on, ask her for a box." She pushed at me with the polished toe of her shoe. It wasn't a kick exactly but it got me moving.

I don't know why I did it. I always did what Rhonda told me to. She had a way of making hideous plans like this seem normal. I knew it was wrong, but according to Rhonda, we deserved this money. In a way, we were working for it. It wasn't like we were just going to walk in and demand that Inez give us fifty dollars. We actually had to plan and lie to get this money. That was work, wasn't it?

I walked into the store. It was dark and stuffy. Inez stood behind a low counter. Boxes of candy lined the wall behind her. She looked up at me, squinting her eyes to see who I was. She didn't trust me. She never had. She said I was a wop, and a good for nothin' wop at that. "What do you need today?" she asked. Her question was an accusation. Why don't you shop somewhere else?

I stopped in front of a shelf of cleaning supplies, laundry soap, floor wax, bottles of furniture polish. I picked up some laundry soap and studied it. "I need a box," I muttered.

"Speak up, child, I can't hear you." Inez moved to the end of the counter. I stood not more than ten feet from her. The smell of the soap filled my nostrils, powdery, sweet. I couldn't put it down. I scratched at the box with a ragged fingernail, leaving small marks around the price tag.

"I need a box," I repeated. I looked out the window. Rhonda had her face pressed against the glass, looking at me. Her nose was flattened against the glass, her mouth slightly open. I saw her form a word with her lips, "Hurry."

I put the soap down and walked closer to the counter. "I need a box." Inez looked at me strangely, her head tilted to the side. I was sure she suspected something.

"Well, why didn't you say something?" she snapped. "The boxes are in the back. How big do you want?"

"A little one is fine," I said. My voice seemed to be coming from somewhere outside of me. I felt disconnected. Inez wiped her hands on her apron and began her slow creeping walk to the back room. I followed.The back room was huge, filled with boxes, sacks of flour, crates of vegetables. The air was sharp and acrid as if ammonia had been spilled there. I had never been back there before, and I was afraid. What if Inez suspected something? What if she had brought me back here only to call the police? Rhonda thought Inez was dumb. But Rhonda thought everyone was dumb. I just hoped she was right about Inez.

I heard the front door open as Inez reached for a small box perched on a shelf above her. I coughed loudly, hoping she wouldn't hear the door open. I began to talk rapidly, wild words pouring out of my mouth. Inez stood before me holding out a small box, staring. I told her I was going swimming that afternoon. We just got a new dog, our old one died. I told her I had gotten straight A's on my report card. I said my parents were going to buy me a new bike. I couldn't hear Rhonda. I just kept talking and all the while Inez was thrusting that box at me.Finally, praying that Rhonda was gone, I grabbed the box, remembered to say thank you, and ran out of the room.

I ran outside, sweating and shaking, surprised somehow that it was still daytime. The sun was still shining and little kids were riding their bikes as if nothing had happened. I felt as if I had been in that store for hours and yet outside, nothing had changed.

Rhonda was sitting on the curb. She looked up at me as I stood there, trying to catch my breath.

"I took a hundred," she said. "Fifty for you, fifty for me."

I clutched the box Inez had given me. I didn't ever want to go back in that store again. Rhonda popped a stick of gum into her mouth. I wondered if she had stolen that too. "It was easy," she said. "We can do it again next week."

Lucy Jane Bledsoe built her first snow cave a couple of years ago in Desolation Wilderness and hasn't quite gotten over the magic of sleeping in it. She loves backcountry skiing and snow camping and writes about it as an excuse to keep doing it. She also loves cycling, which she does most afternoons to stir up the endorphins that get her through the rest of the day's writing.

Lucy writes books for and teaches new adult learners (literacy students), and believes that illiteracy is the root of most problems in this country. Besides teaching new adult learners, she has facilitated a writing group for women in San Francisco's Tenderloin district and edited a collection of their work called Goddesses We Ain't *(Freedom Voices Press). She is currently editing a forthcoming collection of lesbian erotica (Alyson Publications).*

THE BIG CRUNCH

It was dark inside the rented four-wheel drive. Sitting in the back seat, I watched the snowflakes hit the windows. Ahead, in the dull glow of the headlights, all I could see was falling snow and ten yards worth of the snow-packed road. Dorothy drove with her face pushed toward the windshield. She'd just begun growing dreads and the three-inch shoots bounced as she slammed her fist on the steering wheel in a fit of frustration. I couldn't see her face, but I bet she was scowling. She had the fiercest brow, which amused me because it looked so out of place on her face with its smattering of large childish freckles and mouth that looked as if it tasted like blood oranges. Dorothy kept flashing the lights on bright, even honking sometimes, as if she could terrorize the blizzard into submission.

Wanda, sitting in the passenger seat, mumbled something in Spanish. The way she sat with her hands folded in her lap and her long legs crossed, staring straight forward as if we were not in danger, reminded me of stories she'd told about her falsely demure mother. Wanda had said her mother was like a volcano, grand, poised, seemingly dormant. But when something triggered her fire, watch out. Wanda was poised to a fault, but she didn't have much of a temper. When she got upset, she expressed her feelings in Spanish, as if speaking her mother tongue took her to another planet where her feelings of anger or fear were acceptable. I never heard Wanda speak a word of Spanish on campus.

Dorothy pounded the steering wheel of the truck again. "We didn't see one damn mountain. You said the weather would be clear this time of year."

"So, I'm not God."

"Our flight leaves in an hour. Just drive, Dot," Wanda said. She was the only one who got away with calling Dorothy that. "How's Madeleine supposed to control the weather?"

I leaned forward. "We should have stayed at the lodge. I need to say that for the record. We could have taken a later flight."

Dorothy caught my eyes in the rearview mirror. "Look, your life may be on permanent hold, but Wanda and I still have jobs."

"Whoa," Wanda cautioned. "Cool out, Dot."

"Cool out? Oh, right. We just spent a grand apiece to spend New Year's in a frickin' Alaskan blizzard. We could have had a condo in Maui for half the price."

"Sorry," I said. "It's better than being stuck in Manhattan gridlock."

"I'd take gridlock any day," Dorothy countered.

"Well, we're different."

"I'll say."

"Come on, Dot, you can't blame a blizzard on Madeleine," Wanda said. "Let's not get personal again. We're almost home."

"There's something I want to know," Dorothy said slowly. She leaned back so I could see her face in the rearview mirror. She scowled, gripping the steering wheel so hard her knuckles were white. "What color were the guys that stabbed Sara?"

My stomach clinched. "What?"

"Jesus, Dorothy," Wanda said. "Stop."

"No, it's important. Let's talk about it, once and for all. Madeleine hasn't combed her hair the whole six days we've been up here. She refuses to eat anything but junk food. Frankly, she's been a bitch the whole time, as if we somehow <u>deserve</u> her bad mood. And she won't talk about that night. This thing has eaten her insides out and we all keep trying to make nice. I'd like to get to the bottom of it. What color were they, Madeleine?"

"I didn't say."

"Say now."

"White. Does it matter?"

"Yes. It matters."

I sank back into the seat, then lurched forward. "Like if the assholes were Black or Latino, I'd want to take it out on you and Wanda by getting you stuck in an Alaskan blizzard?"

"Racism works in mysterious ways."

"Dot, you're nervous about this blizzard," Wanda said in that womanly voice she used to calm people.

"And you're not?"

"No, I'm not nervous. I'm scared shitless. And this snow has nothing to do with racism."

"Dorothy is losing it," I said. "What's scary right now is her driving. Can we do racism later?"

Wanda nodded. "Madeleine didn't <u>choose</u> a blizzard. This was <u>our</u> idea, remember?"

"Our idea but based on her description of the damn state. How many times has she told us stories about the 'beauty and grandeur' of Alaska, on and on about how the rest of the country is a dump compared to what you can see up here." Dorothy took a deep breath. "Okay, of course this blizzard isn't your fault. And I think I believe that you aren't trying to harm anyone but yourself. But you're very hard to be around. You won't even consider your next move. You've had some bad luck. Everyone does. But you just got to -- "

Wanda reached over and covered Dorothy's mouth with her hand. "Be quiet," she said. "Just get us to the airport."

When Wanda took her hand away, Dorothy sucked in a long deep breath and let it out in one loud blast.

I closed my eyes. The six days had been like this, arguing about the university, our careers, and now even the stabbing. Like homophobia was my fault. Like I was responsible for Sara's death.

So Dorothy wanted to "talk about it once and for all," as if it could be purged, cut out like a cancer. She didn't understand. When a person dies, the atoms that make up her body remain in the universe. She is still here. She never goes away. The difference is, she no longer has meaning. It is worse than nothingness.

*   *   *

I don't blame everything on Sara's murder.

I am by nature a negative person. I was raised by my evangelical parents to believe in a cataclysmic end to the universe, and while I abandoned their religious ideas by the age of six, their hellfire was burned into my consciousness.

Science attracted me because it attacked my pessimism. Hard facts and evidence, proven through meticulous labwork, chipped away my anger. As a youngster I adored Einstein. I loved his vision of a harmonious and orderly universe. It was the beauty of science, the way its answers deepened and deepened until you looked into the face of a creation so much more profound than the one of my evangelical parents, that led me to major in physics and then enroll in the PhD program.

I clung to theories of order even as I began working at the university with high-powered physicists on the concepts of randomness and chaos. I was the one who kept asking the hard questions, and my colleagues valued me for that. But the answers came swiftly and still I did not shift my allegiances. I let desire for order overpower scientific evidence. Everyone saw it. Asking hard questions is a good thing to do; ignoring hard evidence is not.

Sara's murder was the hardest evidence of all, and it confirmed everything I'd been trying to deny. The universe is a place of hostile, random chaos.

*   *   *

I met Dorothy and Wanda four years before Sara's death, just when my problems in the physics department were beginning. The philosophy department, full of archaic white men who wore bow ties and drank port, hired Dorothy to teach aesthetics and Wanda to teach logic, including the freshman course Proofs for the Existence of God. I knew their resumes must have been explosive. I got crushes on them both at first sight.

Wanda was a gorgeous five foot ten inches tall. She wore her hair like a straight girl, long, black and glossy. She had small eyes and a very large mouth full of big white teeth. I loved how she accented her wide mouth by painting her lips scrumptious fruit colors. She could easily pass for straight. In fact, it looked as if that was exactly what she was doing in her tight pedal pushers and spike heels, but Wanda made a point of coming out in just about every conversation she had, especially to the straight men who pandered to her.

Then there was Dorothy of the curling eyebrows and petulant blood orange mouth. Dorothy was one of those cranky, hard-thinking women with a brain like a butcher knife. I'd still be hearing the tail end of a question and she'd be cutting it up five ways and asking which way the speaker meant. I've always had a weakness for smart, cross women.

But my appetite for Wanda and Dorothy cut deeper than simple lust. Philosophy seemed to be the only discipline, other than physics, that aimed at understanding the entire universe. I wanted to know what philosophers thought about, how it was different than physics, a world view that was beginning to fail me, and how it was different than Christianity, a world view that hadn't failed me because it'd never supported me, but nonetheless ruled my psyche. I could tell from a distance that these two philosophers accepted no shoddy half-truths. If anyone had answers, they would.

Befriending the Philosophers turned into a year-long project. While we were all PhD candidates, they were rising stars, already teaching, while I was struggling to stay in my program. I dogged them at functions for gay graduate students. Each time I introduced myself Wanda was gracious, shook my hand, and moved on. Dorothy never remembered me from the last time.

I finally conceived of an interdisciplinary course called Proofs for the Existence of Goddesses. I spent an entire month of my nonexistent spare time putting together a syllabus. I combined physics texts with Rene Descartes, Luisah Teish, Zora Neale Hurston, and even Susan Sontag. I threw in Thomas Pynchon's *Gravity's Rainbow* and a couple of magical realist novels, like Isabelle Allende's *The House of Spirits* and Toni Morrison's *Song of Solomon*. I presented Dorothy and Wanda with the syllabus early that summer and explained my idea. They were knocked out. So were the students we taught the following spring. We alternated lecturing every third class and it was the most exciting academic experience I've ever had. One of my lectures was on the northern lights, a combination of science and mythology. Dorothy and Wanda said it was my best, like poetry. I spoke of the aurora borealis with so much reverence that they were amazed when I admitted that I'd never actually seen it. "Before I die," I told them.

We published our lectures collectively that year and made a medium-sized splash in feminist literary circles. The philosophy and physics departments trashed the book. Dorothy, who wanted a tenure-track position more than any of us, began a very traditional aesthetics project. Wanda applied to divinity school. And I kept plugging away in the physics lab.

That year, the one after the goddesses course, was our best time. We spent hours drinking expensive red wine and talking about ideas and women. We voted Wanda Most Likely to Succeed because she did everything gracefully, even turning away men's advances, even pressing her points in department meetings. She was a born diplomat. From dealing with her volcanic mother, she always claimed. Dorothy was the obvious choice for Most Brilliant. But men didn't like her. They called her overbearing, strident, hard, all the words used for smart women, especially ones who had no use for men. I was sure she would succeed but it would take a long time, there would be scars.

I knew from the start that I was in a different league than Dorothy and Wanda, but that became more obvious over time. About a year before the stabbing, I published what turned out to be my last paper and proudly gave it to the Philosophers to read.

"You've got to harness it." Wanda's apparent frustration with my work surprised me.

"What do you mean?" I asked.

"Your ideas. They're starting to veer. You aren't in the driver's seat."

"Am I veering in this paper?"

"Yes. You're all over the place. The ideas are wonderful, but..."

That shook me. Our hours of insightful discussion led Wanda to divinity school, motivated Dorothy to work even harder to wrest a place for herself in the philosophy department, but I was veering.

Wanda knew she'd been harsh. She also knew I wanted only her most honest appraisal, no matter what. The three of us sat in silence for a couple moments.

Dorothy spoke up softly. "I love this paper. It's vintage Madeleine. You put all the parts together, girl. Madeleine is our Visionary."

I grunted. Why did her compliment sound like charity? She spoke too kindly. Like being a visionary was a liability, at least in my case. In my heart, I knew what she meant. I've always had too much imagination to be a good scientist, and too little imagination to be a great one. I got the feeling I'd just been voted Most Likely to Fail.

That month Wanda was admitted to Harvard divinity school, Dorothy was offered a tenure-track position, and my department head volunteered the information that any kind of teaching job was highly unlikely in my case.

Of course I had known all along that my physics colleagues were right: disaster is more natural than order. It takes only a rudimentary understanding of astronomy to get that. We are nothing more than a fleeting collection of beings living on a tiny rock spinning around in an infinite universe. A universe that is exploding, self-destructing this very moment. Billions of planets in billions of galaxies have come and gone and will continue to come and go. We are nothing.

The problem was I couldn't see any scientific beauty in these ideas. I saw only holocaust.

"Don't you see," Dorothy argued, "that if the Big Bang is ongoing, then that only means that *creation* is ongoing!"

Philosophers are good at if/then statements, but I was way past logic. I realized that my parents were right. *Something* created that speck of matter that exploded in the first place. And destruction was nothing more than itself, destruction. Furthermore, we were all participants. My version of original sin.

Then I met Sara. Everything Sara did was somehow false. She wore black leather, but wasn't into S/M. She lied constantly, even about things that didn't matter to anyone, like whether or not she had a cat. She was either independently wealthy or stole for a living because she never had a job in the six months I knew her. She intrigued me because she absorbed experience, all kinds, indiscriminately, as if all values were equal. She talked to anyone, ate seaweed and wheat juice religiously one month, then nothing but corn dogs and fried pork rinds the next. Sara moved fast, very fast. And she looked like Susan Saradon, only blonde.

Dorothy and Wanda couldn't stand her. Dorothy claimed she was an FBI informant, but I think she flattered Sara. Wanda said, "Well, Madeleine. I think you've entered your Faux Life period." They tried lecturing me, about my drinking, about Sara's bad influence, about my declining career in spite of what they considered my talents. I avoided the Philosophers as much as I could in the six months I dated Sara.

Exactly a year ago, Sara and I walked out of a bar into a cold dark night. It was early for us, not even midnight. I had angered her by flirting with a friend of hers in the bar. Now she pushed me up

The Big Crunch - Lucy Jane Bledsoe

against the brick wall of the building and shoved her hands up my shirt. We made out, hard. Her teeth bruised my lips. Cars cruised by slowly. She pressed her pelvis against mine. I began to get nervous. Women got harassed leaving this bar. I didn't want to aggravate the situation. I tried to pull away but she had me pinned against the brick wall. She felt my resistance and let go, flinging her blond hair. All her mannerisms were exaggerated.

I didn't love Sara that night. I was sick of her. I wanted her to quit trying so hard.

"Let's walk," she said angrily.

"It's cold. I want to take a taxi."

"I'm walking," she announced and took off with big strides. "You take a taxi."

I ran to catch up.

She surprised me by turning and smiling at me. I took her arm, glad to not have a fight.

A car pulled up to the curb. One boy hung out the back seat window, another out the front seat window. "Hey, look at the lez's. You like the taste of pussy?"

I remember so well what her face looked like right then. She wasn't afraid. She was angry. That, I suddenly realized, was what attracted me, her anger.

"Suck my dick, bitch," one of the boys called out. He hefted himself out of the window and pulled his cock out of his jean's fly. He wagged it at us.

I started pulling Sara back towards the bar.

"What dick?" Sara jeered. "Get me a magnifying glass so I can see it."

The boy in the driver's seat turned off the ignition. All three boys got out of the car, slamming doors. I yanked on Sara, but she wouldn't move. She stood her ground as if an army of dykes were marching right behind us. She was the heroine on the front lines, a modern day Helen of Troy.

"Leave me alone." She shook off my hands. "I'm tired of them. I'm so fucking tired of them."

"Jesus, Sara." I was so scared I thought of running, just leaving her.

"Sara?" one of boys said. "Nice name for a dyke." The boys surrounded us.

"What a joke," Sara said. "What a big fucking joke. What are you boys, thirteen, maybe fourteen?"

They did look like children, too young to drive. But they terrified me. I fell when one kicked me and whimpered, "Just leave us alone." I stumbled to my feet and pulled at Sara again. One of the boys tried to tear me apart from her and I kicked him in the groin so hard he doubled over groaning.

That's when the other boy pulled out the knife. Sara thrust back her shoulders, pushing her soft belly at him, and said, "Oh, yeah, go ahead, big boy."

"Sara, no one cares if you die!" I don't know why I shouted this, except that it was true. Her family disowned her when she was a teenager. Her friends were all back in the bar having their own dramas. I wanted her to know she was not Helen of Troy: nothing would change, not one tiny thing, if she died.

I was wrong, of course. I would change. But I wasn't thinking about that then.

The boys stood stunned as the blood instantly soaked her T-shirt and then her leather jacket. "You fucking goddamned idiot," one of the boys screamed to the one who had stabbed Sara.

"Me!" the kid whined. "Me the idiot?"

Their voices were adolescent now, no longer menacing, just scared. As scared as me. Cursing, Sara fell to the cement. I dropped down to cradle her head.

"You stabbed her!" the one who'd been driving said. He was crying. Big sobs heaved out of his mouth.

"Come on." The other one grabbed him. The two boys jumped in the car, leaving the boy with the knife standing over Sara and me.

Then he took off at a dead run. I could hear his panting and sobbing half a block away. Finally, he was gone. It never occurred to me to look at their license number. Later I couldn't tell the cops anything about their faces, either, just a blur of redneck hatred.

I screamed for someone to call an ambulance. Though no one stopped to help me hold her, someone did dial 911. By the time the ambulance arrived, she had quit cursing and lay still, hot steam rising from her wound.

Sara died a few minutes later in the hospital.

I never told anyone that it was my kicking that boy in the groin that escalated the attack to murder. They didn't kill me because I kicked out of fear not defiance. It was the defiance the boys had to kill. I was left with the fear.

Right after the stabbing, I took a leave of absence and went to stay with my folks in New Jersey. I stayed through the summer and had little contact with the Philosophers. They both called several times, reporting on their busy lives, Wanda preparing for Harvard and Dorothy preparing her new lectures. In the fall I returned to the university and pretended to work on my dissertation until the department head suggested I find another calling. I left the program and took a job at a Copymat. Wanda was in Boston by then. Sometimes Dorothy and I had coffee, but we didn't have a lot to talk about.

In early December, Dorothy called me up. "Wanda's in town. We're coming by."

"How's Boston?" I asked Wanda when they arrived.

"Boston's not New York. But I like school. You're a wreck."

I shrugged.

Dorothy scooted forward on the couch. She looked so serious I thought I was about to get another lecture. She said, "What are you doing for New Years?"

"Uh, nothing. I'm working in the Copymat."

"Can you get a week off?"

"I don't know. Why?"

"We're taking you to Alaska to see the northern lights." Wanda beamed.

"Excuse me?"

"You heard the girl," Dorothy said. "You always said you wanted to see the northern lights before you died. So we're going."

"Am I about to die?" I asked.

"Don't be sarcastic," Dorothy said. "I found a lodge about twenty miles north of Fairbanks. We can go for six days. Rent a four-wheel drive and go look at the sky."

I wanted to cry. I couldn't believe this. We were hardly friends anymore. All I could think to say was, "Why?"

"Because," Wanda said firmly.

Dorothy gave me one of her long serious, assessing looks. That look took me right back. How I had coveted her citrus lips and snarly brow! In spite of myself, something deep inside fluttered.

"Okay," I said.

The trip to Alaska was a failure. It stormed the whole six days and we did not see the northern lights. The night before our flight home, we argued about whether to stay or go. I thought it was stupid to set out in an Alaskan blizzard for the airport. Dorothy said that's why we had a four-wheel drive. In the end, I shrugged.

I sat in the back seat, after being held responsible for the blizzard, and listened to the silence. It really wasn't silent. The truck engine was loud. The windshield wipers swiped back and forth. The tires crunched on the snow. And Wanda had resumed mumbling in Spanish. Yet, it felt like the most silent moment of my life.

"I'm sorry, Madeleine," Dorothy finally said. "I'm sorry about the university. I'm sorry about what happened to Sara. This trip was supposed to be a gift. It didn't work out."

"You don't know what it was like," I said, hating how adolescent I sounded.

Dorothy and Wanda glanced at one another. Wanda said, "Madeleine, it's not like we don't understand violence. But you got to turn that shit inside out, baby. You aren't looking deep enough. You're wallowing in it."

"I'm wallowing. That's cute." I watch my girlfriend get brutally killed, and I'm just sinking back into it like it was a tub of warm suds. "Yeah," I seethed. "It feels real good."

"I'm sorry, Madeleine," Dorothy said again, her voice more gentle. I saw her lay a hand on Wanda, like to silence her. Like I wasn't worth the effort. "We tried." She said the words with finality, her voice like the lid of a casket slamming shut on our friendship. And then there was the swishing, crunching silence again.

A few minutes later Dorothy cranked the steering wheel as hard as she could on a right turn. Gracefully, the truck slid forward, across the center line and into the opposite lane. We glided into a deep, soft snow bank, submerging the entire hood of the truck. The windshield smashed right up against the snow. Stunned, no one moved or spoke for about thirty seconds.

Then Dorothy laid her forehead on the steering wheel.

Wanda said, "*Chingada.*"

I crawled into the back and started rummaging through our luggage looking for something stable to put under the tires. Dorothy

The Big Crunch - Lucy Jane Bledsoe

gunned the engine, spinning the wheels. "Don't do that," I told her. "You'll dig us in deeper." But Dorothy always believed she could muscle her way into or out of any situation. By the time I unpacked my canvas duffle bag and got out of the truck to wedge it under a back tire, she'd spun a deep, slick hole. The duffle bag did not help.

Then, for no apparent reason, the engine died. Dorothy turned the ignition, engaged the motor, then it died again. "For God's sake, just leave it," I told her. "Next you're going to flood the engine. Please let me handle this."

Dorothy and Wanda exchanged glances. They'd always acknowledged I had more practical sense than the two of them put together. Still, I guess they wondered if I had any kind of know-how these days. Thankfully, Dorothy didn't touch the ignition again.

I pulled out the sleeping bags we had brought because we hadn't trusted the lodge would be warm enough and told them to cover themselves.

"What are you going to do?" Wanda asked.

"Get us out of this mess," I answered and slammed the truck door after me.

First I used the shovel that came with the truck to dig the snow out from behind the tires. Next I used my pocket knife to carve branches off some nearby trees. It took a good half-hour working in the dark to get enough branches to shove under the back tires. Then I made Dorothy get in the back seat. It would take a certain touch to ease the tires out of their holes, over the branches, and back onto the road.

I turned the key in the ignition. Nothing happened. I pumped the gas pedal and tried again. The engine wouldn't turn over. I knew a few things about car engines, but with the entire front of the truck submerged in the snow bank, I couldn't get under the hood.

I tried to start the truck for thirty minutes, but the engine wouldn't even sputter. It was dead. Dorothy and Wanda, sitting in the back seat, were shivering hard. The temperature dropped quickly at night, and not a single car had passed in the hour we'd been stuck.

"I don't think we can stay warm enough in this truck," I said.

"You're giving up on the engine?"

"There hasn't been one hint of its engaging."

"I'm cold," Wanda said.

"We've got to start walking," Dorothy announced. "How far back is the lodge?"

"Miles," I said. "Believe me. We wouldn't make it."

"Then towards Fairbanks. Surely there're houses or businesses between here and Fairbanks."

"It's below zero. We can't risk it."

"What's the alternative?" Dorothy insisted. "It's too damn cold. This truck has no warmth."

I was thinking very hard, but I wasn't panicked. In fact, I felt at home, dead center calm. Growing up under the threat of the end of the world induced me to learn all kinds of survival skills. As a youngster, I always prepared for the worst case. I could identify dozens of edible plants, knew how to navigate by the stars, how to treat a snake bite, and even survived for a week on food I scavenged from a Vermont forest, just to see if I could do it.

"You're not going to believe this," I said. "But we have to build a snow cave."

The Philosophers stared at me.

"A car hasn't passed us yet. We're still ten miles from Fairbanks and ten from the lodge. We'll freeze to death unless we build a snow cave."

"You got to be kidding."

"We could live a long time in a snow cave. Snow is 32 degrees. Out here it's below zero and getting colder by the minute. Our bodies will warm the cave."

They looked incredulous, like they were trying to decide if I'd gone mad. But I knew what I was talking about.

I made sure Dorothy and Wanda dressed in their warmest clothes and put on their boots. I told them, "We should all work to keep warm, but don't sweat. If you feel yourself starting to sweat, rest. But don't rest long enough to shiver." Thankfully, it had stopped snowing.

Swaddled in down parkas, boots, mittens, and hats we climbed out of the truck. The easiest way to make a cave would be to dig right into the side of the snow bank along the road. Its entrance would be obvious to passersby. As I began digging the entrance tunnel, Dorothy and Wanda used their booted feet and the cut branches to move the shoveled snow out of the way. I worked quickly, slanting the tunnel uphill to allow cold air to flow out of the cave. It was good snow, soft but not too powdery. The hardest part was lying squeezed inside the tunnel trying to dig the beginning of the main chamber. Wanda wasn't much help on her turns, but Dorothy surprised me with her strength. I got excited when the chamber was big enough to sit up in while digging.

After another hour of shoveling snow out of the cave, mostly lengthening the ends for Wanda's long legs, it was almost ready. I shaved the top into a dome, smoothing it as much as possible to prevent dripping. Finally, I used a long branch stripped of its leaves to poke two ventilation holes in the three-foot thick ceiling.

Then I sent Wanda and Dorothy to get the things we'd need from the truck and hand them in to me. I covered the floor of the cave with a blanket Wanda had stolen from the airplane and zipped two of the down bags together. I threw the third bag over the top like a comforter. I had them get a jug of water, a candle, and the sandwiches we made for the airplane. Then I crawled out of the cave and told them to go ahead and get into the sleeping bags.

Wanda looked frightened and Dorothy looked blank. I'd never seen that look on her face before and realized it must be fear. They obediently dropped to their hands and knees and crawled up the tunnel.

Once they were settled inside, I stuck the shovel at the entrance and tied a red sweatshirt to it so that people would know we were there. Then I crawled back into the snow cave. There was plenty of room on either side of the "bed" where Dorothy and Wanda were already tucked in. I carved a small ledge for the candle and lit it. Light leapt up the icy walls and glowed. My friends' eyes looked wild with disbelief. I felt calm and sure. I felt a gravitational pull to center, a place in myself I hadn't touched in months.

"Get between us, you must be very cold by now," Dorothy said.

"Don't worry," I joked. "I haven't been combing my hair much, but I do still wash regularly."

"I can't believe you," Dorothy said. "We're at death's door, and you're in the best humor you've been in for months."

I crawled into the bag, between the two of them. Three women in two down bags is a tight squeeze, but their bodies felt good to me. We lay still for a long time.

Finally, Wanda said, "It actually is warm in here."

Dorothy said, "What happens next?"

"We wait for someone to find our truck and see the shovel."

"And if they don't?"

"They will."

"Your body is hot," Dorothy said.

"Thanks. It's been a long time since a woman has told me that."`

"I can't believe you're cracking jokes. I meant, like temperature-hot."

"That's because I've been doing most of the work."

"You like it that way," Wanda put in.

"I do," I admitted.

"How do you know about all this?"

I laughed. "Applied science is my forte."

"What now?" Dorothy asked again.

"Would you please quit saying that?" Wanda begged.

"I feel like a bear," I said.

"Is that supposed to be comforting?"

"Just a fact."

"How long could we live in here?"

"Dorothy," Wanda said. "For once in your life, quit asking questions."

"It's important."

"What isn't important to you?"

"We could live a long time if we had to," I told them. "We can melt snow to drink. As long as we stay warm."

"I'm pretty warm," Wanda said snuggling up. "Tell us a story. You used to tell great stories."

I turned my head to look at Dorothy expecting her to object. She was scowling, but she put an arm around my middle.

"This is a true story," I began. "It happened the first time I was in Alaska, when I was 18."

Wanda also wrapped an arm around my waist. Great shadows, coming from the small candle, swelled and receded on the cave ceiling, making me think of prehistoric people. I wanted this. To be in a snow cave in a sleeping bag with two friends. I wanted this badly.

"Me and my friend Linda were backpacking in Denali. We'd found a nice valley tucked between ridges. It was beautiful and warm. I'm talking August. So we decided to not set up the tent. I was madly in love with Linda, of course."

"Why 'of course'?" Dorothy asked. I looked at her, expecting the scowl, but her brow was soft and smooth.

"Because she was eighteen," Wanda answered.

The Big Crunch - Lucy Jane Bledsoe

"When you're eighteen, you are madly in love with any woman you're with?"

"Uh huh," Wanda and I answered in unison.

"So I was trying to see how close I could push my sleeping bag up next to hers."

"But it wasn't that cold," Wanda said.

"No. So I didn't have much of an excuse."

"Did she want you, too?"

"Is this going to be a sex story?" Dorothy asked.

"She was straight," I said in answer to both of their questions. "Linda said that there were too many rocks under her and she decided she'd be more comfortable sleeping on another part of the meadow, about twenty yards away from me. She moved and fell right to sleep."

"Straight women are so cold."

"I was too agitated to sleep. So I lay there looking up at the sky, feeling, oh, you know, exquisitely tortured. Then I heard a little snort. At first I thought that Linda farted in her sleep. I was embarrassed, and also relieved it hadn't been me. Then I heard it again. It was not coming from Linda's direction. Next I heard some rustling in the nearby brush, like something rooting around. I sat up quietly in my bag and scoped out the scene. Then I saw it. A cinnamon grizzly about twenty yards from where we were sleeping. I could see it perfectly in the starlight."

"No," Wanda nuzzled in closer to me. "You're lying."

"I didn't know what to do, but I got out of my bag and stood up, thinking I would scare her away. I know better now, but then I thought making eye contact was a good idea."

"You made _eye_ contact?" Dorothy asked.

"With a grizzly," Wanda said. "Are they out here now?"

"They're all hibernating now," I comforted.

"Go on," Dorothy said.

"As soon as I stood up and made eye contact, _she_ stood. You know, rearing up on her hind legs, just like they do on TV nature shows. She swatted the air with her enormous right front paw. In the starlight I could see the black claws were a good two inches long.

"Then she lunged."

Both Wanda and Dorothy flinched in the bag. We all scooted closer to one another. Lying on my back, I cradled both their heads on my shoulders.

"I collapsed to the ground, face first, and covered the back of my neck with my arms. She stood on all fours over me, pinning me there and nuzzling my back with her nose. She made horrible snorting sounds and her breath was foul. I must have smelled bad to her too because soon she just ambled off into the brush."

"Madeleine, is that true?" Wanda was incredulous.

"Jesus," was all Dorothy said.

"What about Linda?"

"She slept."

"You didn't wake her up then?"

"No. I felt... I don't know, good. Sort of whole. And special. Sought out. Denali is an enormous, wild, beautiful place. Beauty is about something much deeper than harmony and scenery." I felt embarrassed telling an aesthetics professor what beauty was.

Dorothy wasn't offended. She brushed the hair off my face and pressed her lips against mine. "Madeleine," she said real softly.

"Are you scared out here?" I asked.

"Yes," Dorothy answered at the same time Wanda said, "No."

"This is amazing," Wanda said. "It's way below zero out there. And we're toasty. Honestly, how do you know all this survival stuff, Madeleine?"

"There is new evidence," I said, "that the universe is not going to expand forever. There may be enough invisible matter in space to create a strong enough gravitational force to pull the universe back together. There will be this cosmic moment when the expansion slows to a stop and then reverses itself. The opposite of the Big Bang. It's called the Big Crunch."

After a long silence, Dorothy said, "You've never told us what happened that night with Sara. Not really, not the details. It's not like you to hold things in."

"There's nothing to tell," I said, trying to kill the waver in my voice. "She mouthed off and they stabbed her." I didn't want them to notice my tears, but my breathing got ragged. When Wanda started rubbing my chest, I couldn't hold back the big sob anymore. Then I cried, really cried. As my body shook and shook, I felt as if I were being held from every direction, our three pairs of legs twisted together in one thick vine. Their hands stroked my back, my neck, my arms. I cried until I was too physically exhausted to cry anymore.

When I finally stopped, Wanda's cool lips touched my forehead. I moved and met her mouth in a brief kiss. I pulled Dorothy in closer, too. The three of us lay like that, wet cheeks together, touching lips softly, like baby mammals. The light on the ceiling of the snow cave sputtered and burst, sputtered and burst. Then suddenly it went out. It was very, very dark.

"Jesus," Wanda said into the utter blackness.

"I love you guys," Dorothy whispered. "I really love you."

Then we fell asleep. It was the nicest sleep I'd had since Sara's stabbing.

Some time later Wanda woke up saying, "I have to pee."

"Hold it," Dorothy mumbled groggily.

"I can't. I really have to go."

"You shouldn't have drunk so much water."

"Madeleine said to drink a lot."

"Yeah, it's good you did. And it's not a good idea to hold it. Holding it lowers your body temperature. I'll go with you."

"Go where?" Dorothy asked.

"Outside to pee."

"You're crazy."

"I really have to go."

"Stop talking about it. You're making me have to go."

"You better come now," I said. "Or you'll be going alone later."

"You're really going out in the cold?"

Wanda and I had crawled out of the bags and were pulling on our boots. I surveyed the domed roof of the cave. I'd made the perfect amount of ventilation. We were toasty but there wasn't a single drip. I had good instinct for that kind of balance.

"Shit," Dorothy said, kicking out of the bags.

We crawled down the entrance of the snow tunnel, me first. I figured I'd pee fast and then scurry back into the cave. I plunked my mittened hands on the snow outside the tunnel entrance and straightened up. Wanda and Dorothy came shoving out after me like triplets being born into the universe.

"My God," Dorothy whispered.

"What is it?" Wanda asked grabbing my arm.

The edges of the sky were cloudless and black, with so many tiny stars they looked like a mist. Directly above, a storm of green and yellow flared up, then swirled like an enormous genie. The colors suddenly disappeared, as if the sky had sucked them up, and then purple bars began dancing overhead, followed by a ribbon of green lacing through the purple bars. "The northern lights," I whispered. "It's the fuckin' northern lights."

We squatted in a circle and peed on the snow while the chaos of color flowed overhead. After buttoning our pants, we stood with our necks bent looking up at the sky.

"Tell us again the scientific explanation," Dorothy said. Puffs of steam followed each word out of her mouth.

Wanda jumped as a disc of red exploded into the sky.

"You all are the philosophers. What's your explanation?"

Neither woman answered and I didn't mind. While they stared at the sky, I stared at them. Dorothy's black eyebrows were curved and sleek, like two ravens. Her lips were swollen from sleep. Wanda stood with her hands on her hips, her pelvis thrust slightly forward, her eyes full of tears. "*Chingada*," she said, "*chingada*."

Kerry Hart was born and raised in Memphis, TN, and lived in Portland, OR and New Orleans before settling in Philadelphia. She would like to dedicate "Reed" in the memory of Lanny Phillips, who, like all the others, is distinctly more than a statistic - with love and thanks for being there during the scary, sexy seventies when it all began for both of us.

REED

The first time I saw Reed I loathed her, immediately sizing her up as an insufferably stuck up rich bitch. She glided into the classroom wearing lemon-colored Levi cords. I stared as she moved, her small breasts bouncing haughtily beneath a neon pink tank top, to a seat in the row by the windows. Her long hair was a shiny brown with glistening gold highlights, but it looked hippyish, out of time. She was deeply tanned and she walked effortlessly like a nocturnal animal, her boot heels tick-tacking on the linoleum floor. Her hands were venous, her fingers long and decorated with rings.

It was September, 1977-- the beginning of my junior year. Reed moved with feline pretension and I guessed right away that she was a dyke. Me in my torn Levi's and baseball belt, paint spattered sweatshirt and hightop Adidas', judging Reed with her slim hips, high cheekbones, aquiline nose and her long hair and lemon pants.

On Halloween I turned twenty-one. The days shortened, the temperature dropped, and with November came grey skies and ice flecked rain. I was desperately plateaued in the middle ground of my college career, bored with the city I was born in, and I hadn't had a boyfriend in a year and a half. My future looked bleak. The boys I had liked had turned into men I didn't. I had to get out so I did the only thing I thought might work. I called my sister in New Orleans and told her I was moving down right after Christmas.

Less than a week later a series of events began that would break my tedium more quickly and in a way I never could have openly anticipated.

It was a crisp, clear November night. I was in class, in a depressive stupor, pondering my life without regard for anyone else-- wondering how I could get done with this semester and get to New Orleans with my sanity intact. I was sitting and thinking, then just sitting-- staring blankly, when I began to focus my eyes and saw to my right and one desk ahead, Reed's left breast. The heat was up and Reed had peeled off two layers, down to a plain white muscle shirt that hung low at her armpit and exposed something I had somehow never seen before, although I had two of my own. But Reed's was different and I stared unashamedly until the thought washed over me how I wanted to touch her small nipple with the tip of my tongue and suck and feel my cheek against her soft chest.

I put my head down on my forearms for a moment, then I looked up to see Reed slump forward and turn her face toward me, her silky hair swinging down -- and at that moment a great gust of wind sprayed sleet-speckled rain from the eaves roughly down onto the closed window. An inexplicable current of air, perhaps created by Reed's movement itself, brought from her to me a fine scent of sweet yellow apples and ice blue soap. Her freshness overcame me, defying the restraints of the depressing season, and our eyes met and her brow furrowed as she whispered, "Oh, poor baby."

Later I was leaving the library and Reed was standing at the bottom of the steps. How did she find me, I thought. She walked me to my car and when I said goodbye Reed asked me if I wanted to come to her house for a drink. She pointed out her apartment, right across the railroad tracks from the school. It was hard for me to say no, and I didn't want to.

Reed's living room was lavishly furnished with antique oak. Persian rugs covered two walls, healthy plants hung from large baskets in front of the windows. Soft tungsten light from one forty watt bulb created a fireplace effect. Reed's kitchen, which was the only other room I saw in her apartment that first night, was oddly illuminated by another low wattage bulb, this one green. I remembered Mama telling me that red lights meant whores-- blue, witches. I wondered what Reed was.

Andy Warhol slept curled contentedly atop Reed's coffee table which was a solid core door laid across two wide cinder blocks. His snow white hair was full and fluffy-- his blue eye was open, his green one closed. Reed asked me what I would like to drink. A moderate pot smoker since age twelve, my experience with alcohol was limited to a glass of Mogan David with Christmas dinner and sips of Busch from Daddy's can with our Saturday night popcorn. I crossed my legs, leaned back in an overstuffed rocker, and said, "Scotch on the rocks."

Reed took two engraved silver cups from her freezer, filled them with ice, put gin, tonic, and lime in one and splashed Chivas into the other. I choked down my drink by coating my taste buds with Marlboro Lights.

As we tired of talking, Reed picked up her six-string and asked me if I sang. I said no, and she began strumming the opening chords of "Mr. Tambourine Man", a tune I knew well. "Sing along if you know this," she said, and I didn't sing but listened to her. I watched her fingers move along the strings-- right ones brushing and plucking, left ones pushing and gliding-- watched her eyes close and her lips whisper, "In the jingle-jangle morning I'll come following you." We talked some more and I told her I was moving to New Orleans. "I will miss you," she said as I left for the night.

As I drove home I thought about changing my plans. My heart beat faster just thinking about seeing Reed again. But you don't change your life plans for a friend. I was twenty-one and moving south to a time and a place that was going to change my life forever.

On December twenty-third a friend of ours threw a Christmas party. I called Reed on the twentieth and asked her if she was going. "Are you taking me?" she asked, and I laughed.

"Yeah," I said. "Be ready at eight."

The night of the twenty-third was frigid. The steady drizzle from the day was becoming bits of stinging ice and the moisture on the streets was freezing. I approached Reed's back door and saw it was ajar. I knocked lightly and called her name. No answer. "Yoo-hoo," I said a little louder as I started toward the living room. I didn't want to startle her. I stepped into the living room and looked toward the hallway beyond which lay the bedroom, study, and bathroom. The lights were off. I turned back toward the couch, beginning to think Reed had stepped out, and I was admiring a colorful photo of sea anemones when I simultaneously heard one footfall and felt a strong arm snake beneath mine, splaying a veined hand across my right breast. I heard a click and instinctively lifted my chin, glancing down to see a pearl-handled switchblade protruding from Reed's right hand and laying neatly against my pale throat. "Ooooh, shit," I laughed. Reed released her hold and spun around in front of me grinning, and brandishing the blade.

"I haven't shown you my knife collection, have I?" she asked, retracting the blade and tossing it onto the coffee table. She lit a joint and we shared it as she bundled up in her calf-length Navy coat. She grabbed two more joints and a bottle of gin and we headed for my car. The last night of the first part of my life had begun.

We left the party sometime well after midnight and sped around Memphis for a while, slipping lightly across patches of ice that dotted the streets. I brought up the subject of homosexuality and while my line stayed cerebral and theoretical, Reed's became personal, confessional. She hung her head and spoke of a Boston prep school-- of an adolescence marked by indiscretion. She told me of a woman she loved there.

At three a.m. I was stopped at a red light near Reed's house. She was quiet and still as I looked at her, then with penetrating finality she said, "I want to make love to you."

When we arrived at her apartment we sat for a moment, my VW idling loudly. I waited for Reed to get out and she said, "You wanna come in for a nightcap?"

"No," I said. "I've really gotta get home."

She sighed. "I'm sorry, okay? Just a little nightcap, okay?"

Once inside Reed didn't stop at the freezer for the iced cups. She walked ahead of me and flung her coat over the rocker as I dropped my jacket onto the couch. She turned around and in two long strides she was standing in front of me. "Come into my bedroom," she said.

Before I could say anything, Reed grabbed both sides of my collar and pulled my shirt apart, ripping several buttons off and exposing my bare chest. I stood in shock as she put her mouth on my nipple. She sucked, and my clit twitched, and I couldn't let this happen. My cunt pounded and Reed went lower, fumbling at my belt, my zipper-- and I squeezed her wrists, digging in my thumbnails. She tackled me to the floor. What was she saying? Sweet breath in my ears, cool and wet from her licking. Reed whispered, "I wanna fuck you 'til you can't walk. Don't talk," she said, putting her fingers to my lips. "I wanna see you come for me."

I struggled to rise and she pulled me over on top of her-- held my face tightly, her fingers draped across my ears. Quiet for a moment, and tender-- her lips brushed mine, then a small kiss, then another and my lips responded. "Take my tongue," she said and I did.

Then panic, resistance-- and Reed was angry again. She bit my lip and it bled salty, and then I was angry and I pulled free. I left disheveled and confused.

The next day was Christmas eve and my last day of work. At ten minutes to closing the roses came. "Who is he?" my co-workers teased. "You wouldn't believe me if I told you," they thought I joked.

On Christmas night I was terrified. I couldn't see Reed again. Things could only go one place from where they were now. I left my grandmother's house at midnight. The streets were frosty and deserted. I was almost home when I heard a horn and a shout, "Hey!", and I looked over to see Reed sailing west in her Austin Healy. On a side street Reed pleaded with me to take a ride with her-- just to talk, she promised, one last time. Tears welled in her eyes. We were going to be out in the middle of nowhere on a brutally cold night. What, realistically, could happen?

Reed said nothing as we made our way out of Memphis. Once past the city lights, she pulled onto a winding country road, dropped the pedal, and said, "You're not going to believe what this baby will do!"

We made it to a heavily wooded area in five minutes. Reed whipped the small car down a foot path and we got out just as fat flakes of snow began to fall. A high wind whistled through tall pines and a full moon blued the sky. I stood stiffly, face to face with the person I was most afraid of in the world.

We sank to our knees onto a bed of damp pine needles, snow dusting our hair and clinging to our eyelashes. We kissed passionately. I kept my hands above Reed's neck and hers fell to my waist. I felt the base of her thumb pressing against my crotch and I kissed her harder. When her other hand entered my pants I stopped kissing her and sat up, shaking my head. "I can't," I told her. "I'm leaving for New Orleans in two days."

"I will follow you," she said.

I had been in New Orleans for two weeks and in my own apartment for two days when Reed arrived. We made out constantly. She stayed for four days and we slept each night crushed together on my sofa that I refused to expand into a bed. My cheeks and chin were abraded, my jaws ached and my nipples stung. Reed told me she loved me and, naked, masturbated against my leg. I never took my pants off. When we said goodbye we stood on my balcony overlooking the lush courtyard and we sobbed and I held onto both sides of her unzipped leather jacket, tugging her toward me, kissing her again and again. I apologized and said I didn't know what to do and she said, nothing-- you don't have to do anything and she kissed my ears and licked tears from my sore chin. I invited her back for Mardi Gras.

It was February 2, 1978. I was walking through the French Quarter when I saw Reed on the corner of Royal and St. Philip. She was three inches shorter than me and slight of build but as we met she reached around my waist with one arm and lifted me off the ground. I knew right then that no one had ever loved me like this and no one ever would again. Inside my apartment Reed made a pot of apple tea and I took a very long hot shower. When I emerged from the bathroom with a towel wrapped around my waist, she was lounging on the sofa bed that I had not folded back up, sipping from a steaming mug. She took a deep breath and I stood frozen. I watched her place her tea on the bedside table. The dim light of the grey noon sky filtered in my balcony doors through enormous leaves of banana plants in the courtyard.

Reed sat up and I remained still as she delicately opened the fold of terry cloth at my waist. We said nothing. She slid her fingers across my ears and into my hair, curling and damp from the shower. I moved closer to her. The tips of our tongues touched. She gently bit my lip and I smiled and shook my head. No, no, not again-- and she lowered her eyes in mock apology. We kissed, then Reed encouraged me down, onto my back, parted my legs and knelt between them.

"I've wanted to taste this for so long," she said.

She gently opened my lips with her thumbs. Everything felt painfully precipitous. I vacillated between bursting into tears and laughter. Reed drew her face closer, studied me for a moment, then looked back into my eyes-- wordlessly enabling me make the connection between my cunt and my mind.

Reed lowered her eyes again and prodded my inner lips with her aristocratic nose. She inhaled deeply and exhaled slowly. I instinctively clenched my muscles against the onslaught of serious pleasure and I raised my knees to protect myself. Reed cocked her head and said without speaking-- our eyes are open, it is not dark, you are here. Then she whispered authoritatively, "I'm gonna make you come for me."

36   *Reed - Kerry Hart*

I clutched a pillow to my chest as Reed's tongue touched me for the first time. Then, she kept her promise.

Reed was a versatile lover. I knew that then and I especially know that now. We only stopped when I could take no more. She tenderly sucked my clit until it stayed swollen and I was near orgasm constantly from the friction of my jeans. She fucked my cunt until I could barely walk, and my asshole until I could hardly sit-- and she used my pain as an excuse to keep me lying down. Before we fell asleep at night she ministered to my soreness with aromatic oils, inserting her long fingers until I could not resist responding. I spent the next five months going back and forth to Memphis to satiate my desire for my lover, and when this madness that dominated every inch and ounce of me became too much, I moved back home.

Reed and I were lovers on and off for the next three years. As time passed our romance lost its sequence and became episodic- but it never lost its powerful passion. A hundred times Reed stole my heart and broke it. Her personality was kaleidoscopic and she seized every opportunity to show me her brilliant colors.

....

It is a frosty winter day and I have a bad cold. I leave my class and go to Reed's apartment across the tracks. She takes me to her antique cherry sleigh bed and cuddles me down under a mountain of hand sewn quilts. She takes my temperature and gives me aspirin and sings me to sleep. When I awaken she brings me chicken soup and rye crackers and cinnamon tea. When I am ready to sleep again for the night she prepares steaming hot whiskey, honey, and lemon to soothe my throat and calm my cough. As I drift off she runs her fingers through my short brown hair and says I'm her teddy bear baby. Reed is the loveliest woman I have ever known . . .

I am sitting in my garage apartment on an early October evening. Multicolored leaves slap against the locked screen door. I've not returned Reed's phone calls for three weeks because of some wrong she has done me. The autumn wind rises and howls and I hear footfalls on my steps. I stop and listen and I hear Reed's voice. "Let me in." I say nothing. "Goddamnit," she says, and I hear ice tinkling in a glass. "Answer me!" Wham. A boot cracks against the old wood.

Wham, slam. Another crack and the door flies open. Reed storms in as I giggle and stand. "What the fuck's your problem?" she asks. She waits for an answer and when she doesn't get one she throws her gin on my shirt.

"You know you want me," she says, and she's right. Reed yanks down my pants and begins to make love to me. Six hours later I am about to have my sixteenth orgasm and I can't stand anymore. I take control, frantically trying to get away from her mouth and I fall off the bed. Reed does not lose contact and I come and she looks up, cheeks and chin shimmering, and says, "Oh, baby, you won't ever have it this good," and she is right, again. On the seventeenth orgasm there is a snap and Reed dislocates her jaw. We laugh about that for days although it hurts her to do so. Reed is the most dangerous and irresistible woman I know . . .

It is a sultry August night and Reed rolls the Austin-Healy's top down and we head for the country. She knows of an old woodshed, and we make dirty, sticky love on its floor for hours. Near dawn, covered with grime, we drive to a place where Reed says there are horses. She wants to teach me to ride. The sun rises and the gentle animals stare at us as we attempt to scale the barbed wire fence of a penal farm. I am crazy, but I am never bored when Reed is a part of my life . . .

It is late afternoon on a breezy spring day and Reed's window is up. A train rumbles down the tracks, its whistle blowing in the distance. We lay naked on her sleigh bed, partially draped by a blue flannel sheet. We are eating fresh strawberries and drinking cold white wine. We watch the sun set and as the darkness threatens to shut the sight of us off from one another Reed lights a candle. The flame licks up and casts our shadows on the wall. "I love you," Reed says and slips her hand beneath my shoulders. "Oh God, I love you." We kiss, we run our hands across each others' bodies. We make love and our scents and tastes mingle with those of the berries and the wine. This for me is love, for the very first time . . .

....

I haven't seen or heard from Reed in years. I know where she lives, and that place is far from me. She may now be settled down with a woman who brings in the morning mail that they read over coffee. They may kiss the cat goodnight and sleep soundly in a well-furnished house that is their home. But I doubt it.

If I saw Reed again I would ask her out for a hearty roast beef sandwich just to see if her jaw still pops. Then I would invite her to my house and, once inside, I would throw my hands up like a woman at gun point. Reed, you can never have my heart and never have my mind again, but the rest, oh god, just take it. I think I could live with that.

Woody Blue, S.E., was born and raised in NE Ohio. She has withstood several careers, including engineering, carpentry and general odd jobbing. For several years she was involved with the Seneca Women's Peace Camp in upstate New York.

Woody is currently a writer and massage therapist in Gainesville, Florida. She believes in r\evolution, radical change, and disrupting the patriarchy whenever possible.

THAT DAY ON HIGHWAY 62

The needle on the temperature gauge rose imperceptibly as the bright red Toyota camper raced across the barren Nevada desert highway. Neither the driver nor passenger paid it any attention; they were too embroiled in the heat of a lover's quarrel, one that had started three days earlier and had no end in sight.

"It's just too bad if you don't like Steve," Daphna ranted at Barb from the passenger seat. "You can't just quit a good-paying job, because he's an asshole. Not unless you have another one lined up." Daphna turned her head from Barb and stared out the window. She didn't want Barb to see the tears that blurred her eyes.

Meanwhile Barb concentrated on the road in front of her but she wasn't fooling either of them. Daphna had seen that Barb's lips were compressed into a thin, red slash across her face, and the tiny lines around her eyes were deepened into dark grooves, a sure indication of a coming tantrum.

"Look," Barb retorted. "Don't tell me what I can or can't do. I'll do whatever I want to." She took a deep breath, then exhaled slowly. Her knuckles, gripping the steering wheel, turned white. "I'll quit my job if I want to. That's my decision, not yours. And if you don't like it, you can leave." Barb continued, "And furthermore, the only reason you want me to keep my job anyway is so you stay home and have a baby."

The temperature dial inched upward another notch. It had definitely crossed the halfway mark and was wiggling towards the lower red line that meant trouble. The glaring sun glinted relentlessly off the Toyota's windshield, heating up the inhabitants inside.

Barb's last remark hit home. Having just turned thirty, Daphna was feeling a bit frantic about having a child. She had tried to be patient with Barb, tried to give her time to get used to the idea. Lately she'd begun to set up realistic timetables, but Barb had been hedging.

Now, sitting in the hot truck, it dawned on her that Barb might never be ready to help her raise a child. When Daphna next spoke, the frustration had left her voice, replaced with the cold edge of anger.

"I didn't realize you were so opposed to having a baby. You should have let me know before. Like years ago when I first mentioned it."

When Barb started to protest, she cut her off curtly. "Oh, don't worry, I understand completely. Go ahead and do whatever you want. That's what's really important anyway, that YOU get to do whatever YOU want."

"Oh, don't be ridiculous," Barb started to say, but Daphna had turned her head back to the window, determined to shut Barb out of her sight, her hearing, her life. Barb didn't try and press her point. She knew it would be useless at this stage. She would wait till Daphna was ready to talk.

Five minutes passed and then Daphna murmured something.

"What?" Barb queried leaning over sideways to hear better. "What'd you say?"

Daphna turned her head to her lover, speaking crisply and defiantly. "I said, would you mind pulling in at the next rest stop?"

"Sure," Barb said, quickly, not quite sure what happened to the argument. She knew she had hurt Daphna's feelings, and she was sorry. But pride got in the way, so she drove on, subdued, and rationalized her anger to herself.

No more words were exchanged till they reached the Sam McCafferty rest stop. By that time, Barb had taken note of the temperature gauge, and was eyeing the jumpy needle nervously. She pulled over to the restroom building and Daphna jumped out. "I'm going over to get some gas and cool down the engine some," she shouted to Daphna's retreating back. Daphna turned her head briefly and for an instant, seemed about to say something.   Barb waited, but then Daphna looked away, very abruptly, and continued down the walk towards the bathrooms.

Barb turned back to the truck, feeling shut out. She drove over to the hose that dangled from the outdoor faucet, parking in the shade of the building. As she ran the cool water over the hood of the car, she began to feel better, thinking about the possibilities of making up with

Daphna, and working out some of their problems. She squirted the hose through the grill, directly at the radiator, cleaning off the thousands of bugs that had dried there.

Concentrating on the job in front of her, Barb paid no attention to the whoosh of air brakes being released, paid no attention to the grumbling of an engine going through its succession of lower gears. After checking the oil, she slammed the truck hood down, just as a brightly colored semi truck pulled past her, heading for the highway. She happened to glance up at the passenger window, and caught a flash of freckled hand pushing back a strand of stringy blond hair. It sorta reminded her of Daphna.

She hooked the hose onto the faucet, climbed back into the truck, and pulled it over to the gas pumps.

It was while Barb was pumping the gas and staring at the rest stop doors, wondering why Daphna was taking so long, that the image of that freckled hand popped into her head. Her brain moved forward slowly, dreading the direction her thoughts were taking. Could it have been Daphna in that truck? She wouldn't do that. She wouldn't go off with some strange man. She knew better. It was ridiculous.

And then Barb's own words came back to her. "I'll quit my job if I want to," she'd said. "And if you don't like it you can leave."

"Oh fuck," she said out loud, oblivious to the man next to her, cleaning his windshield. "Shit!" she said even louder, as the reality of the situation hit her. She yanked the pump out of the tank, and shoved it back into its slot. Her mind was racing over the details of that freckled hand, that backward look of Daphna's, that anguished tone in her voice.

She hurled herself into the truck, fumbling with the seat belt, steering wheel, and gear shift while her mind raced. "What kind of truck was it? Grey? White? No, orange. It was an orange truck, yeah, I think that's what it was. I hope I'm not making this up. Oh let it be an orange truck."

Barb was in third gear pulling out of the service station when she became aware of the shouting and waving behind her. "Damn," she hadn't paid for the gas. She saw a man in the rearview mirror scribbling on a pad of paper.

"Double damn," she swore to herself and filed it away in her memory. At this point she didn't care about anything but that orange truck.

She brushed away the small nagging thought that she hadn't really seen Daphna in the truck, just a freckled hand like Daphna's. Perhaps she was back at the rest stop wondering why Barb was driving away. Well, if that was the case, then they'd probably hold her hostage for the gas money. But if she was in the truck, Barb didn't have a minute to lose.

"They must have been gone ten minutes already," Barb thought. "Shit, I gotta catch 'em." The Toyota swerved onto the blacktop and sped off, the accelerator pedal pushed to the floor. The temperature gauge needle rose from cold to 3/4 of the way to danger and then settled there, seemingly unsure of what to do next. Barb, eyes focussed on the road, played out future scenarios.

"Shit, Daphna, what are you trying to prove, anyway? You trying to get fucked by that truck driver or what? Is that how you're going to have that baby?" That train of thought scared her so she tried a new one, "Oh Daphna, I'm sorry, I didn't mean a word I said. Please don't go off like this. I love you, Daphna. I can't live without you."

With these thoughts tears came to her eyes and her foot lifted a little from the pedal. The resulting slowdown snapped her mind out of that line of thinking. Between clenched teeth, she said, "I'm gonna find her, she can't get away from me."

Hunched over the steering wheel, she pushed the brave Toyota to its limits, until it trembled with the exhaustive effort. Fifteen minutes later, she spotted an orange semi in the distance far ahead of her. "Yes," she cried, punching the air with gladness, feeling hopefulness soar. It took another ten minutes to close the gap.

The truck loomed in front of her, roaring at a steady 75 miles an hour. Barb didn't know if this was the right truck or not. All she could see were the massive steel doors in front of her. She followed at a discreet distance of twenty feet while she tried to come up with a strategy. Looking down at the temperature gauge she saw that it hovered just below the red zone.

She ignored it. What she wanted was to see if Daphna was in the truck without appearing too obvious. She inched the Toyota over to the shoulder side of the road trying to peer into the passenger side mirror of the semi. Her tires crossed over onto the gravel and she swerved dangerously. So much for trying not to be obvious.

The truck screamed on maddeningly, not speeding up or slowing down. Barb made a plan. She'd pass the truck, then look in her rearview mirror at the passenger. If she still couldn't see, then she'd slow down and let the truck pass her. Then hopefully she'd be able to see.

Barb crossed over to the passing lane. She pushed her foot down harder on the accelerator, ignoring the shuddering engine. Slowly and steadily she inched past the rear of the truck. Now the massive wheels churned beside her. As she neared the cab, she watched the driver from his mirror. She judged him to be in his late 30's, immense arms browned by the sun, sunglasses covering the eyes, mouth thrust forward.

Barb kept an impassive look on her face as she edged towards his door. Her speedometer read 80. Both trucks, the small camper and the mammoth semi, rolled forward in space and time, speeds briefly matching.

Then the Toyota began to fall behind, little by little, as the huge truck picked up speed. Barb's heart sank. She couldn't go any faster, the Toyota was at its limit. The larger truck passed her and she slipped into its backstream. From ten feet behind she could follow in its wake. Mercifully the truck settled on a speed of 85, and Barb clung on.

Officer Joe Kimble had just finished his Big Mac when he received the dispatcher's call. "A 701 out at McCafferty's Station," came the scratchy voice of the radio. Kimble sighed and wiped his mouth and fingers with the paper napkin before picking up the radio to confirm that he'd gotten the message and was on his way.

He stuffed the greasy wrappings and used napkins into the paper sack and drove over to the trashcan, juggling the coffee cup in his left hand. After fourteen years on highway patrol, he just couldn't get too excited about someone skipping out on paying for their gas, even if it ·was his friend's gas station.

Once on the road he called the dispatcher back to ask if any ID on the vehicle was available. Charlie was way ahead of him. "Red Toyota Camper, license # 2-4-0-george-henry, that's 2-4-0-george-henry; heading east on 62, pulled out about fifteen minutes ago. Do you read? Over."

"I read, that's 2-4-0--george-henry, red Toyota camper, heading east on 62." Joe looked at his watch and did some figuring in his head. "Switch to Channel 8. Over."

Once on the scanless radio channel, Kimble explained. "It'll be tight but I think I can make it over to 62 by way of Devil Skull Trail. What's the ID on the driver, Charlie? Over."

"Caucasian woman, 25 - 30 years old, 5'7" or so, kinda stocky, short dark hair, sunglasses, red shorts, white t-shirt, earring through her nose. Over."

"What was that? Earring through her nose! This will be one easy snag. I should be at 62 in another twenty minutes. Over."

"You want backup? Over."

"Who's close? Over."

"Daniels and Kupansky are over by Tombstone. Over."

"Put 'em on standby but I doubt I'll need 'em. 10-4."

Kimble adjusted his seat belt and flipped on the lights and siren, determined to head the Toyota off at the pass.

He was just north of 62, on the outskirts of the dusty mining town of Sierra Vista. Up past the next curve, he could get on Devil Skull Trail and lop off a few miles. Gritting his teeth, he passed a nervous motorist, then screeched onto the dirt road in a cloud of dust. Immediately the car started bouncing in the deeply pitted road. "Oh, damn," Kimble thought to himself. "Maintenance crews haven't gotten here for awhile." He slowed to 35 for the first two miles. Then the road evened out and he sped up to 50, his frown changing to a grin as open country flew by.

Daphna chewed on her fingernails as the huge semi roared through the desert. What had begun as an impulsive act to teach Barb a lesson had changed to worry and regret a half hour later. She watched furtively in the side mirror as the Toyota valiantly caught up with them and then hung there as if attached by an invisible rope.

When Daphna had first seen the camper she'd silently cheered. She'd eagerly faced the driver to say, "OK, let me out. I'm sorry I took up your time. It was all a big mistake."

But the words had died on her lips when she glanced over at her self-chosen protector, a diesel dyke from the word "go."

Back at the rest stop, when Daphna had spotted Leonie getting into her truck, she'd made up a story about being a battered woman and played the helpless, desperate wife. Leonie had quickly agreed to take her anywhere she needed to go. Daphna had accepted Leonie's protective arm as she guided her into the passenger seat. It had all been so easy, and had somewhat of a thrilling air to it.

But now Daphna felt quite intimidated by Leonie. It wasn't just the wildcat tattoos that decorated Leonie's neck and arms, or the chains that hung off the back of the driver's seat. And it wasn't just Leonie's swaggering personality, or the thick sensuality that poured off her.

No, two things kept Daphna from asking Leonie to stop the truck and let her return to the camper. The first obstacle was how to explain to Leonie that she'd made up her story, about being helpless and battered, not to mention heterosexually married, in order to get Leonie to participate in her scheme.

Daphna was embarrassed by the political incorrectness of it all, sitting here next to this obviously out, very radical and sexual dyke.

The second obstacle that silenced Daphna was the idea of explaining it all over again to Barb. Much as Daphna longed to be back in the Toyota, she also cringed at the thought of Barb's anger and resulting lack of trust.

Daphna knew that the longer she waited to speak up the harder it would be. And so she made the plunge. When she spoke, she was frustrated to find that her childhood stammer had crept back into her voice.

"I ap-p-preciate your help, Leonie," she started.

"Oh, honey, just forget it. It makes me feel good to be able to help you out," Leonie answered, nodding. "You know, in this business, there just ain't hardly any women. And I have to spend a lot of time with these macho assholes. And sometimes they tell me how they treat their wives. I mean, you wouldn't believe the ATT-ti-tudes." She shook her head and pressed her lips together tightly like she was afraid something might escape from them.

"O-o-ooh, I can get mad just thinking about it. I mean, that's one of the reasons I decided to buy my own truck, so I wouldn't have to work for fuckin' men all the time."

Daphna didn't know quite how to respond to this. She didn't want to talk about Leonie's truck, or men's attitudes. Out of the corner of her eye, Daphna caught a flash in the side mirror. It was the sun glinting off the Toyota's chrome bumper. The effect it had on her was like a giant finger nudging her on the shoulder. She lowered her eyes to her hands on her lap. The fingers twisted nervously like a knot of worms trying to get loose.

Daphna felt a tap on her knee. Leonie was holding out a pack of spearmint gum towards her. "Here," she said. "You chew?" Daphna smiled faintly and shook her head. She couldn't think about eating OR chewing at a time like this.

Like an unwanted stray dog, Barb's Toyota sniffed relentlessly at the heels of the huge semi in front of it. Barb's eyes were glued to the two orange doors, oblivious of the arid desert that stretched out on either side of her. Thudding heart and thudding engine kept time with the slap of the tires against the asphalt. "What do I do? What do I do? What do I do?" singsonged in Barb's head mile after mile after mile.

A subtle whistling began to accompany the song and dancing steam mixed with the desert dust. Barb drove on. Percussion, in the form of a knocking engine joined the impromptu orchestra, immediately followed by a series of hissing hoses. Barb closed her ears and set her mouth and held her foot down on the gas pedal.

As if in a dream, the orange box in front of her broke its grip and started pulling away. Barb and the camper became enveloped in billowing steam. The knocking, whistling and clattering engine rose into a shuddering crescendo and stalled. Almost in tears, Barb let the truck roll onto the shoulder. An intense sizzling pushed against the hood.

Before the truck had stopped, Barb was reaching into the overstuffed glove compartment, digging for paper and pencil to jot down the Nevada license number she'd memorized.

"N-M-6-5-1-F, N-M-6-5-1-F, N-M-6-5-1-F," she repeated as her fingers waded through old receipts, batteries, maps, and plastic eating utensils. Finally, she snagged a sticky pencil with a dirty eraser. Choosing a piece of paper from the crumpled pile on the seat, she began to write the number. "N" - SNAP! The pencil point broke before she'd finished the first letter.

Clamping her jaw together, Barb pulled the lead off the pencil and finished writing the number holding the lead painstakingly between her thumbnail and first finger. It was difficult and time-consuming because her hand was shaking from anger, panic, and a heavy-duty adrenalin rush.

When she finished, Barb put the paper carefully on the dashboard, closed her eyes, took a deep breath and tried to swallow the thick lump in her throat. Tears pushed against her eyelids and she let them come, covering her face and snuffling silently, as if she were in a crowded room rather than a vast empty desert. She sat like this, shaking and sobbing for several minutes.

Eventually, the storm was spent. Barb pulled her hand slowly down her face, wiping her tears and nose with one movement and then brushing the palm of her hand against her pants leg.

Raising her head, she began to look around her, taking in her desolation. Nothing moved so far as she could see. Barb gazed into the rearview mirror. The shimmering desert stared back at her, mocking and empty. She wondered how long it would be before a car would appear. The answer turned out to be 2 minutes and 42 seconds.

While the car was still small on the horizon, Barb opened her driver's door and jumped out. She walked to the front of the camper and yanked open the hood. Then she pulled the red bandana from her back pocket, shook it out, and, as the car approached, began to wave it in the air frantically.

Officer Joe Kimble had made record time on Devil Skull Trail, and was now easing deftly onto the eastbound ramp of 62. Through a complicated set of mental calculations, in which he assumed that the Toyota was doing between 70 and 80 miles an hour, he'd figured that the vehicle as some miles ahead of him. Bubble lights on, he pressed the pedal to the metal. Cactus and mesquite trees melted into a blur as the speedometer needle rose past the 85 mark, the 90 mark, and bobbed erratically between the 95 and 100 line.

"I'm onto you now, Ms 2-4-0-george-henry, earring through your nose," Joe muttered to himself under his breath.

Within minutes he spotted the camper pulled off to the side of the road, engine smoking.

With the practiced grace of a professional smoky, he pulled the patrol car onto the shoulder behind the dusty vehicle, looking for signs of the driver. No head bobbed into view from the cab or the back, no legs stretched out from beneath the car, no figure moved from behind nearby scrub. A wrinkled frown line puckered Joe's forehead.

He eased himself cautiously out of the car, scanning the landscape, uncertain of the amount of danger involved here. On one hand, he was dealing with a woman who'd skipped out on paying a five dollar gas bill, a pretty minor offense. On the other hand, Joe had just watched Thelma and Louise last week, and though he thought the whole movie was some feminist's outlandish sick fantasy, he also feared it might have planted some wild ideas into the general female public.

In his imagination, he could see Ms Earring-through-her-nose lying flat on the front seat, waiting for him to approach the driver window, a cocked Smith-and-Wesson at her side.

He studied the situation for a brief moment and then slid back into his seat. He picked up the radio transmitter and barked softly into it. "838, this is 1734. Over."

Charlie's voice sputtered loudly in the stillness of the wilderness. "I'm here. Whatcha got? Switch to Channel 8. Over."

Kimble turned the dial to channel 8, then said, "I've located the camper on the side of the road, about thirteen miles east of the exit. Looks like the engine overheated. I can't see anyone in or around the vehicle. I'm wondering if it's an ambush. Over."

"Well, Daniels and Kupanski are west of you, heading your way. Over."

"Tell 'em to step on it, and keep their eyes peeled for the suspect. I'll check out the car while I'm waiting and get back to you. Over and 10-4."

"10-4." The response echoed off the shimmering heat waves.

Joe had kept his eyes shifting between the truck and the surrounding desert this whole time. Still there was no movement that he could detect. Dammit, where was that girl anyway? Why couldn't this be simple? Fear and adrenalin had begun to interact with the Big Mac he'd just eaten and a stab of indigestion filled his chest.

Joe considered waiting for the other patrol car but after a minute or two he got bored.

"OK," he said to himself. "I can do this." He picked up his billy club, unstrapped the safety on his hip holster, and made sure his handcuffs were on his belt.

He approached the back of the Toyota with step by step precision. Quietly, he peered through the grimy back window. Nothing threatening there but a few rumpled blankets and some motor oil.

He crouched his way over to the passenger window. He exchanged the billy club for the gun before seizing the door handle and yanking it open. He found no one hiding in the cab, and he let out the breath he'd been holding in a long audible sigh of relief. Another stab of indigestion made him tighten his stomach and he lowered himself onto the seat. Messy. The glove compartment door was open and the jumbled contents strewn on the seat and floor. He picked around until he found the registration.

According to the slip of paper in his hand, the 1985 Toyota was registered to a Barb Scott as of Feb 10 of that year. Well, that helped.

Joe's eyes combed the cab, looking for more clues. They strayed over the pink triangles, the silver labryses, the "goddess bless" and "AMAZON" bumper stickers that decorated the interior. A Madonna postcard and a flyer announcing a moon circle potluck at a ranch outside of Reno gave him the shivers.

"Weird," mumbled Joe. "Probably a dyke, for sure a feminist. Possibly dangerous," he added, rubbing a Dead Men Don't Rape button.

Joe wiped the top of the dashboard with his hand and found a piece of paper. It was an auto repair receipt and on the back was scrawled in shaky big letters "N-M-6-5-1-F." He shoved the paper into his breast pocket.

Back at his patrol car, he reached for the radio.

"Hey, 838, this is 1734. Over."

"838 to 1734," the voice exploded from the radio. "Are you all right? Over."

"Affirmative. Go to channel 8," said Joe, almost nonchalantly. On the private line he continued. "This girl's not anywhere around here. But I got a name on the truck registration. And I also got a possible license plate number to check. Over."

"Go ahead, and by the way, your backup should be there in a matter of minutes. Over."

He gave Charlie the information and also requested a tow truck. Then he rummaged through his pockets till he found the Tums. He popped two in his mouth and sat back on the seat, listening to the rumbling of his stomach and planning a strategy to catch his man-hating nemesis.

Daphna's moment of truth had come. She was staring wide-eyed at the side view mirror when the Toyota fell behind enshrouded in smoke. She turned resolutely to Leonie and spurted, "Leonie, there's something I have to tell you."

Then she faltered and in a quieter tone, added, "It's not too easy for me to say."

Leonie had also watched the Toyota disappear as if by magic, and her foot eased from the accelerator a bit bringing the speed down to 70. She glanced encouragingly at Daphna and announced, "I'm all ears."

Daphna wished she could think of a good starting line. She tried, "Well, do you remember when you picked me up at the rest stop..."

"Fool!" she thought to herself. "Of course she remembers. It wasn't even an hour ago." Out loud, she said, "Well, I mean, I know you remember, but when I told you about my husband, like the way he beats me up and stuff, well, I didn't tell you the exact truth." She paused. Leonie kept silent, waiting.

"Well, for instance, he's not really my husband, for example," Daphna fumbled, cursing herself silently and wondering why the right words wouldn't come out of her mouth. "Well, what I mean to say..." Daphna went on gamely.

Leonie could no longer stand Daphna's fidgeting and discomfort. "Look, honey," she interrupted. "I don't need to be involved in your domestic problems. I'm happy to help out and eager to take you where you need to go. And, believe you me, darling..."

"Leonie, I'm a lesbian," blurted Daphna. Then she stopped, waiting for Leonie's reaction.

After a couple of beats of silence, Leonie grinned and said, "Well, that's fine by me. I am too. And you're not the first woman who's ever left her husband because of that. I know of several places where I can take you where you'll be safe. You got a lover?"

Finally, Daphna had an opening line that worked. "Yeah. That's what I wanted to say. Barb's my lover and she and I had a fight. So that's when I ran into you and told you my husband beat me, so you'd take me away and teach her a lesson." Now that the confession was said, Daphna felt relieved and elated.

But Leonie's face was sad and she shook her head.

"Yeah," she said slowly, "I keep reading about lesbian battering all the time. It's hard to know exactly what to do. It's good that you left her," she said, turning to Daphna and nodding resolutely.

"Lesbian battering?" declared Daphna quizzically. "What are you talking about? Barb doesn't beat me up. We just had a fight, that's all. No, not a fight, we had an argument and I was mad. I just made it all up what I told you."

Now Leonie's brow wrinkled impatiently. "You made what up? What are you talking about? Are you a lesbian or aren't you?"

"Yes I am," answered Daphna.

"And did you fight? Did Barb hit you?" asked Leonie.

"No, she didn't hit me. And I want to go back to her. Look, stop the truck and let me out. She's back there by herself and she needs help." Daphna turned in her seat and put her hand on the door handle as if she were going to jump out.

"Hey, wait," Leonie said, startled. "She's miles back there. You can't just get out in the middle of the desert and walk."

"I've got to get back to her," Daphna stated loudly, as if Leonie had somehow misunderstood her. "Stop the truck. I want out of here."

"Slow down, Daphna. I heard ya. You want to go back there. But we're at least ten miles away. Look, we can call the highway patrol to go check on her."

"No, I want to go back there." Panic gripped Daphna and the only thing she could think of was Barb stranded on the highway. She desperately needed to know that Barb was OK. All of a sudden nothing was important to Daphna except that she get to Barb as quickly as possible. "Can't you drive me back?" she asked.

"Drive you back?" asked Leonie. "I don't know if I can drive you back. I'm on a schedule and I've got a ways to go yet. And besides, we can just call the highway patrol and you can wait for her at the next exit." Leonie's emotions were skipping around from confusion to anger, to wanting to help out, to wanting to get away from the whole situation. She felt manipulated by Daphna and she was also concerned about her. The woman was obviously a little wacky. Leonie wondered what Barb was like.

"I don't want to drive all the way to the next exit, if you're not going to drive me back. Now stop this truck so I can get out," Daphna said, decisively pushing against the door to emphasize her words.

Leonie was alarmed that Daphna might jump out of the truck while it was barrelling down the road. She braked quickly and pulled the truck off the road.

When the truck had come to a full stop, Daphna jerked open the door and climbed down. Still shaken and panicky, she yelled "Thanks for the ride," to Leonie and then started trotting down the highway.

Leonie wasn't sure what to do. Daphna would start dehydrating if she ran very far in this heat. And that was only one of the dangers out there. She wondered why Daphna didn't want her to call the highway patrol.

Leonie's eyes fell on her CB radio.

Thoughtfully, she drummed her fingers along its shiny smooth surface. From her side mirror, she could just make out the diminishing figure, settled into a heavy jog. Daphna definitely needed help. For that matter, so did her lover, Barb.

Leonie had a sudden brainstorm. She reached for her briefcase behind the seat, and pulled out a folder marked, "CONTACT DYKES, BED AND BREAKFASTS, HELPFUL ROAD ALLIES." She scanned the pages rapidly for 'Nevada'. From beneath her feet she pulled out a state map. After a few minutes of studying and comparing the lists and the map, she picked up the CB transmitter, and spoke into it.

"Howdy, my name's Leopard and I'm looking for Chicklet. Is Chicklet out there?"

Barb stretched her neck back against the dingy vinyl seat, closed her eyes, and with both hands rubbed her sore tense shoulders. She was lucky this Alfred guy had picked her up and agreed to continue the chase. It must have been the hysteria in her voice that managed to convince him her little sister had been kidnapped by a truck driver.

Under the guise of stretching her neck, Barb opened her eyes to slits and took in the details of the car and her accommodating driver. It was a scrubby 1973 baby blue Chevy Caprice with matching interior. Car clutter in the form of crushed Diet Pepsi cans and crumpled snack food bags littered the floor beneath her feet. The seat belts were crushed into the folds of the seats, apparently rarely used by Alfred or his passengers. Boxes of what seemed to be computer hardware were stacked in the back seat, covered with a sheet of clear plastic.

Alfred himself appeared to be an aging hippie defiantly hanging onto wire rim glasses and long curly hair. The thick lenses made his eyes seem huge and bulging on a face that was somewhat long and narrow with pinched cheeks and a pointed chin. The whole effect reminded Barb of some kind of strange bird.

In the first few moments she'd been in the car, Barb had breathlessly poured out a half fabricated story. Alfred, intimidated and horrified, had obeyed her instantly when she'd urged him to drive as fast as he could to catch the truck. Once he'd gotten the car up to a good 90 miles an hour, she'd calmed down a bit.

Now that she was somewhat more relaxed, he ventured to question her a little. He started out slow. "So this is an orange truck we're looking for?" he queried.

She turned her head to look at him, took a deep breath and answered, "Yes, it shouldn't be too far ahead. It was going about 80 miles an hour when my radiator blew."

"And how old is your sister?" asked Albert.

"Ten," answered Barb glibly.

"Oh, how tragic," replied Albert gently. "Why do you suppose she went with him?"

"Uh, she's blind," replied Barb, saying the first thing that came to mind. "The poor kid probably didn't know what was going on. Who knows what he said to her to get her to go with him!" Barb felt herself getting in deeper and deeper, but didn't know how to stop.

Alfred tried to imagine the scene at the rest stop. An evil truck driver comes across a blind ten year old girl wandering in a restroom area. He immediately says something to coax her into his semi. As Albert's mind was working on this scenario, Barb grabbed him by the arm and pointed to the side of the road.

"Look, there she is. Stop. Stop the car." Barb was pointing to a skinny blonde-haired woman who was striding down the shoulder of the highway. Since Albert was going 90, they passed her in five seconds. Barb's hand squeezed his arm painfully and shook him violently. "Stop, I said 'stop!' That's her."

"All right, let go, ouch," wheezed Albert, grabbing Barb's hand and pulling it off his arm. The car swerved, throwing the two of them off to one side. Albert grabbed the steering wheel and took his foot off the accelerator. The car spun now in the opposite direction, tires squealing and threatening to let go of the road. Alfred pulled on the steering wheel. His foot found the brake and pushed down hard, as he struggled to straighten out the car. Now the car went off the road past the shoulder, and then onto the bumpier surface of the desert floor, finally coming to a stop.

Barb was slammed sideways into the dashboard, cracking her head on the windshield, and then was thrown to the floor. She lay silent and stunned, amid the trash. Alfred sat hunched in the driver's seat, fingers locked onto the steering wheel, eyes shut tight, breathing heavily. Both seemed frozen, unable to move, or make a sound. A dust

That Day on Highway 62 - Woody Blue

cloud rose into the air around them and then slowly drifted back to the ground.

Barb let out the air in her lungs. "Are you all right?" she asked, raising her hand to the lump that was swelling on her head. There was no answer and Barb hoisted herself off the floor and nudged him. "Hey," she said, "are you all right?"

Albert finally turned his head to her, swallowed deeply, and whispered, "Don't EVER do that again."

"Sorry," said Barb. "Are you all right?"

Albert continued to stare at her, his eyes bulging and his wire rims tilted on his face. "Yes, I'm all right. Why did you do that? Who is that out there?"

"That's my girlfriend, Daphna," Barb faltered.

"Your girlfriend? How did she get out here? I thought we were looking for your sister," said Alfred, still talking in a half whisper.

Barb flushed and felt her ears turning red with embarrassment. "Oh, Alfred, I'm sorry. I meant my girlfriend. I really didn't mean to cause you any trouble. I was really stuck. Look, I gotta go get her. I'll bring her back, OK, so you can meet her." As Barb spoke, she began scrambling around on the seat until she found the door handle, and yanked it open. Clumsily she crawled out, before Albert could respond.

It had only been an hour since Daphna and Barb had last seen each other, but when they approached each other there in the desert, it felt like years.

First they looked at each other with uncertainty, wondering which of the several emotions whirling within would express itself first. Relief? Anger? Joy? Pain? Love? It was all there, swirling around in their eyes and in the set of their mouths.

So intense was the moment that neither of them could decide how or what to say to each other. After a full three minutes of saying and doing nothing, neither of them daring to move closer or step farther apart, Daphna finally spoke the one word that came to her mind. "Well?" she asked.

Barb's eyes got huge and she sputtered, "Well what?"

Daphna's eyes were soft, vulnerable, and strong all at the same time. "Well," she said, "What do you want?" Barb stared at her, rage and tenderness seesawing back and forth within her.

Eventually she found her voice. "I want you, Daphna," Barb said brokenly. "I want you and me to be together for a long time. That's all I know." Her eyes met Daphna's for a moment more and then she turned her back and stared at the desert through an ocean of tears. She stood stiff, proud, and alone.

Daphna scuffed the ground with the toe of her shoe. "I get so mad sometimes, Barb, cuz I don't know if I'm living my life or yours. I can't let go of my dreams, Barb. I can't ignore what's inside of me, or change it just because it doesn't suit you."

Daphna continued softly. "I want us to be together too, Barb. And I want a family. And I want to know from you if it's possible to have both. We have to talk about it and we have to make some choices. Barb, I love you. Talk to me."

The desert stillness was unbearable. Finally Barb shifted and then turned to Daphna, arms out. "Hold me, honey," she said tearfully. "Hold me a little while, and then let's go home and talk."

EPILOGUE

Officer Joe Kimble, followed by Officers Daniels and Kupanski, found Daphna and Barb miles from any vehicles, holding each other and sobbing. Alfred, thankful he was still alive, continued on his way. Leonie left the scene after talking the matter over with Chicklet, the dispatcher at McCafferty's Rest Stop. Chicklet and Leonie cut a deal and the five dollar gas bill was paid. Chicklet contacted the highway patrol and told them to bring Barb back to McCafferty's where her truck had been towed. Thus, Daphna, Barb and the brave Toyota were safely reunited.

Laurie Fitzpatrick: I was born in 1962 in Ancon, Canal Zone. The family moved to Knoxville, Tennessee in 1965, where I lived for the most part until the age of 24. I hold a Masters in Fine Arts from Tyler School of Art, and am self taught as a writer. It is my desire to document, expose and elucidate the concerns of women, lesbians, and gays, using the South as an obvious metaphor for dualistic, oppressive and nurturing social forces. I grew up in the South, and believing the environment shapes the individual and prompts their actions, I write about what I know the best.

MY HAIRCUT

I shiver, leaning against the brick wall of the barber shop, more from anxiety than cold on this February afternoon. My discomfort grows with the awareness that what I want is childish: to prove something to Mom and Dad after five years of struggle to become my own woman.

This shop is on the first floor of the Parker Hotel -- a place that smells of disinfectant and rents mostly to old men -- located on 13th street amid pornography shops, strip joints, and the city's most disreputable bars. My best friend Dan told me about this particular shop, where he gets his hair cut in a very short, ordinary masculine fashion. I want my hair to look like his, instead of long and limp, an apathetic statement. Best of all, a haircut from this place costs a mere six bucks. However, Dan warned me this barber traditionally serves only male customers.

I shudder, thinking maybe it won't be so impossible up here in the North, especially in this neighborhood where money can buy anything.

The message my mother left on my answering machine this morning sings in my head, taunting me, "Andie, me an' Daddy have been a prayin' you'll come home for your birthday. To help Jesus out some, we already bought you a plane ticket. We wanna show off our 'big-city-girl' at church next Sunday. I'll call later with all the details. We love you, Honey."

I laugh, recalling a favorite drunken chant from my high school party days that we screamed until our throats were raw, "Beat me with your Bible Belt. Cover me with Bible welts."

Of course, this morning was the first I heard of our little birthday celebration. I managed to avoid returning home to see my parents mostly by ignoring their repeated telephone calls. Last year they got really desperate and pulled the ticket buying stunt. I made them pay for their guilt trip by ignoring them, and they lost five hundred dollars.

This year, however, I am ready to face my parents, but on my terms. To do so, I will get something I have wanted since I hit puberty: a man's haircut from a barber in a barber shop. I could have my hair cut by a stylist for twenty dollars or more, but I would end up with an androgynous look, at best. Only a barber shop cut will do: short, devoid of feminine elements, guaranteed to shock the folks back home.

I gather my courage and peek into the shop. In the center of the window, upon a dusty stool sits a small hand painted sign that reads "Enjoy Barbering As Did Your Dad." I inhale deeply, filling my chest with sharp cold air, steeling myself against the rejection I have encountered before.

I was fourteen the first time I tried to get a man's haircut, back in my hometown of Newport, Tennessee. My dad coaches the high school football team, the Newport Black Panthers, and as a result is best friends with every man in town. To uphold his tough and competent image, Daddy wore his silver blond hair in a Marine style buzz cut. As a proven football expert, Daddy's views on other aspects of rural life were sought, such as what is the best caliber of bullet to kill a deer, the optimum age to castrate a bull, or the sturdiest American truck money can buy. Daddy was generous with his opinions, which were widely repeated and discussed. Nobody, however, spoke of the numerous times he was spotted in his Chevy truck on the highway, weaving dangerously in and out of traffic, drunk at the wheel.

The people of Newport followed our family's trials and tribulations as though we were the Royals of England. They knew all about my mother's miscarriage in '67, how she became born again in '68, and Daddy too in '75 following tricky prostrate surgery. Likewise, everyone knew what a disappointment and behavior problem I had turned out to be. A few went so far as to say I should have been born male, and not female; but seeing as how God never makes mistakes, the blame always fell back on me. A footnote to this ongoing drama was how my father insisted I wear my hair long and have it lightened to a platinum blonde sheen. He was oft quoted as saying, "My little girl should look as pretty and feminine as she really is inside."

I would spit when I heard this, saying, "What he knows about me inside could fill a thimble without spilling over."

The town barber, Mr. Cook, had a son who played quarterback for the Panthers, and was of course best friends with my father. One Saturday morning, I strolled casually up to Mr. Cook's shop, where he leaned against the door jamb squinting his tiny blue eyes against the sun. I stopped just short of the threshold to his 'male only' sanctuary and he straightened up, effectively blocking my entrance.

Clearing my throat, I imitated my dad's friendliest request, "Good morning, Mr. Cooke. I wonder if I might get a hair cut today?"

He deflated me with one quick stab of his sharp eyes, then smiled and said, "You have such pretty hair, you don't really want t'get it cut off. Besides, its against health rules for me to cut a woman's hair in a barber shop."

"What health rules?" I asked impetuously.

"Them." he said, pointing his black plastic comb toward the shop window, at his Draughn's School of Barbering diploma he received in 1943. He said, "Now git before someone sees you hangin' around here."

I ran off, resenting my father more than ever.

Touching the glass of the shop window, the cold seeps into my fingertips until they hurt. Just beyond the sign the barber works on a customer. He is old and he moves slowly, calmly trimming the thin silver hair of an even older man. I think, no way is this guy going to cut my hair.

The barber pulls the brown apron away from the customer's wattled throat, shakes the silver fragments of hair on to the floor, careful not to spill any on the old man's shirt. I duck out of sight when the barber looks my way.

I say to myself, "The man hasn't said no to you yet. And he might just say yes." Suddenly, the door swings open and hits me, but I am too scared to flinch. Straining to remain invisible, only my eyes move as the old customer feebly emerges, his silver hair trimmed neat, short, and very butch. I desperately want my hair to look that good.

As the shop door closes and locks itself, I pull away from the wall and tap shyly on the window. The barber shuffles over, unlocks the door and looks up at me, puzzled.

I blurt out, "Would you please cut my hair?"

The barber frowns then cranes his head to see if anyone is behind me, waiting in ambush.

"Please?" I ask, almost begging.

"Yea, OK." His gaze falls to my shoes and he steps back from the door. I pass and he mumbles, "As long as you don't want anything fancy."

I sit in the only chair in the room: an enormous green vinyl lump that could serve as a prop for a Frankenstein movie. The barber disappears into a small room in the back of the shop. Turning in the chair to face the mirror, I pull a strand of hair, enjoying a twinge of pain as I pluck it out. In the mirror I watch the old barber come up from behind carrying a brown plastic apron in one hand, and a stiff white collar in the other. He covers my chest with the apron and pins the collar around my throat, then asks me what I want done.

I say, "Make it half an inch short all around, but leave it an inch long on top."

"No problem." he says while slowly shaking his head 'no.' He leans over my shoulder and pulls a black plastic comb and a pair of scissors from a jar of green fluid on the shelf, then says, "I have to rinse these off," and leaves me again.

I cannot relax knowing full well he might change his mind. I close my eyes, anxious to be initiated into a ritual of the male world that they take entirely for granted: the barber shop haircut. I think, 'Old magician, I give you six bucks and you work some magic that'll change my life. Make this reparation to me and I won't come back to embarrass us both with my need for revenge.' I am determined to sit here until he tells me to leave.

I mark the old man's progress by the noise he makes. He mumbles to himself, then runs the tap. He comes up from behind, the rinsed instruments clutched in his bony hand. I smile encouragingly at him in the mirror, the muscles in my jaw as tight as corset straps.

He says, "It's been forty years since I cut a woman's hair, and that was my wife's hair."

I maintain a polite smile and my silence prompts him to act. He lifts the comb and sinks it into my hair, pulling it down from the crown

My Haircut - Laurie Fitzpatrick

of my head, covering my face and creating a mask he cuts away the next instant.

As I relax, the warm vinyl sighs, gives in and I sink into the chair. His thin silver scissors chew at the hair, devouring a type of beauty I could care less about.

This will be the second time in my life that I will wear my hair short. The first and last time I got it cut was by my drunken aunt back in Newport.

One spring morning in my senior year of high school, I talked my two best friends, Lydia and Marie, into skipping school to ride around in my new car, a 68 Dart convertible, an early graduation present from my dad. When Daddy handed the keys to me, he emphasized that the car had a V-8 engine under the hood with only 40,000 miles on it, and that it was not a toy.

But a joyride on a bright spring day was not all I had in mind. I made sure that Lydia sat next to me in the front seat, leaving Marie to hang out the passengers side. As we barreled down the back country roads, I would pull the steering wheel hard to the left and make Lydia slide into me. I shivered with excitement as her body pressed fully against mine. My car stunt frightened her, so after doing it two or three times, I stopped the car, stroked her bare knee and reassured her I would not do it again. She giggled then punched my arm; and we took off again, squealing tires spitting gravel like buckshot, showering trees, bushes, an occasional mailbox.

I felt ten feet tall and in control of everything behind the wheel of that car. Fortified, I proclaimed my determination to do the one thing that would truly free me and shock everyone we knew: I would get my long blonde princess hair cut short.

Lydia challenged, "Just how short?

I said, "I'll get it shaved shorter than one of Daddy's Panthers."

Marie chimed in, "I'd give money to see that. No way would anyone in their right mind do it for you."

"Well," I drawled slowly, "we have two choices. Either we can drive for three hours to Knoxville and I'll have a beautician cut my hair, or we can find someone in town who isn't in their right mind who'll do it." I smiled confidently to Lydia, then to Marie, countering their skeptical expressions, "I know just the person. We're gonna pay a visit to my Daddy's own little sister."

We drove to town, to my Aunt Starlette Horner's Hollywood Hair and Expert Dog Grooming Salon.

Opening the door, we were assailed by hairspray vapors laced with the sickening odor of scotch. Aunt Starlette had laid herself out on a pink vinyl lawnchair in the back of the shop, with a red satin pillow beneath her neck supporting her head just right to protect her hair from getting mashed. She lifted her head up slowly, balancing her freshly combed and lacquered cotton candy yellow bee-hive hairdo, and called out, "What you girls doin' here at this time of the day? Shouldn't you be in school?"

I did all the talking. "No, not today." Lying was as easy as breathing, "Its a religious holiday. Flag Day."

"Oh well, that's nice." She took a drag on her cigarette, blew the smoke out of her nose and said, "What you girls want?"

"I need me a real short haircut for summer." I explained, "When it hits ninety, this hair feels like an old wet dish rag wrapped around my head."

Aunt Starlette reached up, grabbed the towel rack above her head and let out a long groan as she hoisted herself off the lawnchair. Lurching toward us, she had to keep pushing her feet into her tattered blue slippers so they would stay on. A cigarette hung from her lip, a simmering white stick glued in place with spit. Squinting at the three of us from inside a cloud of mentholated smoke, the cigarette wagging up and down, she said, "I don't believe your daddy would like that."

"Oh, he won't mind," I chirped reassuringly. "You see, he gave me twenty dollars so I could get it done in Knoxville, but I thought it would be just as good to get it done here and support our local economy." I pulled two tens out of my pocket, money hoarded from Christmas, and waved the bills in Starlette's face. Smiling, I said, "It's yours, if you want it."

She snatched the money out of my hand, stuffed it into the elastic waistband of her polyester slacks and said, "If your Daddy said it's OK, then I guess it is. You sit there." I took my place in the powder blue vinyl styling chair. Starlette assumed a business like stance as she ran her fingers through my long blonde hair. She mumbled, her lips flicked ashes into my hair, "It's a shame t'cut it, but if your Daddy said so, well ... I'd better use the poodle shears to get it even all over." She dropped my hair and wandered off toward the back of the shop, looking for the shears.

My Haircut - Laurie Fitzpatrick

Lydia moved close to me, flashed a half empty pint of scotch and whispered, "I fished it out of the spider plant by the front door."

I took a swig, handed the bottle to Marie who took a sip. She gave the bottle to Lydia to swallow what was left.

Marie burped and told Lydia, "When Starlette gets back, go back'ere to the lawn chair and see if there's some more."

Aunt Starlette returned with the shears, plugged them in, switched them on, and plowed the whirring blades into my hair. The blonde strands fell in graceful ribbons and collected in piles on the floor. Working the shears deftly for a knock down drunk, Starlette mumbled over and over, "It's a shame, such purty hair, such purty hair," but in less than five minutes my head was shaved close to bald.

All four of us stared at my reflection in the mirror, our mouths hanging open, stunned by what Starlette had done. As Starlette's jaw worked up and down, a drop of spittle crested her lower lip, releasing the cigarette. It tumbled through the air and landed in a small hair pile. Starlette dropped the shears and began to whine, "Oh Sweet Jesus, what did you girls make me do? What's Jack gonna do to me when he sees this?"

"Dammed if I know," I said as I jumped out of the chair and kicked more hair into the smoldering pile. "Look at the bright side, you can sweep up that hair and sell it to make a fine wig." Marie stood by the front door holding it open, signalling me to come on, and Lydia patted the outline of a second pint hidden under her T-shirt. We cut out fast, leaving Starlette to pass out in her lawnchair.

We drove to the lake, passing the bottle and taking long, hot draughts of scotch. I needed time to figure out how to present my new haircut to Daddy without getting killed.

I parked the car on the grass next to the water, and remained behind the wheel brushing my hand over my short hair. It felt furry, like petting a baby animal. Lydia and Marie sprawled out on the grass like cows, in the shade of a tall oak that leaned over the lake. Lydia took a mouthful of the amber colored booze, swallowed then gasped, "You should walk right into the house and tell the old man to go straight to hell. That's what I'd do!"

"Like hell you would," I said. "I can't go home tonight, it's that simple."

Marie took the bottle and sucked down the last of the scotch, coughed then offered, "You can stay in the carriage house out back that we fixed up for Aunt Leet. She died of a stroke in there, though."

I laughed, "I suppose I'd have to stay there about two years until the hair grows back, and I think my daddy would suspect something."

"He might think you got pregnant and ran away outta shame." said Lydia.

"Never," I said quietly, gazing down at her reclining figure, along her perfect plump legs and round ass. Lydia looked up at me, caught my eyes on her and smiled. I looked quickly away, staring with great interest out over the water at the flickering spot the sun burned on the lake's calm surface. I said flatly, "Get rid of that bottle. I'm ready to go home."

Somehow, I managed to drive them home without killing anybody or getting pulled over by a state trooper.

I eased my car onto the crumbling asphalt road that ran the last two miles to my house. This was where my dad taught me how to drive, so I knew every dip, pothole, and curve in the road by heart. I loved to take it as fast as I could, my personal record stood at 86 MPH, but if I hit a pothole, or did something worse like fishtail the car, my rule said to slow it down.

I gripped the steering wheel and pressed the accelerator pedal to the floor, -- eased it up to sixty as the car bucked and swerved around this pot hole, then that one. The curve by McGhee's farm came up fast, and I took it at 70, easy -- then on to the straight-away. My breath came hard, and adrenaline cleared the fog from my head. I only reached 78 MPH, but the power surging through my nerves gave me plenty of courage to tell Daddy I would never let my hair grow longer than an inch.

I pulled the car up into the yard in front of the house, parked it, jumped out and slammed the door. I heard my father's voice coming from behind the house and stormed toward it. He was inside the ramshackle barn out back, talking to his dog. His speech slurred -- obviously he had tanked up as well -- as he said, "You like Mighty Dog? You do? Well, I think I got some here that you can have."

My dad named his dog Lil'Boy because it had been born the runt of the litter, with all white fur and human looking blue eyes. Daddy hand raised the puppy and trained it to point and retrieve. I was present the first time Lil'Boy heard a shotgun blast, and watched as the dog keeled over in a dead faint. My dad poured a cold beer on the Lil'Boy, resuscitating him. The animal jumped up, ran back to the barn and never dared to venture outside its four walls again.

But somehow, Lil'Boy's overwhelming fear of the world made my dad love the dog all the more. He would say, "Lil'Boy is the smartest child I ever raised." I hated that stupid dog because it got more love from my dad in one day than I got from the man in a whole damn year.

My fingers curled around the cool metal of the latch on the barn door. The cold touch jarred the bones of my fingers, hand then arm, made my heart leap and prevented further action. Instead, I peeked through an open knothole in the door and saw Daddy swaying in the dim light, leaning over the small pen where the agoraphobic dog lived.

Because it is impossible to open this door quietly, I tried opening it slowly, hoping to make less noise. The effort failed -- the rusty hinges released a protracted scream, announcing my entrance to God and everyone. I tried to back out, but it was too late -- Daddy turned, saw me and bellowed, "Oh my loving God, what the HELL did you do to yer hair?"

I slipped, fell in what I hoped was mud, scrambled to my feet and ran into the house. I flew past Mom who stood at the kitchen stove cramming a huge chunk of meat into a steaming pot. She called after me as I disappeared up the stairs, "Andie, is something wrong with the dog?"

I locked my bedroom door behind me, fell to my knees and vomited into the Snoopy wastebasket next to my desk.

An hour later, the three of us sat at the dinner table. Daddy ignored us for the most part, except to stare at me occasionally and slowly shake his head from side to side, to state silently that 'he just did not know why.'

My mom attempted to make the peace by lying outright, "Andie went in to get her hair lightened today, and well, your sister was in her usual condition. She accidentally left the peroxide in too long and it burned th'hair right off."

Daddy cast a dead fish-eyed look on her to let her know that he was no fool, then sipped his beer, seeming to prefer it to the pot roast and baked apples Mom had fixed. Pretending not to be annoyed, she used her smooth as butter voice, "Jack, it's only hair and it will grow back in time."

To which I replied, still drunk, "Not if I can help it."

My dad jumped all over this, yelling, "All I want is for my little girl to look beautiful."

"Oh big news flash," I cried, "as if you haven't told me that every day of my God-damned life!" I pulled the car keys out of my pocket and slung them across the table at him. They crashed in his plate, knocking a hot slice of gravy soaked meat into his lap. We both jumped up, and I screamed at him, "I don't want your stupid car!" then ran to my room.

My dad did not to speak to me for three months, up until the very day I boarded the Greyhound bus bound for the Northeast, where I chose to go to college.

I stood slumped against the bus, my hair a medium length shag, fingering the peeling decal of the skinny gray dog. Leaping, a smile on its face, it could be the ghost of Lil'Boy making his way to freedom on what would be his luckiest day. My dad took a minute to recite a tired farewell speech, "If you come back to Jesus then maybe you'll find that happiness you knew when you was a little girl. You will always be my little girl. Now don't ever forget that."

He kissed my forehead then patted my cheek. I wanted to bite his hand.

Five years later, I still see his pot bellied yet overpowering form, dwindle as the bus carried me away, until he looked like every other fat old dad in America. When the bus turned onto the highway, Daddy disappeared from my view.

The old barber trims and shapes my hair, perfecting his work. Gradually, he combs it more than he cuts it, then he stands back and asks, "How's it look?"

I briefly examine myself in the mirror, and say, "Looks great."

He brushes bits of hair away from my neck and shoulders with a tiny broom, unfastens the collar and expertly peels off the apron. I climb out of the chair and hand him six dollars.

Walking home, I notice how my head feels lighter, but strangely I can still feel my old hair hanging around my neck and shoulders. The air bites my ears, so I hurry to my apartment.

I examine my new hair in the bathroom mirror, looking closer at myself than I dared to in the barber shop. I do not look masculine, nor any less feminine. I look more like myself, while not looking like me anymore: my eyes seem bigger, the bones of my face more angular and pronounced, and the full strength of my chin is revealed. On the outside, my face and hair reflect the way I truly feel about myself.

But on the inside, I am aware of a strangeness between two who knew of each other for years and have only just met: the one I felt my self to be who is now the one I look like.

I suddenly realize these two are one -- they are me -- and I am whole.

Janet Mason: I am thirty five years old and live with my lover, Barbara, and cat, Midnight, in Philadelphia where I walk dogs and give nature walks (for fun and money), ghost write articles and speeches (just for money), and write fiction and poetry (mostly for no money and lots of fun) as much and often as I can. "Waiting for Liftoff" was written after going to a lesbian bar and meeting a young dyke who asked me to shoot a game of pool with her, and then proceeded to scratch on the eight. Obsessing about what her life might be like brought me to terms with my own emotional reality of being torn between two different worlds.

WAITING FOR LIFTOFF

If anyone cared to add up the hours, they'd know I've spent plenty of 'em in this place. Even more in places just like it. Dim lights. Hazy air. Shiny red stools. Pool tables with quarters lined up. Barmaids with too much makeup or none at all. Thick glass bottles stacked up like Christmas presents. Sometimes I just sit and stare at those bottles. Think how my life is like 'em. Slow Gin. Chivas Regal. Wild Turkey. Gordon's Gin. Blackberry Brandy. Sweet sticky love. So sweet, I stay far away from it. Cool dry afternoons. Drinks over ice that slide away from me quick as a cue ball from the stick.

But most of my days come right out of the tap. Rolling Rock. Budweiser. Coors. Nothing light. Nothing sweet. Nothing exotic. Just steady streams of time. Predictable. Endless. Like me walking into this bar every afternoon. Four-thirty on the dot. The TV that's always on. The same songs played over and over. The only thing that changes is the weather. And the way I feel. Some days I walk into the bar and the beery smell of stale smoke feels like coming home. Other days I want to choke. But I don't know where else to go. So I walk in. Sit down. Order a beer. Check out the crowd.

It's kinda like work. Walking in the same back door everyday. Turning on the same Xerox machines. Lifting the same reams of paper. Saying good morning to the same faces. Sometimes it feels like I never went home the night before.

At least here the faces are different. There's not so many regulars as my neighborhood bar. This place is special. Mostly girls come here. And don't think it's like ladies night at the other places. No sir. These are girls who like girls. All kinds of 'em. Butches. Fems. The in-betweens, like me. My hair's just as short as the rest of the butch girls. But I always wear something fem too. Like my tight jeans with the open zippers up the backs of my calves. And I do look pretty good in 'em. Twenty-four waist. Slim hips.

Now, don't think I'm stuck on myself. But even my friends in the neighborhood say I'm a looker. Fact is, I'm surprised more girls don't buy me drinks. Or at least come over and talk to me. 'Cept that lots of 'em come in twos or small groups. All clustered together like they don't wanna know anyone else.

But it's not all their fault. I am kinda shy. But don't go round telling people that. I'd rather do anything 'cept ask a girl to dance. And, like I said, I don't know why more don't ask me. Sometimes I think I'm too butch for the butches and too fem for the fems. My friend Amy, from work, tells me that's the old way of thinking. But I tell her, that's what I see.

That's why I play pool. It's easy to put a couple of quarters on the table. And if nobody's playing I go right up to a girl and ask her if she wants to play. Doesn't matter if she's by herself, in a group, or with another girl. Though I do try to stay away from those couples who look all stuck together like the epoxy glue commercial.

None of that stuff for me. I've only been with a woman two or three times. And never for more than one night. I say two or three times 'cause I woke up with a strange woman one morning and didn't remember what happened. My head was pounding. And I sure as hell was embarrassed. So I just grabbed my clothes and caught the first bus home.

Now, don't you be spreading no stories about me not being able to handle my liquor. Maybe when I was younger. But not now. I'll be turning twenty-two in a couple of months. And most times I remember everything the next morning. The thing that makes me saddest is when I scratch a good game of pool. I do it almost every night. Then I know I've had too much to drink and it's time to go home.

Playing pool is my kind of flying. Amelia Earhardt had her airplane and I have my green felt sky. I rack up that gleaming triangle. Scatter all those colors with my break and off I go.

I get real relaxed during a game. Sometimes I'll even start talking to the girl I'm playing with. Most often, I'll ask what her sign is. I don't want to ask nothing personal like where she lives or works.

I guess being gay is special, but it sure ain't easy.

When I was sixteen, my best friend, Mary Ellen, got caught making out with another girl in St. Mary's locker room. Fortunately, it wasn't me she got caught with. Even though I made out with Mary Ellen in that locker room more than anyone else did. It just so happened that she got caught with Sylvie instead.

At first I was jealous. Mary Ellen was kinda cheating on me. But it wasn't like I never sneaked around the locker room with nobody else. So I decided to let things be. Then I found out that her parents tried to put her in reform school. Reform school. Like she tried to rob a bank. It turned out they couldn't send her to reform school. But they did send her far away to live with her great aunt in some little coal town. The last I heard she was married and on her third baby.

After Mary Ellen got sent away, I didn't make out with anyone in the locker room no more. And it wasn't till last year that I found this bar. Amy told me about it. She had me pegged right away. She comes in here once in a while, too. But most afternoons, she's too busy with all her activities. When I ask her what she's been up to, she sounds like one of those overworked goody two shoes candy striper girls I used to stay away from in high school.

She's involved with all kinds of things. Spending time with AIDS patients, helping girls get abortions, picking up trash. She's just like those candy stripers. Always trying to get me to go with her. "You do what you want," I say. "I'm gonna shoot pool with the girls after work. If you wanna come along, that's fine."

One of Amy's projects was to get me to stop drinking. She was sticking pamphlets in brown paper bags and bringing 'em to me at work. I told her to watch out. "People are gonna be thinking you're the one with the problem," I said, "carrying those bags around like some wino."

Then she told me she did have a drinking problem. That she doesn't drink any more but still craves it. The only thing that stops her, she says, is that she hit rock bottom almost four years ago. Lost her job and ran outta friends to borrow money from. "If it wasn't for Sobriety Sisters," she said, "I'd still be drinking now."

Waiting for Liftoff - Janet Mason

Sobriety Sisters sounds to me like a real goody two shoes group. But Amy says it's for girls like us who drink too much. Says it saved her life. Even though she quit drinking three and a half years ago, she still goes to meetings. Makes her feel good about herself, she says.

After I heard her story, I broke down and looked at a couple pamphlets. Almost made me feel sicker than a hangover. Pictures of car accidents and twisted up livers and stuff. Finally, I just told her to stop bringing them in. I don't drive and far as I know my liver's fine. To my surprise, she stopped bothering me. Sometimes she even comes with me after work. Though she only drinks cokes since she's a sobriety girl.

She did get to me though. I have to admit. 'Specially when I go from the bar downtown straight to my neighborhood bar. Sometimes I've been drinking so long, I forget what I was drinking. And the next morning I always feel like hell.

That's how I started my day this morning. More than a hangover was hammering at my head, though. It all started yesterday afternoon when me and Amy came in here together and she started telling me about some parade she went to.

"I went to the Gay and Lesbian Pride March in New York last year. Did you ever go?"

I was in New York once to see the Radio City music show when I was a kid. But I didn't think that's what she was talking about. So I just said, "What's that?"

"Every year, hundreds of thousands of lesbians and gay men go to New York and march in a big parade. It's wild. People carry banners about how proud they are to be gay and lesbian.

"And there are huge floats, too. Some of the women drum and dance and some of the men even dress up like women. It's been going on for twenty years. It's a tradition, just like the Thanksgiving Day parade in Philadelphia. But it's a lot more fun."

"Twenty years? That's almost as long as I been around," I said.

Amy laughed. "Well, I been around about five years longer than you but I still think it's amazing."

"It sounds like fun," I said, "but I don't know why people have to go out and talk about how they feel. And I don't know about that word. It kinda makes me embarrassed."

"What word?" Amy looked at me like she was concerned about my health or something.

"You know that word...lesbian. It sounds too much like lezzy to me."

Amy reached over to where my hand was resting on the bar and put her hand over it. I was shocked. Amy and I are pretty good friends. But we don't go around touching each other or anything. But then I got used to her hand being there and started to like it.

"Maureen." She looked into my eyes. "The best thing you can be is a lesbian. It means that you love women. It means you hold yourself in the highest regard."

"Well...maybe." I was far from convinced. But I did like the way her hand felt on mine. Right out in public. And with me not being real drunk or anything.

"You know where the word lesbian comes from?" Amy's brown eyes were still staring right into mine.

I shook my head from side to side.

"A long time ago there was an island named Lesbos. In fact, it's still there today. Thousands of years ago mostly women lived on the island. And they all loved women. That's why we're called lesbians."

I wondered if she was making this up as she went along. An island with all women? Sounded a bit off to me. But I didn't want to be rude. Besides, I liked the way her hand felt on mine.

"Who lives on the island now?" I turned on my stool to face her a little better. But I made sure my hand stayed in the same place.

"Both women and men live on the island now. It's part of Greece. And not all the women love women. But everyone is a Lesbian. It's their ethnic identity."

"Even the men are lesbians?" Things were starting to get real confusing.

"I have a book about it in my apartment. If you want to come over some time I'll show it to you."

This was the first time Amy invited me to her apartment and I was real flattered. But I'm not one to give away my feelings so I looked back at her and said, "Sure. Why not. I'll come over and take a look at it."

Amy seemed to suddenly realize that her hand was on top of mine the whole time. She took it away real shy like. Then we just sat quiet for a few minutes.

She had to go to a meeting and I promised my gang I'd meet them in Sam's Place, so we left the bar and caught separate trolleys.

Twenty minutes later I was across the Avenue. Girard Avenue to outsiders. But those of us who were born in the neighborhood call it Jaahaaahrd. A long drawn out word. Lots of row homes and cobblestones between the beginning and the end.

There was a time when I hardly ever left the neighborhood. I used to work in one of the mills there after high school. But not anymore. My friends told me I was crazy leaving a job in the neighborhood to work downtown. With bus fare and all. And I don't make that much more money than I used to.

My friend Peg said maybe I thought I was better than the rest of 'em. Now, I like my neighborhood. But taking this job at the print shop was the best thing I coulda done. If I stayed in the neighborhood I wouldn't have met Amy. Like I told Peg, just 'cause my family worked in the mills for three generations doesn't mean I have to.

The sun was going down when I got off the trolley. Grey pink haze reflected off the small glass window squares as I walked up to the bar. The first thing I always look at when I go into Sam's is the Coors sign on the wooden wall. You know the kind I mean. With the orange letters and the white neon mountain behind 'em. I always get a kick outta that sign. Maybe 'cause the closest thing around Sam's to a mountain is the El tracks that run high above the bar.

Sam was inside, bending over the sink, wiping off some glasses. When he heard the door bang behind me, he stood up. "Hey Maureen. How ya doing?" He waved at me with his white towel.

Peg, Ceil, and Linda were at the back of the bar, gathered around the dart board. When I walked up to 'em they all slapped me on the back.

After we sat down at a table, Peg started in about her ex-husband again. "That damn faggot left me just so he could hang out with his faggot friends," she said.

She eyed me suspiciously. "Guess you see lots of 'em downtown."

My gut clenched. But I can be real cool. "Well, I'm not exactly looking for 'em," I answered. And that's half true. I hardly notice any of the guys downtown, gay or straight.

Most of the time, when Peg starts in on faggots I let it slide. Not that it doesn't bother me. I'm just not one to get riled up about things. But my conversation with Amy was still in my head. I was thinking how lesbian is 'sposed to be a good word. And how I should be proud.

I know Peg's still my friend. But sometimes she can be downright bitter. One time, when she was still married, she started asking me why I never date anyone. I told her I didn't intend to have nobody telling me what to do and using up all my money at that. I knew Fred took Peg's money to buy drugs.

Peg narrowed her eyes and said, "What's the matter with that? You sure you don't like girls, like those lezzies we heard about in school?" Now I didn't know what she heard about anyone else--or me for that matter. And I wasn't asking. I just said, "Well, you ain't heard me ask you out for a date now, have ya?" The girls hooted and Peg shut up.

Most often, I have a good time hanging out with my crowd in Sam's. I get to catch up on the news about the mills and the people in the neighborhood. Seems like someone's always dying, getting married, or having a baby. And once in a while, someone goes to jail.

But ever since Peg's ex-husband left her, she loves to start in on faggots. The other girls always laugh. Seems that they think making jokes about faggots is a good way to pass the time. I think they like to call 'em faggots just cause the guys are always walking out on them. Used to be that they talked about black people just as bad.

Now, I don't have to be no goody two shoes like Amy to know it's not right to put people down. And I told 'em so. But they didn't listen. Just laughed and said that working downtown must be getting to me.

Then about a year ago, Ceil went and got herself a black boyfriend. She's still with him, too. Not that she ever brings him into Sam's or even into the neighborhood. You never know what could happen. But she told us all about him. How she loved him. How she was afraid her father might keel over if he found out.

It took a little while, but the crowd did stop talking nasty about black people. 'Cept that Peg made snide remarks every now and then. But the rest of us ignored her. Or told her to shut up.

I thought about this a lot. I wondered if I could do the same thing Ceil did. Like maybe I could just say, "Hey, remember when Peg asked me if I like girls. Well I do. And I'd 'preciate it if you'd stop with the faggot jokes." Sometimes I think I could do it. 'Cause we're tight. Like sisters. We help each other. But then I don't know. Even though Ceil's boyfriend is black, he's still a guy.

Every time I think of telling 'em, I remember Mary Ellen. The way she got sent away and never came back. Never even wrote me either. Then I think about my family. How embarrassed they'd be if word got around. I do have my own place now. A one room apartment over the Fourth Street diner. But my parents and my brothers only live three blocks away. And I got cousins, aunts and uncles all over this neighborhood.

Sometimes when my crowd starts with the faggot jokes, I take a deep breath and say to myself, this is it, I'm gonna tell 'em.

Then I get a knot in my stomach and my jaw gets stiff. And I can't say nothing.

But I can't laugh either. That would be like laughing at myself. I guess I'm kinda like a female faggot. I'm a girl who likes girls. When I think about the way it used to be with me and Mary Ellen, doesn't seem like there's anything wrong with it.

Just two girls who like each other a whole lot. Doesn't seem so bad, does it? But the way people carry on about us. Calling us lezzics and queers. Saying we're sick. Kinda makes me afraid to get to know a girl better.

I thought about that parade going on for twenty years. I was just two years old and people like me were being proud in New York. It made me happy. But at the same time it made my blood boil. All those years of holding in my feelings. The nuns in high school never told us about no island called Lesbos. They just told us homosexuals were sick. That's why Mary Ellen got sent away.

So instead of sitting there not saying anything, I got up and ordered a beer. When I got back to the table Peg was making her wrist limp and talking funny. Then she got up and swished her hips from side to side. Ceil and Linda were laughing like it was the funniest thing they ever saw. When Peg sat down she narrowed her eyes until they were two little mean slits.

"There's nothing in the world I hate more than a Goddamn faggot."

I gulped down my beer so I wouldn't throw it at Peg. Then I stood up and looked down at her. "You don't know what the hell you're talking about." My voice got louder and louder. "Fred ain't no faggot. He's slept with just about every woman in town who'd let him."

My arms and legs shook as I talked. But I didn't let that stop me. "Furthermore, you don't even know any gay men. And you'd be a whole lot better off hanging with them than you were with Fred."

I flung my arm down and it knocked my beer glass clear off the table. Nobody moved an inch. Peg, Ceil and Linda were staring at me like I just came down from some other planet.

I glared at Peg as I spoke. "You know what you are. Let me tell ya. You are so pathetic, you're disgusting." Then I looked at Ceil and Linda. "And you two are just as bad for laughing at her. Don'tcha realize when you make those jokes, it's as good as calling me trash?"

Peg's eyes were as wide as her mouth was when she was making fun of faggots. Linda and Ceil were both sitting more still than I had ever seen 'em.

I grabbed the back of my chair and gave it a good shove against the wall. "And one more thing." My voice was lower now and tears came to my eyes. "Don't any of you ever think about how much it hurts me. Don'tcha have any idea what my Goddamn life is like."

I ran out the bar and down the street. When I heard Ceil calling my name I ducked down an alley. Damn I felt terrible.

My head was pounding. I knew it wasn't just the beer. It was the whole night. It was my whole life. I thought I was gonna puke up every Goddamn faggot joke I ever heard.

As angry as I was, I was sorry I said anything. Hell. Sam's was my second home in the neighborhood. And after everything I said, it was gonna be real embarrassing to show my face in there again.

At the downstairs door to my apartment, next to the diner, I decided I would go upstairs and call Ceil. I figured she'd be the most likely to understand, 'cause of her boyfriend. As it turned out, I didn't have to. When I got inside, the phone was ringing.

It was Ceil. And you know something, I was right. She did understand. She said she had thought for a while that I was gay but didn't want to pry. I corrected her and told her that I was a lesbian and told her the story about Lesbos. I don't think she believed the part about the men being lesbians, but then I'm not sure I believe it either. Before we hung up, she apologized about going along with Peg and promised to talk to the girls.

Just sitting here thinking about talking to Ceil last night makes me feel good. 'Cause my gang and me are tight, and I'd hate to lose them. Maybe the girls in this bar did come from Lesbos. And maybe

I'm related to them in some way. But I know where I come from. It's the place my family's lived and worked in for generations. Even if I move downtown, I'll always go back to my old neighborhood.

I'd even miss Sam if I didn't go back to his bar anymore.

There's something about his calling my name when I come in the door that makes my life feel permanent. I always know when I leave that I'll be back. Sure as I know that I'll be at this bar downtown, shooting pool with the girls after work.

Amy promised to stop in tonight just as soon as she's done with her meeting. I can't wait to tell her what happened with my gang last night. And how Ceil understood about me being a lesbian and everything. Even though Amy's a goody two shoes, I like her a lot. I think we could be real tight, like best friends. I wouldn't even mind if she put her hand over mine again.

I told her at work today I might go with her to one of her events. It has to be something fun, though. Not a candy striper's job. I might even go to a sobriety girls' meeting with her if I think I can stand it.

Maybe sometime soon I'll do that. Someday soon. Meanwhile though I'll be right here. Resting on my stool. Looking across the bar at those bottles. Just thinking about my life. It's a miracle all those bottles never come crashing down. Maybe me sitting here staring at 'em is helping to hold 'em up. I don't know.

But I do know that I'll be here. Maybe you wanna come in here some afternoon and shoot a game of pool with me. Like I said, I'll be right here. Warming up my engine. Getting those quarters lined up. Just biding my time till liftoff.

Nancy Tyler Glenn was born in Los Angeles, California on February 12, 1938 at 8:05 P.M. The first lesbian she knew was her mother, Dorothy, who filled her earliest years with fantasy and song. Her novel Clicking Stones *(nominated for a Lammy) was published in 1989 and since then she has had short stories included in three anthologies. She currently lives and works in Tucson, AZ with her two cats, ZahZee and Cooper. Her novel in progress,* The Collaborators, *and a collection of short stories, are scheduled for publication by Willoworks, in 1995. She loves to hear from her readers, PO Box 435, Bisbee, AZ 85603.*

THE SWIM

Judy had said she might be late and I didn't see her car in the driveway of the Tudor house where she was house sitting. I parked my VW Bug, grabbed my towel, and walked to the iron gate that led to the pool.

I felt pumped up after my workout and enjoyed just sitting, watching the ripples in the water. After a while I looked around, then stripped down. I tested the water with my toe, dove in and did an underwater breast stroke to the other end of the pool, kicked off and tried to make it back. I couldn't do it. I was out of breath, so I surfaced and gulped air.

When I went under again I thought I saw something. I wasn't even near it when I realized it was a naked woman sitting motionless in a full lotus with her eyes open. Her dark hair floated eerily around her head. Fear gripped me. She had to be dead.

I surfaced again, swam as fast as I could for the edge of the pool, and got out. I didn't know what to do. I should call the cops, but fear turned to terror--my terminal paranoia set in. What if it had been foul play and they thought I...?

I heard a splash and whipped my head around. The woman had surfaced and was walking slowly through the water at the shallow end of the pool. She climbed up the steps to the deck before turning around.

She saw me and waved. "Hi," she called. "I didn't know anyone was here." She walked around the side of the pool toward me.

I was still in shock--but not too numb to notice her perfect small breasts, concave belly, and the swell of her mons with tight black curls. She walked with the grace of a cat.

Then she was facing me. Her face was a perfect oval with eyes of the deepest blue I'd ever seen and thick dark eyelashes. Her eyes pierced right through me and it was all I could do to restrain myself from grabbing something to hide my nakedness.

The corners of her lips turned up ever so slightly. "I'm called, Serene." She reached down and brushed the inside of my limp hand with her soft fingertips, then reached behind me for my towel.

I watched her bend over and begin toweling her hair. I looked and then found myself staring at her beautifully rounded tight buns.

She turned her head and looked up at me with a sly smile, then went back to drying her hair. She finally stood up and shook her head allowing her luxurious black mane to fall over her shoulders.

I was still in a state. My little pea brain couldn't take in all the events of the last few minutes. I finally managed to find my voice-- somewhere higher in my throat than I prefer. "What were you doing down there?" I pointed toward the pool with my head (my arms were still lifeless stumps).

Serene spread the towel on the lawn, taking her time. When she was lying, propped up on her elbows facing me, she finally answered. "I was meditating...well not exactly meditating, though I do meditate. But meditating requires breath." As if to illustrate, her abdomen moved in and out in a rhythmic pattern. "And I've never learned to breathe underwater."

"Could have fooled me," I wisecracked.

She ignored my remark and continued. "I was fantasizing about sex."

I turned my ear toward her and moved closer. "Sex?" I echoed.

That sly smile again. "Sex."

"How long can you stay underwater?" I wanted to know.

"As long as it takes to come."

My body was beginning to wake up. I licked my lips. "You mean you masturbate under water?"

She shook her head slowly from side to side--never taking her eyes off my face.

"Then, how...I mean...if you don't...?"

She shifted to her side and propped her head in one hand. With the other hand she plucked a blade of grass and began biting on it. "I just fantasize until it happens."

"You come."

She stretched out on her back and pumped her legs to her chest a couple of times before relaxing them. "Hmm Hmm."

I moved closer and sat on the grass so I wouldn't be towering over her. "What kind of fantasies do you have?"

She closed her eyes. "She was a handsome lesbian--about five foot seven, tan all over. She had amazing green eyes with specks of brown. Her body was well defined--not just her torso, arms, and shoulders--but her butt and legs too. Her pubic hair was golden and her hair was dark blond streaked with gold from the sun." She opened her eyes and turned her head toward me. "And her breasts...."

The muscles in my abdomen tightened. She was describing me. I mean--the actual facts. I *am* five seven and my eyes *are* green, etc. I noticed my jaw was a little slack. I closed my mouth and licked my lips again.

She reached over and put her fingertips on my bare thigh and began making little circles. "Do you want to know what we did?"

I didn't trust my voice.

She turned on her side and began caressing my thigh again, this time with her hand. "Well," Serene looked at me. "By the way, what is *your* name?"

I cleared my throat. "Rush."

She stroked from my knee to just short of my pussy. Once or twice she snatched a few tufts of my pubic hair and gave a little tug.

I wanted to stop her. I mean, I'm no stone butch--but I'd say at least 70%. I couldn't stop her though. I couldn't even move--except for the involuntary things like deeper breathing and I knew my pussy was sopping wet.

Serene spoke as though in a dream. "I was in bed. It was a hot night so I'd thrown the sheet off of me and pulled my nightgown up to my waist." She moved her hand to my abdomen and began kneading and stroking, then brushed against my pubic hair and began stroking my thighs again.

I looked at her. Her eyes were glazed and she seemed to be staring intensely at something just a few inches from her face.

She continued. "I'd opened the window and heard the rustle of the trees even before I felt the breeze between my legs." Serene moved next to me and rested her hot face against my left shoulder. Her fingers began kneading my right shoulder and back. "I began undulating and opening myself more and more to the breeze." She turned her head and I could feel her teeth sinking into the flesh of my shoulder--just short of breaking the skin. Then she licked the mark she'd made and caressed it with her face.

She pushed me onto my back. I went with it, not wanting to break the spell. I'm not saying I wasn't hot.

"I almost felt I could come. I raised my knees to my chest and spread the cheeks of my buttocks and rocked from side to side." Serene's hand cascaded over my body like a waterfall and when she brought it back up she entered me. I groaned at the sharp feeling of pleasure. She moved her fingers slowly in and out. I gasped and pulled her against me. She smelled like the sea.

Serene's voice was full of emotion. "I knew my clit was hard and ready to burst. I wanted to touch it but didn't want to disturb the agony of wanting it."

She was still moving her fingers in and out, but had increased the speed and pressure. I was moving with her, pushing against her thrusts. She pressed her breasts against my arm and her pubic bone against my leg.

Then she was still for a moment. "I opened my eyes and Rush was standing at the foot of the bed."

I jolted when I heard my name.

"She just stood there with her thumbs tucked into her belt, staring down at me." She began moving again--very slowly. "Then, deliberately, Rush kneeled on the bed in front of me, pushed my legs apart, and took me into her mouth."

Serene moved so quickly I didn't realize what was happening. She turned around and put her pussy near my face and her own head in my crotch. I pulled her down to my mouth. She followed me like a dance. Every time I sucked her clit, she sucked mine. When I circled her with my tongue, she did the same to me. If I pushed against her with my tongue, I felt her pushing against me.

I could have gone on forever, savoring the taste of her, and feeling the exquisite sensations between my legs, but the more frenzied she got the more frantic I became and we were both groaning and licking and sucking.

I've come at the same time as my lover before, but nothing like this. We got higher and higher. At some point I couldn't tell if we were doing the exact same things to each other. Her fingers were digging into the flesh of my thighs, and I know (even though I tried to be careful) there were times when I clawed at her back. Then she started screaming--it was muffled because of where her mouth was, and I was so wild I started doing the same, feeling my clit ready to burst and then I knew she was coming--and I was coming and I felt the ground move under me and I shot out to the stars. I don't know how long I was there, but after the explosion I began drifting slowly back to earth, holding onto Serene for dear life.

When we landed, we didn't move for the longest time. Then Serene pushed herself up and lay next to me. She was so beautiful--so soft. I knew I was in love with her and would be for the rest of my life. I caressed her, touched her face-brushed her lips with my finger tips. "Who are you," I asked.

"Judy's cousin," she told me.

She curled up against me. I thought she was falling asleep. Then I heard the clank of the iron gate, and Judy's voice yelled, "I'm back, Rush."

We sat up and I turned toward the sound. Behind me I heard a splash and felt a cool spray over my hot skin.

"What have you been doing?" Judy asked. "You're all sweaty and red as a beet."

I smiled, "I've been getting to know your cousin."

"Cousin?" Judy looked puzzled. "I don't have any cousins."

"Well, whatever she is then, wait a minute." I went to the edge of the pool and dove in. I breast stroked to the place where I'd first seen Serene. She wasn't there. I turned and began scouring the bottom of the pool. The more I looked the more she wasn't there. Finally I surfaced. "She isn't here?"

"Who isn't here?"

"Serene."

Judy said. "I don't know any Serene."

I swam to the edge of the pool, pushed myself up, and sat with my feet dangling in the water. I shook my head. It was a dream. I must have fallen asleep. I must have fucking sun stroke. I looked out over the water. I wanted to see her. I wanted her. I loved her. How could I love a dream?

Judy came over and sat at the edge of the pool with me. She touched my shoulder. "What's this?"

I looked where her fingers were. Serene's teeth marks. "Shit!" I said.

"Damn!" I said.

Nancy Picard is a poet and writer who has lived overseas for more than seven years, most of her adult life. She is interested in internal and external landscapes, mapping, and restoring values that have been lost, or rather, that she feels she still needs to discover. She is a dedicated journal writer, and has been writing for magazines and newspapers, international development agencies, and anything and anyone else for the past ten years. This is her first work of published fiction.

VIOLENT LANDSCAPE

When you first begin to tell a story, you begin with new. A settling down, then the next breath. When you first begin to write, you also begin with new. A new piece of paper or a new white blank computer screen or a smooth slice of sand, snow, upon which you trace your experience. You begin.

The hysterics used to write on themselves. Silenced, given no access to public language except of the body, they stood, palms forward, like angels falling from the clouds. And if not bound, they screamed and tore their flesh and hair. Long ago, they were called possessed. Later, simply "female." It was the pre-historic, or rather, pre-hysteric, for which I had been searching; back before the possession of scripted meaning that was withheld. When symbols spoke the loudest in the image of the female. And the female was whole.

We had not gone far into the Göreme Valley. We had not gone far along the arid brown earth, a surprisingly stark contrast of nothingness to the monuments of guidebooks detailing the ways in which visitors are welcomed. Always a surprise, this gap between the text and what one sees, the reality of the present.

No one can define a relationship if they are in it. No one can say exactly what is happening until it is over, and only then can one say for sure, what is happening now is that being over is *happening now*. No one, never, no matter who you ask. For once you begin to see what is going on between you and something else -- be it a person or a cat or a wall of rock -- as a relationship, you begin to be a reader of yourself.

And can you read yourself? Not truly, for there is always a second meaning, a third, a fourth. And each one changes the other.

Try it. Go look in a mirror. The best would be the kind with three or more angles. Turn, twist, look forward and behind. Have a silent dialogue with yourself. But above all, do not speak.

I have said nothing about screaming.

I met Tanya, who was a Peace Corps environmental volunteer, at a time when connecting with the Earth was becoming a spiritual quest. To me, she had connected in this way more than anyone I had yet met. She had not travelled much in Europe, though she had cycled, kayaked, canoed all over the United States, and had even camped on a glacier. I thought this was especially admirable.

However, all of her experience had not prepared her for Turkey. "I think you should wear a hat to cover your hair when we're there, " I said referring to the predictable and constant, sharp stone stares from the men at foreign, blond women. Although my hair is a kind of nondescript brownish red, I had cut it off in preparation.

My hair, the way I dressed, my whole outer persona reflected an inner need for safety that would carry over to the image I presented while traveling. Tanya, who cared nothing for her outer image, was unaware of its effect on others. People in Hungary always stopped and stared at her, as they did at anyone or anything different from themselves.

Everything in Hungary was muted, subversive, hidden too deeply for my needs. I had gone to Hungary to see a new conception of myself. I had wanted the difference around me to throw back a new self-reflection, to spring me from my societal-self-imposed trap of cultural conditioning. But instead, I found myself digging at dirt, finding bones with no flesh and skeletons that would not speak. For two years I had been searching, and with a simmering kind of frustration, I was beginning to realize that I had stepped into Hungary's world of stunned silence, and that I was still enclosed.

I talked Tanya into the trip to Turkey. Just the thought of being there warmed my skin inside out. Here would be the music and dark possibilities of the beginning of the history of worship, of human gathering and living, as far as I knew it, or wanted to believe it. After two years of living within painfully narrow confines of thought and action and belief, mirrored around me in huge slabs of concrete and forced housing, beliefs that had kept alive the walking dead, I was aching for the difference of choice. For the difference of people who had willingly come together.

Tanya agreed to the trip only after reading about the hiking possibilities. She brought maps, checked trail guides, and even consulted her compass in the middle of the city. But I came for the first collected half-moon shards of obsidian. The Goddesses.

My thoughts as I write this are scattered because I know what he must have been doing at this time. He must have sensed we were coming. He is thinking of us now as I write. This I know, as well.

On the bus to Istanbul, I fidgeted the whole way, so unsure of my feelings, thinking only that Tanya looked more precious to me than ever and why? Why? As if I were going to lose her. In Istanbul, Tanya talked to the men who approached us on the streets, and I said to her, "I do not want to be friendly." She said, "Why do you always get to make all the decisions." It was not a question.

In Istanbul, we toured the dusty Topkapi palace with its harem of whispers. We walked through the brooding Hagia Sophia, and later, in our socks, through the Blue Mosque, built up in pillowing steps to God. We crossed into Asia over the Bosphorous, oily and full of small fishing boats.

I checked the guidebook and read aloud to Tanya. "It says here that we should stay in at night," I told her. So we did, practicing our Turkish numbers and basic sentences as we sat on beds that sank in the middles. But we had to venture out to take the night bus to Ankara, after fighting among crowds of men shouting prices and destinations. By this time, Tanya had started wearing a hat.

We toured the Ankara Museum the next day. Encased in glass, beyond our touch, sat the first female figures, the women I had come to see. Long, thick breasts resting on bellies, arms along the backs of leopards, strong necks. "I need to be outside, where they were, where they worshipped," I told Tanya. "I need that."

We are always making history. We are always telling ourselves, we will do this not because we want to, but because we have not done this before. When the iron curtain parted, I wanted to be one of the first people backstage. First, always first. I wanted to see where the first Goddess had been worshipped. I wanted to walk freely on the land that had been painfully turned. We had escaped from Istanbul to Ankara, and now we were escaping from Ankara to Göreme. We were finally arriving. Travelling on the smaller bus to Göreme, formal waiter-dressed staff poured fresh lemon tonic on our hands after every stop to protect us from the heat. We rode in the front seat as if we would arrive more quickly by watching the pencil-flat brown road. We passed donkeys pulling wooden carriages; one man in front, three woman behind, all dressed in the white heat and light of September.

We left the bus at the main Outdoor Church Museum. Everything fell below us. You do not enter the Göreme Valley slowly, you drop into it like a bird from the sky seeking prey. Magical cones and towers appear, shooting upwards, like dripped upon sand castles on a wide stretch of beach. Windows, shadows cut and carved in unusual rectangles, are the only faces of a somewhat random order. Here no one asks for something authentic. Everything is as it was, so there is no point. "Unspoiled", the guidebook writers remark.

We chose a cave hotel, a room with thick and permanent scars of digging. We took showers and put on our appropriate clothes. Tourists we had seen along the roads and hiding in the shelter of shade had displayed arms and legs of red, exposed skin. We were startled at their lack of respect for the traditional dress. We covered our bodies. We did not protest.

The Göreme Valley hides secrets. Underground cities had once hid thousands from persecuting pre-eighth and ninth century invaders. The towers, by the thousands, stretch in crooked yawns toward expanses of blue sky. "We have never had any problems here, " the woman chain-smoking at the Tourist office told us later as I watched her fat, brown fingers tap the ash away. "Never."

On the left side of the road, the Valley stretched forever, dotted black-holed towers receding. Small moving flashes of color, hikers and wanderers, appeared now and then against the brown upon brown. Tanya took pictures. On the right side of the road, the Museum huddled along the side of a tall ridge. The churches inside were looped in protective barbed wire and surrounded by chunks of collected, broken stones. At least twelve or thirteen churches, all bearing a name and theme, had been carved centuries before inside towers in the sequestered section. The colors of despised and persecuted saints painted in all forms of martyrdom were still visible. More primitive churches were splashed with red dusty markings of circles and waving lines, a collection of the pagan and christian. Symbols tattooed the rounded frames of windows and ran along the chiselled doors. In the more intricate churches, layers of people died horrible, though colorful deaths. Perhaps they would have escaped their fates if they had been given the chance, but the century old paint held them fixed to the walls in permanent agony. All the while we were there, the dust swirled upward in the light from the entrances' mouths like the breaths of the demons, who were clawing the walls, scratching at flames.

We looked past other tourists in three or four towers, but we preferred instead to be outside, to scramble on top, running our hands along the rough outsides of the cones, checking for heartbeats.

I walked high up, past where Tanya's slick-soled shoes allowed her to go, to be alone. The Valley had been carved out by the insistence of an angry and persistent river, which had not been able to wear down certain sediments in the soil and instead had to move on, move around them, until it dried and left the sediments as the pointed, tower monuments. I stared out over the Valley and again felt unsure. Everything around me was a miracle of nature. There were no windows here, only sky, so why did it not get through? Why was I not hearing voices, not feeling the slightest message from the stones? No birds, no sound, only silent and hot sun. Tanya said on the way down, "Let me take your picture." I flinched as she clicked the shutter.

On the way out of the Museum gate, a man remarked on Tanya's "Women's Trans-Antarctic Trek" shirt. "Did you do that?" He asked, laughing. "No, but I support them," she said. "They have only just started." He looked away.

We were walking back toward the town when I said, "I want to go to see where they lived."

"Who?" She pushed her camera case up on her shoulder and stared toward the town, then into the valley, shading her eyes with her hand.

I looked at her, "The people. Where they lived, not where they worshipped in persecution, but where they lived, died, loved, fought, ate, shit." I stared into the valley, where the towers and caves held secrets for which I had come miles and years.

"O.k.," Tanya said reluctantly. She followed me off the road. Later I would say that we had read the guidebooks, the signs on the walls of our cave hotel, everything that admonished us to take a walk through the lovely valley of Göreme. Later I would say that it was the afternoon, that there were people around, tourists everywhere. Later I would say that we were only 100 meters from the road. But I only remember that I said these things later.

The rasp of a boot along gravel. The sharp intake of breath before Tanya says, "He's got a gun." Immediately I see my boot in the sun moments before, a lizard scurrying, scraping by. I see the field we have just passed, the road, the people, and I turn to see the mouth of the first small tower cave we have just now entered obstructed by the dark shadow of a man, the gun raised stiff armed at Tanya's temple, and the scream begins entering my throat. It is a snake, and I am choking on it.

he is grabbing at my breast what is he doing grabbing at my breast keep my skirt down must keep my skirt HE'S CHOKING ME HE'S CHOKING ME slap and run to the front of the cave WHAT DO WE DO I think I can I think I will let THE GUN him rape me so that HE'S PUNCHING ME JUDITH WHAT DO WE DO I try to kick him see him pull her face down to kiss her WE HAVE AIDS AIDS WE ARE SICK YOU DON'T WANT US SICK SICK he is using his tongue i see his see her grimace THE GUN IS AT MY FACE THE GUN then feel the shove JUDITH HE IS CHOK he is pushing us back and I am screaming money money do you want money and that stops him, he holds THE GUN to my head, takes the money and then JUDITH HE IS TEARING MY CLOTHES WHAT DO I DO WHAT DO WE DO I DON'T KNOW he is slamming us THE GUN against a solid rock wall TANYA I DON'T KNOW I DON'T KNOW he is grabbing me THE GUN hurting TANYA

she is running.
she has grabbed the gun and she is running for the mouth of the cave.
he has turned from me, from pushing his face against my neck and he grabs her.
they fall to the dirt floor. clouds of dust in the edge of sunlight.

GET THE GUN JUDITH.

I am not in Turkey. I am not trapped in a cave. I am ten years old, my hands itching for the football. I see my brother in the backyard after Thanksgiving dinner. He is motioning to me. Falling. Waving his hands as he screams to me to come and

and I start running forward, knees bending. I can see it, there, in front of me, in a mass of arms writhing. I want this. Badly. I am diving forward, parallel to the earth. I am not thinking of landing, only my want. And in my head I don't know if I am or someone else is screaming, but I hear

GET IT GET IT GET --

"Imdat!!!! Imdat!!!" Tanya has gone, her clothes gathered to her like a child. She has run as he has run, both of them splitting off in separate directions. I stood alone in the cave, and dumbly looked down at the gun in my hand, and then up again to see him tearing down into the valley. I did not think to shoot but instead to run, a mad animal in crazed circles, back into the cave to see if we had left anything. Once inside, I realized with terror that I was still in the cave.

I ran out again shouting "Imdat!" -- the echo of myself propelling me forward. Tanya appeared around the corner. She was covered with dirt and fear underneath the blue, blue sky. "Help us, Help us!" Some tourists, at first stupefied mannequins in the distance, soon ran up from the road. They had not understood my call in Turkish, only our stricken looks and torn, dirty clothes. Mutely, I showed them the gun.

"This never happens in the valley," the woman at the Tourist bureau said as she translated for the police between deep draws on her cigarette. At first the men, perfect, hair oiled and combed, sat tucked into their uniforms while they listened politely and took notes. "Where is the gun?" one asked, and I opened my backpack. There, inside next to a sandwich in a zip-locked bag, a small pistol gleamed black and brown. I held the backpack forward and allowed the chief officer, the one asking all of the questions, to take out the pistol himself. He gave a low whistle as he turned it over in his handkerchief and stared at the other man with him. I stared behind them at the dusty, faded tourism posters plastering the walls.

The police closed the streets leading to the Valley and searched. "You must look at the men we find," the chief officer told us. Tanya resisted, but I went outside, heart pounding, to stare into the angry eyes of each of the captured seven men as they stepped out of the police van. All were dressed in the blue shirts and jeans of our description, but none had the face of the man who had attacked us.

"We need your passports," the police insisted, but Tanya and I said no, we're sorry, it's impossible. Someone suggested photocopying our pictures; the nearest photocopy machine was two towns away. We promised to send them the copies. We never did.

Back in our cave room, Tanya insisted we leave. "I can't handle this," she said. The stares of men, so frequent and annoying before in Istanbul and Ankara, had now become cigarette burns. That night, she slept and I stayed awake until dawn, praying, protecting. We flew out two days later.

In the eight months since we returned, Tanya and I decided to break up, to stop seeing each other, or somehow the relationship decided for itself. I knew though that it had started to crack long before, and Turkey had simply snapped us in two. "We cannot support each other," she told me. "We are both too needy for ourselves." In the end, she wanted to put it all behind her, me included. Her counselor, a man, told her to try and forget everything. I told her, I cannot. I will write about it.

As far as we know, as we will ever know, the man who attacked us is still out there. In the Valley, somewhere, in all valleys, all dark spaces. I had to decide afterwards whose world it was, though, and what it meant, this pureness of survival, one-on-one, or in our case, the strength of sisterhood. The fight. The struggle.

I returned to Hungary, where the struggle was merely overwhelming and exhausting everyday living. It wasn't just the loss of Tanya, or the loss of our trip that eroded me. It was the noise. Skeletons constantly rattled windows and shook open doors, hid behind trees and jumped from the throats of dogs. I shunned the outdoors to such a point that I had to decide if I would give up and stay inside always. I spent months taking taxis everywhere after dark. Darkness meant that I slept with the light on, or rather, slept little at all.

One time, I asked a taxi driver to turn his lights on the front door, so that I could walk in the yellow beams up the walkway. Surrounded by this yellow light, in the limits of its fuzzy edges, I would be safe. The taxi driver swung his car around, but before I got out, he reached into his pocket and gave me the mace that he said always kept with him. "I insist," he said. "It's a gift. This is a dangerous city." I almost took for free the small, silver gray container he offered, and then before I got out of the cab, I paid him for it.

The exhaustion of being constantly aware of myself and everyone else every minute through dusk and into a night I never allowed to be, and darkness I would not acknowledge, slowly wore me down. And in that wearing down, somewhere deep, a hum began. A hum behind my speaking voice, a hum behind eyes I could not seem to close, a vibration: no. No. I woke one night from fitful sleep convinced again that there was a man hiding in each closet, under each bed, behind each dark pane of glass. I cannot live in this fear, I thought, and forced myself to walk the flat in the dark. I let my heart pulse into each corner.

I walked out on the balcony and looked at the lights of Budapest, running along hills. Everything was quiet and I laid down. Just before morning, in the grey light at the end of the bed, a thin in-line of a man was standing. His fury at my existence was complete, blurring the air around him with its heat. I clenched my teeth. I waited for the fear of him to kill me, but it didn't. Instead, my fear turned, just ever so slightly. The man's bones began to swell, and he took on shape and form. He bent down to me, and I started to burn, deep. Deep inside. The fear spun first to ice, then to fire. He grabbed me by the throat, and I reached up, breaking his grasp, and swallowed him whole.

The next day, I began to send for brochures of travel organizations for women, and upon receiving each one, I made a silent prayer of thanks. And my thanks became a mantra, the echo of the voices of all women who have had their deep and essential NO caught, captured, never freed. Within me now, the echo continues, a resonant hum of resistance. It has been a long walk from the mouth of that tower cave, but each step has been toward light, and darkness, and life; the decision to return.

For all of my travel experience, I had never before seen someone's ability to tap into her anger so quickly and readily. I believe it was this ability of Tanya's that saved us from being tortured and killed. "It's a fine line between courage and stupidity," she said later. "What if it hadn't worked?" But I thought of her anger, and I thought of the strength behind it as I slowly built my own strength without her. And as I built, first through sleep and then through entering night spaces, I began to feel capable again. I began to feel not that I had escaped the cave, where my ghost still haunts the entrance and warns young women away, but that by surviving we had perhaps broken one cycle in the violent landscape. And built into my strength, or growing from it, the thought that maybe our resistance meant something beyond even what we could comprehend. I will never know concretely for sure, but I sense this.

A few days ago, Tanya visited me for the day. Though our relationship as lovers and travelling companions has been long since over, she asked before she left, "Would you like to travel together again, maybe? You don't have to say yes right away." We both laughed.

As a present to myself for surviving, I returned to the United States for a vacation and went snowshoeing with one of the women's travel organizations I had discovered. Vermont white, all around. Pure, simple, white. A beginning. I traced my story on the snow as I walked, drug it behind me, and pushed it forward.

Chriss-Spike Quatrone: I am a lesbian, writer, radical, living in Amsterdam, New York. I've had an essay appear in Common Lives\Lesbian Lives, and poetry in: Backspace, Community, Circle of Light, Poems That Thump In The Dark, Yammering Twits, Rant, In Your Face!, Insomnia, Perceptions, and Jejune: america eats its young. I also hike and backpack in the Adirondacks with my two dogs a lot, I have a cat, I love pizza. I am a member of two writers support groups. My poetry and short stories have a surrealistic edge to them always. I believe writing is the best revenge. I am a proud survivor of sexual and physical and emotional abuse.

HOLIDAY DECORATING

Wild Spike No-Cock spit on her hand and then used it to slick her hair back. She slammed her front door shut loudly. A storm of protests erupted from the senior dyke living downstairs.

"Wild Spike, why must you be so damned noisy?" Virginia asked. "And surely you're not going to ride your motorcycle in this weather!"

Wild Spike tossed her head back and laughed. She kicked at the mounds of snow Virginia had so carefully shoveled together into clever piles just that morning.

"Watch me!" she said. "And anyway, I have to go get some ornaments. My winter solstice tree needs balls."

"It took a lot of work to shovel that sidewalk. Ingrate!"

"Don't worry, Verge. I'll put it back." Wild Spike laughed as she stomped towards the garage. She enjoyed the clomping sounds made by her engineer boots.

Pouch. Check.

Machete. Check.

Plastic bags. Check.

Branding iron. Check.

Satisfied, she gunned the engine of her dream bike.

Down the streets of Hiserville she flew, her machine shattering any sense of quiet in that snow-laden afternoon. Kids on bicycles (the latest craze in Hiserville) pedaled frantically out of her way, jumping curbs and slipping on treacherous sidewalks to be safe from her furious path. She narrowly missed a collision with Woody, a grizzled mutt who was happily plowing through the snowdrifts.

"There goes Wild Spike No-Cock!" a small girl named Amanda shouted to her playmates Jackie, Steph, and Roberto. "When I grow up, I want to be just like her."

"Yeah!"

"Awesome!"

"Too cool!" came their answering echoes.

Wild Spike laughed as she flipped off the curb by Recovery Universal Rehab Center. Her bike became temporarily airborne. She felt the crunch as tires met slick pavement once again. She gunned around the corner in screaming high gear, steering out of a tailspin.

She found her target. He was walking away from his expensive car in the rehab lot. She leaped off her bike and applied the kickstand. In one fell swoop of a long arm, she collared a certain Doctor Nygert, plunderer of women. He wiggled and squirmed under her mighty dyke grasp. His feet and legs flew wildly, crashing against the side of his parked car as Wild Spike swung her machete.

"So, what have you got to say for yourself?" Wild Spike sneered at her frightened quarry. Moistness enveloped the seat of his expensive pants.

"Slime!" The machete gleamed thirstily. With an expert practiced hand, Wild Spike proceeded to perform rough surgery on a specific delicate part of Doctor Nygert's anatomy.

"Not my cock!" he screamed, his eyes bulging in mortal terror. "Not them too!"

"Yes, them too!" Wild Spike blithely threw the bloody cock into a snow bank. She deposited the two warm balls into a plastic bag and tucked it inside her pouch.

Doctor Nygert squirmed anew when he saw the brand descending towards his forehead.

"Now do hold still," Wild Spike instructed. "The words will come out crooked if you move." She belted the physician-rapist in the gut. A hot searing pain enveloped his forehead.

She tossed the limp Doctor Nygert by the doorway of Recovery Universal. His brand glistened under the neon afternoon light.

"Good day!" she yelled above the noise of her last-gasp muffler and exhaust system.

Wild Spike took off. Woody loped along beside her, something messy clutched tightly in his mouth. He left her and headed towards a vacant lot.

Amanda and her three friends came running up to the bloody bundle that was Doctor Nygert.

"Stay away from me," Doctor Nygert warned weakly. Steph laughed. Jackie read the message branded on his forehead.

"GUILTY OF HEINOUS CRIMES COMMITTED AGAINST WOMYN," she read.

"What's 'heinous'?" she asked Amanda.

Amanda shrugged. "Don't know. Must be something awful though."

"Worse than homework?" Roberto asked.

Amanda nodded gravely. "Definitely worse than homework."

The four ran along the street, following the tracks left by Wild Spike No-Cock's motorcycle.

Wild Spike spied her fan club in the rearview mirror.She circled around and waved to the children. They waved back.

"Always stand up for who you are!" she yelled.

"Yeah!"

"You know it!"

"Right on!"

Amanda's yell pierced the air. "Kill the bastards!"

That one's going to be a mighty fine dyke, Wild Spike thought as she crashed into her driveway and galloped into the garage.

She jumped off her metal steed and clomped up the sidewalk to her door. Virginia stuck her head out her window. "You missed the news. That nasty man Wayne somebody got acquitted."

"The one who raped his wife and then she--"

"Serves him right too. He deserved it. I'm sorry they found the thing. I think we should all go down there and have a protest."

"A riot," Wild Spike agreed.

"Did you get your balls, Wild Spike?"

"Sure did, Verge. Come on up, why doncha? and I'll tell you all about it."

"Okay," the older woman agreed, "as long as you don't talk my ear off about motorcycles."

"No sweat!" said Wild Spike. She smiled broadly at Virginia in freedom. "I'll make us some hot chocolate. You can help me hang up my new balls."

Catherine Toldi: I live by the Monterey Bay with my partner of thirteen years, and two cats. I work as an organizational development consultant, educator, and writer. After a lifetime of writing--a personal journal, poetry, short stories, assigned papers, a master's thesis, and a novel--I am delighted to start being more public with my creative efforts. Along with this more personal publication, I am a co-author of a book about consensus decision-making, which will also be published this year.

Despite the chaos of turn-of-the-century life, I believe that balance is possible, and try to find mine by attending equally to intellect, passion and spirit. I am greatly helped in this effort by gardening, dancing, zen buddhism, my lover, and my varied interweaving circles of family and friends.

YOUR TRUE VOICE CALLING

Saying Yes to Adventure
There is a lesbian body throbbing beneath this tailored wool skirt and silk blouse, but who would ever know? There is a wild spirit who roams yearning through this maze of mauve fabric office-dividers, desks and phones, but for the most part, I keep her capped like a genie in the bottle of my dogged practicality. However there *is* hope: a perky young dyke starts cruising by my desk with increasing frequency, and somehow her sweet curiosity coincides with Spring pressing insistently through the skylight and vents, and with my long-dreamed schemes of radical change, which are finally coming into focus.

I admire her recent haircut, which she says she got because her hair had been bothering her latest piercing. So a few days later, I figure that I can tell her some of my secrets, too. I whisper to her in the corridor that I have decided to get my navel pierced. She seems surprised at the juxtaposition of this administrative type and below-the-neck piercing, and I like that! I want a witness to my emergence, even under these fluorescent lights, and in these windowless halls.

My partner and I drive up the following week to an appointment with the piercer. A friend has given her this ritual as a gift, a timely marking on her healing journey. But what about me? I say it's to summon my wild woman. She's been dormant for too long, as I've been the good public servant, the good graduate student, the best To-Do List manager in the whole fucking country!!

I say this, but even as we drive, I waver inside, afraid of the pain, unsure of my motives, wondering if this is more about ego and adornment than about my proclaimed spiritual desire. The closer we get, the more reasonable it seems to heed these doubts. But at the same time my stomach turns as I recognize that this is the voice of status-quo caution within my very own soul; this is the voice that weaves the veil that seems so insignificantly light--yet each layer of reasons *why not* have bound my wild woman into paralysis.

And besides, what would I tell my young friend, who seemed so pleased with my announcement, who eagerly advised me to clear my calendar after the piercing so as to fully savor the lingering rush? What reason *why not* would I give? I realize that it is as easy to say Yes as it is to say No, and decide that the time has come to say Yes to Adventure.

So we meet the piercer, and his beautiful Goddess accomplice, and my partner strips down to her striking nakedness: she will go first. We find the right music. She sits in her silence and lets herself be filled by the knowledge of the pain she has endured and how now she is claiming that pain, claiming her body, choosing who and what will touch her and exactly where. Exactly when.

He rings a deep bell; we encircle her. She sits like a peaceful Buddha and receives the piercing in one swift movement, one sharp gasp, his nimble fingers threading the jewelry like a tiny ring of light into her skin.

Such a pure moment. We all savor her beauty, and the clarity of her intention.

The Raw Recognition

Movement, some moments, shift the energy, and then it is my turn, and I'm lying on the table, the Shaman with his silver needle at my left; my partner's hands press against the soles of my feet; the bare-breasted Goddess on my right. I sink deeply into my breathing.

As he pulls up a section of my belly-skin and flattens it with a vertical clamp, adrenalin surges through my system, and I let my mind roam out to the edge of my consciousness, where ideas like "pain" blur into a hyper-aware endorphin acceptance. Slipping off into an empty place I feel the tip of the needle touch my flesh. He waits while I inhale deeply, then pushes the needle through with my exhale. There is a searing moment as the metal pierces my flesh. My psyche releases; I feel relieved, self-congratulatory: "that wasn't so bad."

But they are murmuring. I hear their voices as if through a distant fog. Something is wrong. Somehow it' s not over. *It wasn't so bad*, but only if now I can rest. I don't want to know what they are saying , so I purposely hover out in the formless realms, as fear starts to rise in my mind. My partner is squeezing my feet; I hear the Goddess say, "do it again while she's till high."

But my belly is burning with a relentless flame! I have spent my strength, and am at the limit of my endurance. I must surrender, I'll do anything to escape this fire. Do it again? Do it again? I can't!

But some deeper voice swells up from outside of my mind. A bubble of breath arises from my very bedrock, from the silent dark source, mother of rock and root. My body remembers all of the times I have been here before:

struggling up a granite pass

sitting up through an endless desert night

healing from the loss of love

mile 22 of the marathon

the burning tattoo needle

sitting still in zazen hour after hour with a tyrannical, raging mind...

I have been here before. My body knows how to fully enter this place. It's just intense sensation, that's all. There is this one moment, and then there is the next. All there is to do is feel the feelings. I'm not going to die. Or perhaps this *is* the dying, prying loose the grasp of the one who's held the cork so tightly. I open up every cell, and tears spill out of me, my mouth opens in an uncontrolled moan -- *Yes*, sighs the Goddess -- and the moan becomes a wailing roar, as my wild woman surges out into the open air, released at last.

I float out on a vast emotional ocean. I see my companions' faces wavering through the water of my tears. They are weeping too, with raw recognition.

Winter Solstice

Now that my flaming belly has healed, and the silver-winged bauble dangles like it has always been there, indeed, like it grew right out of my flesh, I can look back and imagine that perhaps my wild woman held the Shaman's hand and pulled the needle straight through my skin, much to his surprise. "Not so easy," she laughed at me, "you need to feel this all the way down into your bones!"

Or, maybe my moment had just come. The bud was swollen on the bare branch, and pierced by the whiff of Spring and the encouragement of helpful guides, it blossomed: nature fulfilling itself, letting the inside out, and drawing the outside in.

But I *do* know that it is a lesbian body who learns how to shimmy her belly to the rhythm of the *doumbek*; who publicly opens her arms to her lover, even when surrounded by mostly heterosexual eyes; who marches in her first ever queer pride parade in her home town. These silver wings dance whether revealed or hidden beneath the administrative costume, the black meditation garb, or the hard-won writer's sweats.

There is an unbounded wild spirit who flies freely from orchid to pine, computer to altar, circling her center, no longer yearning: she dwells here.

Who can ever know what one moment begins? When she tells you to leap, or plunge, or retreat, or let the needle through, let the veil be torn--listen to her, for she is your own true voice calling.

Shelley Anderson's job with an international peace organization takes her around the world. She wants to thank Thai friends, in particular the women of Anjaree, the Thai lesbian-feminist group, for all the long talks over great food. Rural people in Thailand are being pushed off their traditional lands to make way for agricultural businesses and illegal logging. Their daughters are being forced into brothels that service the hundreds of thousands of foreign men, many of them Westerners, who come to Thailand as sex tourists. In police raids on brothels, girls as young as thirteen years old have been found HIV+. This story is dedicated to all the Thai women struggling for democracy and equality in Thailand. For information in English about Thai feminist struggles, send US $10 to Friends of Women Newsletter, 1379/30 Soi Praditchai, Phahonyothin Road, Samsen-nai, Bangkok 10400, Thailand."

LAND OF SMILES

The impatient cars buzzed around the stalled bus like angry bees. Bored tuk tuk drivers either chatted with the customers in the back of their open-air taxis, or turned their radios up even higher. The air was thick with the stench of exhaust fumes, blocked sewers and cooking smells. The sidewalks were as crowded as the streets. Some pedestrians sat on stools drinking iced coffee, while others rushed past to shop or to work. Vendors dropped strips of pork into soup pots, or arranged slices of papaya and pineapple, one row pink, the other moist yellow, on their carts. Peddlers outside air-conditioned shopping malls with windows full of cappuccino machines and silk lingerie debated the efficacy of their amulets with customers. It was midmorning of an utterly normal day. It was chaos, heat and noise. It was Krung Thep, the City of Angels, better known to the *farang,* or foreigner, as Bangkok.

Down Rama I Road, past the National Stadium, an oasis in the midst of all the heat and noise existed. The Hôtel Suprême had fifty scrupulously clean rooms and a quiet garden full of gardenias. The Hotêl's service, from the liveried doorman to the courteous waitresses, was meticulous. A hungry customer could find *escalope de veau à la Provençale* or fried prawns with spicy green papaya salad in the air-conditioned restaurant. Mr. Guan, owner and proprietor, had every reason to feel well pleased with his three-year apprenticeship in Nice. Unfortunately, the hotelier's course had not included dealing with the supernatural. Mr. Guan, like many Thais, offered a bunch of small tasty bananas and incense each morning to the *phra phum,* the spirit of the house. The *phra phum* lived inside the spirit house, the miniature house perched atop a slender pillar outside the hotel. The tiny carved elephants that guarded the miniature door, the incense and the food, were all meant to show enough respect for the spirit so that he or she would be content to stay inside the spirit house and not trouble any humans. The *farang* customers found it charming. Mr. Guan found it wise. In any case, it was not enough to prevent a supernatural being from taking up residence one day in the Hôtel Suprême.

This creature drifted down the third floor corridor, driven by a restless hunger. Any Thai visitor would have immediately recognized it as a *phii gaseu*--a ghost whose insatiable appetite fed on the entrails of human beings. No *farang* would have recognized it. Though raised on elves and pumpkins that turned into technicolor carriages, the *farang* had relegated the supernatural to the mind's garbage pail. There, like refuse not properly disposed of, it fermented and smelled but was politely ignored. The feeling, however, of either Thai or *farang* who encountered the *phii gaseu* was the same: absolute terror.

The first customer who saw the creature was Mr. Schulman, of Shulman's Super Shoes, 216 Alderton Street, Bennings, Kansas. It was two o'clock in the afternoon and he was sneaking out of room 302 to meet Mr. Joseph Albrecht--Joe--of Tylers' Falls, Idaho, in the downstairs lobby. Mr. Schulman--or Ernie, as he preferred being called--was feeling very happy and daring. The air-conditioner had successfully masked the sounds of escape from his sleeping wife. Mrs. Schulman was exhausted from a long morning of touring the Nakhon Kasem market for brass gongs and rattan baskets. Ernie and Joe, after many winks and a big tip to the tour guide, had made their own plans for the afternoon. In a half-hour, barring one of Bangkok's notorious traffic jams, they would be sitting in a dark bar, glasses of Singha beer sweating in their hands, watching an exotic strip tease. The tour guide, returning the winks and pocketing the tips, had given Ernie a piece of paper with directions in Thai for the taxi driver. Ernie fingered the paper in his pocket reassuringly.

Ernie turned from the room door and hurried towards the flock of elevators hovering at the end of the hall. This was the precise moment that the *phii gaseu* turned the corner and floated down the corridor. Ernie, of course, did not know the creature was a *phii gaseu*. All he saw was a human head with a pulsating bloody heart and gray intestines trailing after it, floating in mid-air, headed straight towards him. He screamed and ran back into room 302, where he promptly fainted.

Far away, in another part of the city, an old woman surveyed a large cardboard box with a critical eye. The woman's name was Da and the cardboard box was her home. The roar of the buses, the gas fumes, and the busy sidewalk flow of pedestrians did not disturb her. The fact that her shelter would not survive another heavy rain demanded all her concentration. Seven months ago, when she had first come to Bangkok, she had spent at least a week dazed by the city's frenzied glory. The contrast between her northern village's green peace and the surreal city could not have been greater.

The countrymen she had found lounging outside Hua Lampong train station enjoyed her amazement. Da was neither young nor pretty, so none of the `fisher women'--the plump, chic women who waited at the station to recruit minnows for the bars and massage parlours--had offered her work. Hungry after the 18-hour train ride, but determined to save her dried fish and rice for as long as possible, Da had wandered inside the station gazing at the beautiful shops full of candies, bottled drinks, gold watches and chocolate boxes. The frosted glass of a refrigerator had fascinated her, until an angry shopkeeper pushed her outside. Too tired to be angry, Da sat on the floor and watched the people rushing back and forth.

A newspaper kiosk brought her back to her senses. Da wanted very much to touch the black letters before they flew away, but she was afraid to anger the kiosk owner. There was a pain in her heart. She recognized the Thai script from the books Mae had sometimes brought home from school, to read by the kerosene lantern Da had bought her for her studies. Da had been so proud of her daughter. The whole village had been proud when Mae left for her job as a maid in Bangkok. Perhaps she was being punished now for that pride. Looking at the hundreds of people, hearing the roar of the trucks and buses outside, Da finally understood what others had told her: Bangkok was a giant that crushed villagers like her in the palm of his hand. He

Land of Smiles - Shelley Anderson

swallowed young girls alive. For the first time she doubted that she would find Mae.

Life had taught Da that work brought solace. She found jobs to earn her rice while she searched for Mae. First she had made dumplings for another woman, who hawked them along with other delicacies in front of the station. But the woman had gone home for a holiday, and Da could not stop eating until she returned. She turned to stripping insulation from wires, wires of all shapes and colors, piled like mountains in a sunless room where she sat half a day at a time. But gnarled hands were not as fast as the hands of children, and the boss told her to go. Now she collected discarded detergent bottles, food wrappings and other plastic refuse and sold them for scrap. She wondered where she would sleep once the inevitable rain had finally rendered her cardboard box a sodden, unliveable mess.

Of course, no one back at the Hôtel Suprême knew that Da existed. They had their own problems. At the reception desk, Sunitra smiled as she helped customers make an international call or locate lost luggage, but inside she was very unhappy.

"It's not natural for a girl your age to remain unmarried! When will your mother and I see our grandchildren? Who will take care of you when we are gone?" The conversation from last night played itself once again in her mind. She had called to say she would be home late, because she and Kanita were seeing a movie.

Sunitra felt guilty, wondering if her parents had guessed what was going on between Kanita and herself. Unfortunately, she knew how they would take it. They were already disturbed over her failure to marry, despite several good prospects they had found for her. Kanita was lucky, Sunitra thought, absentmindedly straightening a piece of hotel stationary. Kanita had many brothers and sisters, but Sunitra was an only child. Her parents had helped her greatly during her student days, and she owed them everything. She understood their longing for a grandchild to cuddle and spoil.

The problem was, it was her parent's need, not hers. How to explain Kanita? Their delight in each other, their dreams and secrets? Beautiful Kanita, with her laughter that could set Sunitra's heart to racing double time as she turned down the alley and climbed the stairs to Kanita's house.

Kanita, of course, also lived at home with her family. She had a room overlooking the family's garden. It was small and tidy, like Kanita herself, with a low bed where Sunitra had spent hours lost in wonder at Kanita's shell-like ears and soft, soft skin. In the other corner was the bed of Kanita's younger sister, which was in frequent use as a place to practice guitar, do school work and to read. Kanita and Sunitra wanted a place of their own, but how to get their families to agree to such an unusual arrangement?

Sunitra realized with a start that the switchboard's red light had been on for several seconds. Chiding herself, she answered the telephone, and struggled to understand the gibberish from a very distressed customer in room 302.

Ernie's interrupted tryst created havoc. The Schulmans, Ernie white and shaking, Mrs. Schulman suspicious that her husband had indulged in too much rice whisky, led a trickle that soon developed into a flood. The hotel staff, shocked but still smiling, soothed the remaining guests and promised discounts. Mr. Guan wondered aloud if someone had drugged Mr. Schulman's coffee, as a prelude to attempted robbery.

He paid for a detective to sit unobtrusively in the lobby and for monks to bless the hotel. Exotic fruits like apples were offered before the spirit house and more incense burnt. Neither the blessings nor the apples worked. Two weeks later, the young wife of a Chinese businessman, on a visit to relatives in the city, returned from a boat ride along the canals and spied the *phii gaseu* hovering outside her room. She had studied medicine before her marriage. She observed the creature's slow drift down the corridor, intestines dangling, and wondered if it was some sort of elaborate practical joke. The hairs rose on the back of her neck when she found no hidden wires. She grabbed a fire extinguisher and aimed it at the creeping monster. Her indignant husband phoned the desk, while the guests in neighboring rooms huddled behind locked doors.

A young and very minor member of a small country's diplomatic corps had also encountered the *phii gaseu* two nights before, upon leaving the room of a consulate's wife. As she was not his wife, and as her husband was higher in rank and from a much larger country, he had decided to keep the sighting secret.

Hotêl Suprême was in an uproar. The elevator operator quit. The cook, an extremely devout Buddhist whose wife's cousin was a witch in the south and so knew about such things, threatened to leave. As most of the kitchen staff were the cook's nieces, nephews, cousins and in-laws, who would leave when he did, Mr. Guan was extremely upset.

Sunitra explained the situation to Kanita when they met that night at the movies. "It's horrible. Everyone's scared out of their minds and the tension is giving me a headache," she whispered, squeezing Kanita's hand extra hard. The latest American comedy played out on the screen before them. Kanita gently laid Sunitra's head on her shoulder and rubbed her forehead. Sunitra thought the creature was probably a stray dog, offal trailing from its mouth, who had somehow found its way into the hotel. Kanita, who worked with a environmental group strongly opposed to the official push for industrialization, wondered excitedly if the creature was an escapee from government nuclear experiments. She was secretly proud of the fact that a creature from folklore was turning out to be real.

They left the movie theater and hurried towards a temple, where they volunteered every Wednesday night. Kanita had been the first to come into contact with the radical monk who headed the temple's food kitchen, but it was Sunitra's commitment who kept them both going. The long line of poor people who waited patiently for the steaming rice and thick soup depressed Kanita. Many of the people, she knew, were farmers who had lost their land to loggers. Kanita received their bows courteously, but was sometimes afraid that the despair and anger that rose within her would poison the rice. The lines grew longer every week.

Sunitra's headache returned. While the monks distributed tea, she laid the soup ladle down and pressed her palms against her eyes. Kanita reached over to rub her shoulder.

The old woman waiting for a bowl of rice noticed the gesture. There was something in the caress that reminded Da of the times her daughter had rubbed the old woman's shoulders after a day in the fields. Da stared at the young woman behind the table, searching for a familiar curve, a treasured look. She did not find it, although the face before her was as young and open as Mae's. But Da's attempt made her aware of something else. She saw the miasma of pain on the woman's face.

Da was well acquainted with pain. She understood its shadings and gradations, its causes and manifestations. Best of all, she had much experience in alleviating pain, because she understood the spirits. She had talked to the spirits many times, just as she had walked through the forests many times to gather healing plants, first with her mother, then later with Mae. She knew how to dry and boil and grind plants and stones to release their powers, knew how to massage an upside down baby into the right position for birth, how to cure a bad burn or a hacking cough. Her hands were already tingling, the power collecting in her fingertips.

Bangkok people often laughed at Da's northern dialect. She didn't care. In her peasant Thai, Da asked the young woman if she would like to be released from the headache.

Sunitra hesitated, sure that the old country woman would try to sell her some worthless charm or amulet. But she did not want to hurt her feelings. "Of course," she said. She never regretted it. She was surprised at how soothing the calloused hands felt. Her surprise deepened as relief trickled from those same hands like drops of rain, then swept across her forehead. She wanted to shout with the pleasure and wonder of it.

"You are a witch," she said, a little fearfully, to the old woman.

"Of course," Da answered. "It's a gift from the spirits." She could explain the different rituals to calm a *phii tai tang klom*--the ghosts of women who died in childbirth--or a *phii tai hong*--the ghosts of people who died by violence; and the different diseases different spirits caused, but she doubted the younger woman would be interested. Bangkok people, Da had learned, were surprisingly ignorant.

But this woman and her friend were suddenly looking at Da with intense interest. The friend asked diffidently, "Do you know anything about hungry ghosts?"

Kanita and Sunitra agreed later that this chance meeting was providential. Da was very happy to share with them what she knew: how ghosts are attracted by trouble and unhappiness, how illness was created by ignoring the proper rules of conduct, how healing could occur after harmony was restored. "It is good you are interested. This knowledge should not die with me," she explained. "Too many people are going to Bangkok and are ashamed of the old ways." When they asked if they could visit her at home, to learn more, Da had chuckled and showed them her wet cardboard box. It was then that the gentle conspiracy was born.

Mr. Guan was sceptical, but after a panicked meeting with his accountant, who was seeing too many figures in the red, he agreed to the experiment. Sunitra and Kanita went to bed at dawn in room 302, next to Da's single room. They took showers with their clothes on and then took them off to walk around the room backwards. Such behavior confused the *phii gaseau*, Da assured them. She herself chanted and burned herbs, seeking an ally in the spirit world.

"I have been promoted and must work longer hours at the hotel," Sunitra bowed and explained to her proud parents.

"This is a unique anthropological study," Kanita bowed and explained to her professor father. "I will write it up and make a good name for the family." Her mother, noticing Kanita's new energy and the happy gleam in her eye, smiled and asked no questions.

A full moon came and went and no *phii gaseau* appeared. Da solemnly informed Mr. Guan that the ritual must continue for at least three months--long enough for the rainy season to end. Relieved that the hungry ghost had not been seen for a while, he agreed.

"Of course, it might take longer. Ghosts are tricky," Da told Sunitra and Kanita one night with a twinkle in her eye. She had come to visit them and to see how they had redecorated their room.

"I thought you told us the ceremony was only done once," Sunitra said dubiously. She offered Da a bowl of mangoes, and then passed the bowl to Kanita, who was brushing her lover's hair.

"We must adjust to modern ways," Da said, grinning. She winked at Sunitra and patted Kanita's hand.

"Oh, no," Kanita smiled back at the old woman. She took Sunitra's hand and then reached for Da's hand. "Modern ways must adapt to us." Sunitra smiled into her eyes. She took Da's other hand. "I prefer the old ways," she said softly, her heart full and at peace.

Ann Adams: I live in the Manzano Mountains of New Mexico near Albuquerque, having forsaken an academic career for the trials and tribulations of starting an intentional women's community. I am currently self-employed as a writer, scroll saw operator, and paper-maker. With all my free time, I garden, work on the tirehouse the community started last summer, and help raise a five-year-old son with my partner Bonnie.

GOOD NEIGHBORS

"The fucking cows have been in the garden!" Susan yelled as she burst into the kitchen.

Molly was startled. "What? How do you know?"

"Because they left huge footprints in the beds about 18 inches deep, shit all over the place and kicked the irrigation system apart so the whole damn thing is a swamp," Susan answered angrily. "We have to do something to keep them from coming on again or they'll destroy what's left of the garden as well as eat all the grass and trees we planted. I can't believe that asshole put them on without telling us."

Even in her rage, Susan felt partially responsible for this disaster. Manuel Romero had come to them a month earlier, to say, "I'm putting cows on the land next to yours. Better put up a fence."

But no one in their small, budding women's community wanted to take on the enormous undertaking and expense of fencing a half-mile of land. They all knew that they were responsible for protecting their own land under the archaic range laws of New Mexico, but there was still hope that Romero might provide the labor and cost.

Susan sighed as she went to call fencing companies. She should have known that Romero wouldn't give them more warning, especially after Karen, one of the other land partners, had chewed him up and spit him out. Of course, she had every right, considering that Romero had driven up the hill, past the house, and on to the meadow with no invitation. Karen started screaming at him before he even pulled his 280Z to a stop.

"Who the hell are you? Get the hell off of this property! You're trespassing and you have no right to be here!"

When Romero tried to smooth talk his way out by saying he was a neighbor, Karen told him that if he wanted to talk with the women on the land he could call or visit them down at the house. He replied, "Well, you're a ...." and Karen responded, "That's right. Now get off this land before I call the sheriff."

There had been other signs of intrusion by Romero. He'd been busy "preparing" the land that he'd leased from his cousin. He had hauled a watering tank to the very western edge of his land, which would encourage his cows to wander over the invisible boundary onto the women's land. He also cut down a number of trees along his northern line so that he could shove the brush under the fence where the ground had washed away. Romero didn't care if the cows went on the women's land, but he didn't want them wandering on to the road. In his enthusiasm for his work, he appeared to have missed the red surveyor tape tied to the fence that marked the boundary between his land and the women's. In fact, he'd gone at least 50 feet past the marker.

"He's just pissing on our non-existent fence," Karen commented when they'd spotted the water tank and the downed trees. "He's trying to force us to make our move, but we'll wait him out."

Susan knew that only trouble would come from waiting, because Romero could act whenever he wanted, leaving them scrambling like they were now. But Karen was the oldest and had the most ties to the local Hispanic community, so Susan had followed her advice. Now Karen was out of town on a business trip and Susan had to pick up the pieces. If they'd taken action, at least tried to talk to him again, maybe some kind of compromise could have been reached. Unfortunately, Romero was such a womanizing prick, no one wanted to deal with him. Consequently, they were dealing with his cows right now. Susan wasn't sure which was worse. In any case, Romero was obviously waiting for them to do his work for him. But the cows were his; it should be his money and labor.

As Susan picked up the phone to dial the first fencing company, an idea came to her. Stunned by the simplicity of the strategy, she forgot to hang up the phone until it beeped at her. She put the receiver down and walked calmly into the living room.

Molly had just returned from checking out their devastated garden. "We have to do something, Susan!"

"We will," Susan replied lightly.

"What do you mean? How can you be so calm when the cattle have ruined everything you've worked so hard on?"

"Because I figured out how to solve our problem."

"Well, don't keep me in suspense! Let's hear it," Molly said.

"Okay," Susan began. "Romero expects us to put up a fence so that he can keep his cows on his land and make his money without having to put out a lot of energy. But he's forgetting that once his cows get out on the road through our land and we close our gate, there's no way for them to get back on to his land, especially since Mr. Romero only plays cowboy on the weekends. In fact, I suspect that he's sitting in his home in Los Alamos chuckling about our little predicament right now. Since today is only Monday, we have four or five days to play with his cows."

Molly stared at Susan in amazement while the plan registered in her brain. Then she smiled broadly and asked, "What do you think we should do with them?"

Susan replied, "Well, I'm torn. I thought about losing them in the National Forest but they'd just be grazing free when Romero should be paying a grazing fee... it would take him a lot of time to round them up. I thought about running them down to Perito and out onto State Route 27, but they'd be a hazard. Then I remembered Romero's spring wheat crop. I've heard that cows will break through a five-strand barbwire fence to get to wheat. Since Romero is too stingy to put up a five-strand or even maintain the four strands he has, I say we look for a spot where the cows could get through."

"Let's do it, " Molly said after a moment of contemplation. "I'll check out the fence and you go find out where the cows are and get them to the front of the meadow."

Susan felt the excitement rise in her body. "Come on, girls! Let's punch some dogies," she called out to the dogs lounging on the couch. "It's time you earned your living around here. Just think of those cows as giant black and white spotted sticks to fetch."

Alice, a small Lab mix, slowly lifted her head to consider the possibility, but Gertrude, a Shelty mix, eagerly hopped down, ears raised and ready for action. Alice lethargically followed Susan and Gertrude out the door and up the hill. But once they reached the meadow where cows were scattered all over, she became a great deal more interested in the possibilities that lay before her. As she tensed to run, Susan restrained her verbally: "No, you wait until I tell you or you'll have the herd spread everywhere. Come."

Good Neighbors - Ann Adams

The dogs stayed close to her heels as she skirted the cattle. The cows were clearly used to human attention and only glanced briefly at Susan and the dogs before continuing their grazing. Each time Susan saw a cow drop its head and rip a large clump of grass from the ground, she winced. She knew the cows were only doing what they needed to survive, but not on her land.

When Susan got behind the last of the herd she turned around and regrouped with her eager troops. "Okay, gang. Now you get to do your thing. Alice, you go right; Gertrude, you take the left," she said, gesturing with her arms.

Rather than obeying her command, the dogs took off side by side, like bullets, heading for the nearest cluster of cows, barking furiously and dancing around their heels. Startled by this sudden intrusion, the cows froze momentarily, then crowded together, kicking at their tormentors. After a few moments they started to move off.

Susan noted with relief that they turned to the road. *Of course, Romero used to graze his cattle on this land before we bought it from his brother. He was always herding them onto the road to get from one piece of land to the other. They must be used to this,* she thought to herself. *Boy, he must be pissed he can't graze them here any more. Not half as pissed as I am for getting jerked around. Well, he's going to find out we're not just a bunch of passive females who will kowtow to his every move.*

Susan returned her attention to the task at hand, as one cow tried to escape from Alice's insistent harassment. Susan jumped into the cow's path, waving her arms, and it quickly rejoined the herd, but not before shitting right in front of her. As the odor assaulted her nose, she cursed Romero again.

She saw Molly at the top of the hill and waved her acknowledgement as Molly pantomimed that she would herd the cows out the gate. She was relieved that Molly had considered that problem. With no one to direct them, they would have spread all over the lawn in front of the house.

But Susan realized that the tricky part would be to get the cows down without losing them in the trees that lined the right side of the hill. She'd just have to hope that the herd instinct would do the trick. With the fence off to the left, she ran to their right. The dogs continued barking in the rear.

Susan picked up a stick to wave. The cows were bellowing like air raid sirens and rolling their eyes nervously as they lumbered along. Susan decided to enjoy her part. Yelling "Yah" like Annie Oakley reincarnated, she felt pleased with her success; so far so good. The cows responded to her commands by nudging the calves along in an attempt to avoid separations.

Suddenly, Susan noticed that one of the larger cows was actually a bull. He turned around to face Susan and snorted angrily as he pawed the ground. Drool hung from his mouth to the dust at his feet. Susan paused and glanced around for cover. A little belatedly, she realized that there might be a reason why people herded cattle on horseback rather than on foot.

`Stepping closer to a stout pinon, she decided to call the bull's bluff. Waving her stick furiously and yelling louder than ever, she drove the bull back to the herd. Wiping the sweat from her forehead, she breathed a sigh of relief.

When she rounded the corner of the drive at the bottom of the hill she saw Molly waving the cows through the gate like a tollbooth operator at rush hour. The last one was a stray calf, who had initially thought the chasing game was fun, until it heard its mother's plaintive bellow and frantically ran to find her. Molly and Susan followed it out and closed the gate behind them. Whatever happened now, at least the cows were off their land; the rest was gravy.

While the women paused to catch their breath, the cattle milled in confusion on the road, then began wandering off in both directions. Molly and Susan had to act quickly before they lost control of the situation.

"There's a really weak spot not too far off that way," Molly reported gleefully. "I helped it a little by pushing the wire down with my foot. No finger prints and the cows will wipe out any foot prints."

"Why don't you go back there and I'll drive them to you," Susan suggested. Molly called the dogs and the three of them moved up the road. As long as she wasn't bothering them, the cows were content to graze. Meanwhile Susan eased her way along the fence in the opposite direction to get behind them.

Once in position, Susan easily moved the cows forward since fences lined both sides and they had nowhere else to go. Up ahead Molly stopped and pointed at the fence. As the herd approached, she yelled and waved her arms. Her actions excited the dogs at her side, and they began barking.

With these obstacles in their path, the cattle balked and milled in circles. As the tension, noise and dust increased, several cows saw their opportunity, the sagging wires of the fence Molly had sabotaged. They surged forward, pushing through. The nearest post snapped under their weight and the cows pushed harder, their necks outstretched as they called for their calves. They effectively trampled what remained of the fence, and the rest of the cattle followed. They spread out eagerly once they realized the manna from heaven that lay in front of them.

The women propped up the fence post to cut off the cattle's escape route, and quickly left the scene, tired and sweaty but pleased. As they walked down the dirt road towards home, Molly asked Susan, "So, what are we going to tell Romero when he calls about his cattle?"

"We'll tell him the truth," Susan replied. "We found his cows on our land and we chased them out onto the road. There's nothing illegal about that. Later, when we noticed they'd tromped his fence down, we put it back up. After all, that would be the neighborly thing to do."

***Sara Aletti** worked for more than twenty years in executive editorial capacities at several national trade publications. She currently owns and operates a small New York-based public relations firm. She has published both fiction and non-fiction, and has written one novel, which remains unrepresented and unpublished.*

As a professional photographer she has shot everything from magazine covers to buildings under demolition, and had several one-woman shows during the late sixties and early seventies.

She is old enough to wish she were younger, but not too old to enjoy good, hot, horny and creative sex.

COMMENCEMENT

We sit arm in arm, savouring the spirit of nature. Our shoes are banished as we dig our bare toes into the moist earth. The light green of early Spring kisses the hills and suddenly, somehow, we look at each other. I sink into your eyes, your cornstarch blue eyes, the color of the sea on a sunny day. And I find my lips on yours, just a heart-stopping brush at first. Sharply, I breathe in your breath and it's sweeter than the Spring air.

Our lips touch again, and this time we nuzzle each other. Lips caress lips. Our tongues peep and touch, withdraw at the spark, then touch again. You draw my tongue deep into your mouth with a suction that is slow but so inexorable it threatens to pull the rest of me into your mouth after it. I explore your tongue and teeth, then invite your tongue into my mouth.

We are sitting in the tall grass, just the two of us, as the Spring wind dances in the trees. Then, I find myself being undressed slowly by your tentative, nervous hands, sweet hands so loving. My heart beats so loudly, I nearly swoon as you lift off my blouse and unbuckle my bra, exposing my breasts to the breeze.

My breasts have never seen the sun or felt the wind. My nipples gather themselves up and harden in the air, and I lie back and savour your caress and the electricity you somehow seem to carry in the tip of your tongue. You minister to my nipples, alternately rubbing them with your fingers and polishing them with your tongue. Again, I feel like I am being pulled into your mouth, piece by piece.

You slowly roll down my panties, kissing me everywhere as you go. I feel your lips on my stomach, thrill to the shy dart of your tongue in and out of my navel, ache as you trail your tongue down my belly but cruelly skip over my pubic hair to land gently on my inner thighs.

Slowly, you brush off my bare feet, rubbing off the dirt and the leaves and the grass, and kiss my toes one by one. You nuzzle my arch and rub my foot against your cheek. You hold both my feet together, like praying hands, and kiss them, sucking first one foot, then the other completely into your mouth as your tongue bustles under and between my toes. I have never thought of my feet as erotic. Now I know better, and I long to know more. You will teach me unimagined delights. I am writhing, as the longing in my groin passes beyond rapture and becomes something very close to pain.

You make your way, achingly slow, as if we had all the time in the world, dragging your provocative tongue up my shins and thighs. You gently pull my legs apart and nuzzle my soft inner thighs, kissing and nibbling until you have reached my most intimate lips, which are dripping with honey.

Lips on lips. The grass under my buttocks is deliciously scratchy as I open my legs as wide as I can to admit you. I feel like a flower opening to the morning sun. Oh, your tongue is a revelation, a world in itself of warmth, a wet caress made wetter by my own wetness. You run your strong fingers through my pubic hair, knitting from it little curls, as you take my entire sex into your mouth, sorting it out piece by piece: first lips, then clitoris for your tongue to know, then throwing your tongue deep into my channel.

You move your hands up my soft belly, raking it into goose flesh with your long fingernails as you go, until you find my breasts. They are cold from the air, and your hands are warm and soothing. You roll my nipples between your thumb and forefinger and middle finger. I begin to quiver, fluttering like a leaf in the wind. I suck in the Spring air, my mouth drying as I moan and coo, unable to put into intelligent words how this merciless ministering tongue is pulling a climax from deep within my fundament.

Slowly, from within my bowels, a climax rises. At first it is a tiny spot midway between ache and tickle, the head of a pin buried so far within me I fear it may never be brought to the surface, that it might die inside me, stillborn. But your tongue digs and digs and digs, excavating as patiently as an archaeologist investigating an ancient site, probing thoroughly every sector of my vagina, discovering every trick of my interior geography, and mapping it mercilessly.

My climax grows with each tongue-thrust, growing from that pinpoint to fill the vacuum my body has become with an explosive and unbearable anticipation. I can feel the climax flowing from my toes, from my fingertips, from my scalp. I try to put it off, to savour this moment before the inevitable eruption, to preserve it like an ancient leaf locked in amber. I want it to last forever. I have never been this alive. I have never experienced such pain. I have never experienced such rhapsody.

But as much as I try to hide the climax from your omnipresent tongue, you burrow into my every corner until you pinpoint it and drag it out of me. I become the climax. I scream into the Spring air. My shout of exhilaration seems to shatter the sun, which disappears for the moment, alarmed, behind a wispy stream of clouds. Wave after wave after wave flows out from me, as my body bucks in the wild abandon of pure feeling. I don't care that I scream. Let the woods hear it. Let the sky hear it. Let God cover His ears as my shouts of physical emancipation ricochet from corner to corner of His heavenly abode.

I am unraveled, undone by that probing tongue, and reassembled stitch by stitch. I have been to the mountain. And I will never be the same. I have been touched by the heaven in your hands and your tongue and I am transfigured.

Can I ever recapture this exquisite moment? Can your tongue or any other ever flush me out again like that? I am terrified that I have peaked, that I will never again rise so high, where the air is almost too thin to breathe. I fear that I will spend the rest of my life trying to relive the moment that has just died. I begin to sob.

You kiss the tears from my face. I can smell my own juices on your lips and I can taste myself in your tongue. We have exchanged our essences. You twine your fingers around mine as your lay next to me, pressed so close that we are cemented to each other by sweat. My blood seems to flow from my heart, down my arm and through the palm of my hand and into yours. We transfuse each other as we tighten our grips. I close my eyes and let the breeze stir in me again that feeling.

Oh, you are so soft I want to cry again. I open my eyes to see my own breasts quivering with my convulsions. You roll onto your side and pull me onto mine. Your breasts flatten against mine as your hold me tight to kiss my trembling lips. I can feel your jewel-like nipples harden against mine. You open your hand to span my left buttock, kneading it as one sly finger slips between my cheeks to find my anus. You tickle it with your fingernail, and little sparks go off inside me. I am so wet from my own juices and your saliva that you easily slip your finger inside me to fill me, literally and figuratively, with a profound sense of satisfaction. You pull my buttock hard towards you, and our pubic hairs mingle. Our nests rub together. I part my legs slightly, and you pull me onto your thigh. I ride it to another climax, shorter, softer, sweeter, less disruptive.

I give you a long, deep kiss of thanks, caressing your miracle-working tongue with my own apprentice tongue. I nuzzle my way down your cheek and, after resting for a moment in the hollow of your neck - such a sweet-scented neck, I can feel the big artery pulsing with life against my cheek - I lower myself until I find your breasts. They are so much larger than mine. Wondrous, they fascinate me. They sit like big puddings, clean and pink, with a cherry nipple riding on the rhythm of your breath.

I gather up one big, soft breast in both hands, and squeeze it into an enormous blossom topped by your bud of a nipple - sweet little nipple, pink and puckering with delight at the homage of my lips and tongue. With my first lick it gathers itself up proudly into an erection that feels stiff and rough to my tongue.

At first I just kiss it, over and over, pulling at it with my lips, drawing it into my mouth and sucking gently, then letting it fall back into itself. Over and over, I suck at it, drawing more of the big, fleshy globe into my mouth each time. Eventually my mouth is joyfully filled to overflowing with soft, ripe tit.

You open your legs for me. Your lips part to reveal a tiny cavern, walls moist with syrup waiting for my tongue. I approach your cunt almost prayerfully. With my curious fingers I open you. I have never seen anything this mysteriously beautiful, this deeply intimate. I look inside you and I seem to see your soul.

I kiss your trembling outer lips, which respond by drawing themselves up like angels' wings. My lips stick to yours as I burrow to find your clitoris, which is bold and erect, demanding the attention of my tongue. First I lap your collected honey, which is sticky and warm and sweet beyond imagining. As I dip my tongue into it to savour it, I feel tremors deep with you. You lift your legs and encircle me. I reach up over your belly to find your big, soft breasts. They have become cold so I cover them with my hands, which are as flushed and heated with passion as my face. Your nipples are rough and hard as wood. I dig my long thumbnails into them and your body twitches as you take a sharp breath in response.

I find your little button clitoris, draw it carefully into my mouth and lock onto it with my teeth as I burnish it with my tongue. Oh, oh, oh, you whimper. I can feel your climax growling deep inside you as your abdomen trembles in anticipation and growing excitement. At first, like a dreaming puppy, you quiver and twitch and grunt. Then your climax takes hold of you and of me, and I am tossed like a boat riding deep sea swells as you writhe. Your legs grip me powerfully and push my face onto your vagina, welding our lips together. I am almost driven into you, as if you are pushing me - mouth, nose, face, maybe all of me - into your vagina. You want to ingest me. Sweetest, if I could, I would crawl all the way into you, find a warm, wet, dark hollow deep inside you and lie there forever.

Your climax has its own language and choreography. You mew, you wail, you laugh, you grunt and mutter. You raise your legs in the air and point your toes at the sky, then drop them back to earth and spread them wide, then close them again to lock and press me like a flower in a book into the plush flesh of your inner thighs. Your hips rotate clockwise, counter clockwise, then buck sharply against my face three or four times in quick succession. The soft soles of your bare feet fondle my head as you run your toes through my hair, at the same time pushing my face against your vagina. All the while I hold your pulsing sex captive in my mouth, locked securely in my teeth.

Then the crescendo of your climax is over. Your breasts are slippery with sweat. I bail your vagina with my tongue as my head rises and falls on your gasping breath, which slowly dies down to the point where I hear nothing, feel nothing. You are so quiet as I lie rubbing my cheek against your pubic hair, that I am almost afraid you have died of pleasure. My tongue is proud of its work.

I surface from between your legs. My face is covered with your juice, which nearly masks the sharp smell of the late afternoon air. You splay your legs and I kiss your dripping vagina once more, then crawl

120   *Commencement - Sara Aletti*

up over your body. I nestle on top of you and you close your arms and legs over me. Breasts on breasts, vagina on vagina, we fit like two halves of a mold. We must be made for each other.

You smile as you look into my eyes. We don't have to speak. We are fulfilled. We have tasted deeply of each other and found the taste wondrous. We are enchanted with each other. We hold onto each other, and I doze at your breast while you caress my hair.

The sun descends, turning increasingly deep shades of gold, then orange, then red. The shadows of the nearby trees crawl towards us and, finally, cover us with a chill shade. We kiss again, long and deep. Your lips stick to mine.

I never want to dress again. I want to remain naked, locked in your body's grip forever. I want to take root here. Both of us. I want us to grow, to leaf and flower, season after season, here on this hillside.

How moonlight would become you, I think, and wish we could stay into the dark so I could see you clothed only with moonsilver here on this hillside, your skin blue-white, your pink lips and nipples dark and inviting in the shadows. I wish I could run through the night woods naked at your side, I wish we could fly on the night air like ancient forest goddesses.

But the world is too much with us. We have to dress and go home. How heavy my clothes feel, how confining my bra after my breasts have danced in the sun, how claustrophobic my panties seem after my vagina has tasted sweet spring air, how tight my shoes after my feet have dug into the earth and been caressed and kissed by my lover.

My lips, my breasts, my vagina, my feet will never be the same. I will never be the same. I know what and who I am now.

Commencement - Sara Aletti **121**

Janet Bohac's collection of fiction, Evidence Of The Outer World, *was published in 1992. Born and raised in Michigan, she received her B.A. in Creative Writing at University of Miami and lived in Miami for twelve years. She has also been a Screenwriting Fellow at The American Film Institute in Los Angeles. She earned her M.F.A. in Creative Writing at Western Michigan University and has taught writing as the 1994 Writer-in-Residence at Austin Peay State University in Clarksville, TN.*

LOVE LIKE LAND

My father grew up along the Waccasassa Bay, down a piece from where the Suwannee River mates with salt water. He grew up knowing that ground shifts, that the land one stands on is a temporary gift that can be taken away. Land is a dynamic rather than a static thing. One big storm, rain or hurricane and the view from your window changes. From year to year the channels change. Sand collects, mangrove pods--formerly content to float out to sea--drag bottom and deposit themselves. Soon there is an island, then land, and like the sea, the land becomes one fluid motion.

The colors in this part of the world are green and blue. The sky and ocean are blue; the trees are green. The fresh water springs are both green and blue at the same time and have a nacreous quality like the firey part of an opal or a child's soap bubble.

So the point is, not even the colors remain the same. Like the margin between water and land, there is an ebb and flow between blue and green. Only the clouds, ibises, and people interrupt this continuum.

My father left Waccasassa Bay to work on the highway known as the Tamiami Trail, so named because it was the only road going if you wanted to get from Tampa to Miami. He finally settled in Chokoloskee, a place very much like Waccasassa Bay, where the fresh water of the Everglades slides into the Florida Bay, following the inch-by-inch slope of land and the force of gravity. The important thing to remember here is that the fresh water is pulled by a force it does not need to understand. It is pulled by a force of physics and it must obey. It has no choice; it doesn't need to think, understand, contemplate, make decisions. There is no opportunity for vacillation. The only thing

122   *Love Like Land - Janet Bohac*

that can happen is a larger force, like wind, like a hurricane that will temporarily push the fresh water back into the glades and cause the salt water to encroach miles upstream from where it belongs. But this is temporary and eventually the fresh water will once again find its way through the mangroves and sawgrass and cypress and palmetto.

It will obey in the end.

That is the thing to remember.

So the story I am going to tell you has its origins in this world of blue and green, water and shifting sand, but this story has many possible beginnings.

The important thing to remember is not that this story begins here or has as many beginnings as a channel has islands, but that it has only one ending and the end is here.

One possible beginning of this story is to tell you how my father, who worked on the Tamiami Trail and subsequently became a backwoods guide in the swamps of Florida Bay, married my mother, a woman from Arcadia. Arcadia, a couple of hours to the north, was as static and stable as the coastal swamps are changeable. The only thing of interest there were the summer storms which had a fierceness and drama unlike anything else in Central Florida.

My mother, as solitary and eccentric and leathered by the sub-tropical sun as my father, began to paint watercolors when she moved to Chokoloskee. A gallery or two in Naples and Sarasota carry her work and she has always made enough to keep her in cigarettes and scotch, a drink she uses ritually, only at sundown, to toast the sun on its way under the horizon.

So I grew up in the boat, on the water, in the swamps, but not in the world of people. My mother's idea of cooking was a sliced ripe tomato on Sunbeam bread. My father's idea of cooking was gar or mullet or tarpon or bream fried in a skillet over a campfire.

The important thing to remember here is not that my mother had no culinary sense or that I never ate meat except for the occasional bit of fresh venison, rabbit or squirrel that my father was given when a tourist from up north bagged more than he could use, but that I grew up in a blue-green world of shifting channels instead of the world of people.

Miami, when seen from the shallow water of Biscayne Bay about six miles out, looks like a cross between Venice and *Robocop*. Glass pillars rise out of the water and reflect the blue or grey of the sky. The Metrorail trains scoot up into the sky over the Miami River and glide down into the center of the pillars on a rainbow-colored track.

It looks as stable as any city can get with concrete and glass and asphalt, but it belongs to the coast. Concrete and asphalt were once pourable.

Glass is always in a liquid state.

When I decided to leave Chokoloskee for the world of people, the logical step was Miami. I wanted to be a journalist, but the *Miami Herald* seemed a closed society, and so I ended up writing freelance for the myriad journals and alternative magazines that had sprouted. I covered club openings, who was seen with whom; I did movie reviews and theater reviews for small theaters who needed whatever press they could get. I worked as a dishwasher, hostess, waitress, whatever, whenever I needed money to pay for my apartment on South Beach, and as soon as I had enough money saved to keep me for a month or two, I'd quit.

You could do that on the Beach because it was a boomtown. Every block had at least two restaurants on each side.

In Chokoloskee we were lucky if we ever had two restaurants open simultaneously.

Apparently after the Civil War, the United States had some interests in the Aleutian Islands that had to do with walrus and seal fur. They sent the pelts to London, and this is not important except to tell you that from these furriers in London, Clare McDonough's great-great-great-great grandfather emerged to own a mink farm in Maine.

The family eventually settled in Boston, and Clare, a few generations down the loins, came from a well-to-do family. She was educated at Yale and became a psychologist who specialized in Jungian analysis. Most of her clients were women, and most of these women had to be of Clare's social background in order to afford Clare's analyses of them.

What's important to note about Clare, however, is not so much that she came from money or inherited her father's black Packard when he died or that she used her great-great-great-great grandfather's steamer trunk as a bench at the foot of our bed where she sat and put on her shoes every morning, but that she came from the world of people.

Were you to ask Clare, she would not find this at all significant. She would have no frame of reference, no Chokoloskee, no Waccasassa of her own in which to place this definition of herself.

Maybe it was that Clare and Helena both came from money, or that their families came from islands. Maybe there were a bazillion similarities that increased exponentially, geometrically, or algebraically when factored together.

Helena Anoni's family money came from Trinidad, but I never heard exactly how. Sugar? Salt? Rum? I made a note for myself once to look up the facts about the GNP of Trinidad, but I never did.

I met Clare McDonough at a party Helena Anoni was throwing to celebrate her newest avant garde theater space she called "No Shame." The first production was entitled "Prostitude" and featured four sex workers Helena had culled from Biscayne Boulevard and the escort agencies. The women started off with monologues scripted from their own experiences, but every performance was different, depending on the audience's participation. On opening night, a male volunteer from the audience was spanked after being ordered to drop his pants.

From friends who continued to attend this production of No Shame faithfully during its year-long run, I heard opening night was exceptionally tame in contrast to what came later.

Clare and I became favorites among our friends to tease for our stable , vanilla-sex , no dyke-drama relationship. Clare told people we were "garden variety" lesbians. I always thought she meant this to indicate we were like tomatoes or potatoes as opposed to high-maintenance, hot-house orchids, birds-of-paradise, or passion flower vines. Like one might care for potatoes or tomatoes, we cared for each other with consistency and consideration. There was nothing slap-dash or hit-and-run about how we tended to each others' needs. We always planned evenings together and regarded them as sacred and inviolable. If a story lead popped up during the day, I would let it go if it meant breaking our plans. Clare had no patients who required evening care or frantic suicide watches.

We lived together in this way for four years before Helena Anoni disappeared.

At first, no one was really sure that Helena was missing. While it was totally unlike her to miss the opening night show and reception of No Shame's latest production , it was also just like her to fly up to New York on a whim to stay at her apartment because she missed the City. She had flown on the Concorde just to see a friend's theater piece in London one evening, then flown to New York in time for breakfast. So with Helena, anything was a possibility.

Staying out of sight and incommunicado for two weeks, however, was not.

I began to formulate a story idea, one that was sure to get interest in the local rags, if not something bigger, like *Interview* or *Rolling Stone*. I began to interview people around South Beach, at parties and clubs, and ask them for their theories on where Helena had gone. I started carrying around a tape recorder in my pockets instead of just a small notebook.

From one woman, Penny Anti, a performance artist who frequently appeared in No Shame productions, I got this: "I think she probably sold herself into white slavery, either in Bangkok or Morocco and is presently enjoying being buttfucked about twenty times a day by anonymous patrons. If I catch up with her, I'm going to be her night relief. A girl needs a break, after all, and I'm happy to do it."

From a bartender at the Warsaw Ballroom: "Helena isn't missing, darling. She's here practically every night. We've got every queen on the Beach dressing up like Helena. On Sundays we pick the best one at our tea dance."

Her brother Brian, however, took the matter seriously enough to file a missing person report with the police in Miami, New York, and Trinidad, and when another two weeks went by without any clues, he told me, "I don't know where she is, but this isn't a joke anymore."

I overheard a couple at the next table one morning at News Cafe swapping Helena Anoni theories and scribbled them down later:

SHE: "She joined Hoffa on deserted Caribbean island."

HE: "Actually, it's an island in the Bermuda Triangle and there's a time warp that allows them to be raising the Lindbergh baby as their own."

When I finally got up the nerve as a no-name, no-paper, freelance reporter to talk to the police, all they could tell me was what had been recently released in the paper: Helena Anoni was missing without a clue.

The first time I took Clare to meet my folks, I warned her that all she could expect of the local fare was sliced avocados and maybe some beer-boiled shrimp. On the way down, we stopped the Packard in Everglades City and bought five pounds of stone crabs, some sweet corn and red potatoes.

Clare designated herself the house chef for the few hours she was in Chokoloskee and shooed my mother away whenever she tried to do more than tell annoying stories about my childhood.

We ended up with a feast. I had never seen my parents relish what they ate like they did whenever I took Clare to visit on weekends with the Packard. It was her way of making them love her.

And, of course, they did.

Friends at first joked to Brian Anoni about putting his sister's photograph on milk cartons around the country and about sending out those mailers that have ads for steam cleaners and Roto-rooters on the flipside.

He put up with it for those first two weeks, then anyone who kept at it wasn't invited to the house anymore.

Others took their places at the parties.

It was maybe about this time I noticed something different about our bedroom. Clare and I were undressing for bed and talking about who was obviously no longer welcome at Brian's. Clare had one leg up on the footboard and she was unbuckling the sling on her shoe. Her dress was gathered up enough for me to see the curve of her thigh and I stopped. I stopped undressing and fell to my knees in front of her and kissed that part of her thigh that led to the very heart of her. Then I looked up at her tenderly. She was looking down at me and we smiled, and then she did something she had never done quite like this before. She ran her fingers through my hair, then grabbed a handful and pulled me to her roughly, grinding herself into my face, my lips, and my waiting tongue. As we fell to the floor together, I noticed the grooves on the carpet left from her great-great-great-great grandfather's trunk that had always sat where we now were making love.

"What happened to your trunk?" I asked.

And Clare, who rarely used language harsher than "Cripes!" looked at me and said, "My great-great-great-great grandfather can go fuck himself," and pulled my face down to her.

A mutual friend, Carmen Diego, when asked for her theory on what had happened to Helena Anoni, said, "I think she was probably kidnapped."

"But there's been no ransom request," I reminded her.

"Helena probably just paid them herself."

"But her brother says there's been no mysterious withdrawals since she's disappeared," I countered.

"Then," she replied, thinking, "he's in on it."

"I think it's the brother," a waiter who preferred to remain anonymous told me one night at Bang. "He just wanted her half. He got greedy."

"Do you know Brian?" I asked.

"No."

"Then how can you have this theory?"

"It's classic. It's archetypal. I don't have to know him, or her. Though she was in here once in a while."

The authorities had no suspects and no body, just the absence of Helena. Brian knew they were probably keeping an eye on him, but it didn't bother him. He figured while they were watching, he wouldn't be likely to disappear too.

They dredged the canal behind the house, from the Doral to the Fontainebleu and only found shopping carts and a Chevy Nova.

I asked the director of the current show at No Shame if Helena had planned to be at the opening night of "Macho/Faggot/Madonna/Whore."

"But of course! In fact, she had said she was making a video tape for us to use during the play's run. You know, when the main character is masturbating to the television? Well, since she never arrived with it, we had to send somebody out at the last minute for *Deep Throat* or *I Spit On Your Grave*, but, as it was a Saturday night, there were no copies to be found on the Beach, so we had to go with *Lassie* dubbed in Spanish which actually went over quite well.

Sometimes instead we now alternate it with the forest fire scene from *Bambi*. Both get a good laugh from the audience, but I don't think it's what Helena had in mind."

A particularly dry month and an especially low tide coincided, and one morning when my father was jumping into his airboat with a couple of tourists down from Kentucky, he found Clare's great-great-great-great grandfather's trunk breaking the water's surface under the dock. At the time, of course, he didn't know what it was, or what it was doing there, so he took his clients out for a ride and a day of fishing tarpon in the mangrove swamps.

Later that evening, when the tourists were gone and my mother was enjoying her ritual scotch and cigarette on the porch, my father dragged the trunk by its handle to the shallower water, flipped open the locks, and found Helena Anoni decomposing at his feet.

I spoke to Clare's mother only once on the phone in the four years Clare and I lived together.

She said, "Don't let Clare's dishonesty get to you. She can't help it."

"On the contrary," I said, "I think Clare is one of the most honest , most principled people I know. That's why I love her."

It was true. To me, Clare was the kind of person who, had she been a journalist, would have gone to jail rather than reveal sources, or who, as a prisoner under torture, would refuse to give names.

There was a silence for a few seconds, then Clare's mother said, "Obviously Clare hasn't told you about her father," and hung up.

Obviously, Clare hadn't.

She never did.

I never asked.

For some people, others are interchangeable parts.

For others, life is a brightly colored 500 piece puzzle and every piece must be present, must be turned right side up and snapped into place, and people are those pieces.

There is a third group to which I belong. For us, life is a puzzle. Period.

Obviously, my father called the police, the marine patrol, and the neighbors out to see what had floated under his dock. However, the steamer trunk of Clare's great-great-great-great grandfather was too heavy to have floated. It had to have been placed there.

Once the police and FBI were satisfied that my father and mother had not placed the trunk there, and neither had I, they took Clare into custody and charged her with the murder of Helena Anoni, a charge she responded to not at all. She refused to talk. Her lawyer pleaded not guilty when asked how she pled, but it was clearly a formality, and the jury had no trouble finding her guilty when the evidence was amassed for their edification.

The evidence found was this: scuff marks on the terra cotta tiles of Helena's foyer exactly matched the dimensions of Clare's great-great-great-great grandfather's trunk as did nicks on the rear fender of Clare's Packard. Fingerprints in Helena's house matched Clare's, and when the police searched Clare's office, an untitled video of a pornographic nature was found on her shelf next to *Synchronicity* and *Dreams And Their Interpretation*.

The opportunity to dispose of the body had come just hours after Clare had killed Helena Anoni.

Clare woke me up with a cup of coffee and suggested a drive out to Chokoloskee. She needed to drive and think, and she felt like surprising my parents by cooking a big pan of paella.

The car was already loaded.

All I had to do was get out of bed and get dressed.

When we arrived, Clare sent my father and I off to buy some oysters and shrimp. My mother could always be trusted to stay put in her studio until sundown, and it was then Clare backed the Packard up to the dock, dragged her great-great-great-great grandfather's trunk to the end, and pushed it into the water and watched it sink.

The medical examiner declared the cause of Helena's death to be asphyxiation as far as he could tell.

The why took longer. But this time, I wasn't asking for anyone's theory or following people around parties with my tape recorder in hand.

Instead, the press was following me around.

Only after Clare was found guilty was I able to learn the why.

The Clare McDonough who faced me from behind a shield of plexiglass and stared into my eyes asked no forgiveness. There was no shame.

"I'm only going to tell you briefly," she said, talking into the phone, "what happened. Then, don't come here again."

She waited for a nod or some sign of agreement from me.

"I only want to understand," I said.

"You won't understand, and I don't care if you understand. I don't care if anyone ever understands.

"Helena and I were lovers for six months. We made a show of her being my patient. I even let her pay me, so the secretary wouldn't find anything unusual in the billing.

"It wasn't at all that I seduced her. It was Helena who seduced me, who unlocked in me the key everyone has, but few can turn at will. We made love in my office and I allowed her to turn me into her slave.

"I like giving up all control and she knew it. She used it. She used me.

"The night she died, she invited me to her house. I let her tie me up to the bed. It was something I had fantasized, and she was giving me my fantasy. She blindfolded me and put foam plugs in my ears to make me focus entirely on the love we were going to make. She left me there for a while to anticipate all the things I wanted her to do to me. From somewhere she had got a tank of nitrous oxide, a dentist friend or someone, and she gave me that to make me relax, and turned up the stereo so loud I could feel the bass pounding through my body and when I was completely ready, she came to me and did everything I had asked for, many times over, until I was exhausted and fell asleep.

"When I woke up, she was sitting up in bed watching me. I was no longer tied and when I went to put my arms around her, she motioned mischievously to the television set where a video was playing silently. She pushed the volume control on the remote and the thudding of that music she had been playing earlier rose up.

"There I was, splayed on the bed, having all the things done to me that I remembered Helena doing, only it wasn't Helena performing them. It was some woman I had never seen and would likely never see again, someone Helena had paid to fuck me while she filmed it for the new No Shame play.

"I felt sick and horrified and betrayed and the worst was that I had consented to everything--as long as it was with Helena. She had crossed a line, but worse, so had I. I had had my fantasy, and it was all I had wanted it to be. I wanted it over and over. I wanted to be used up. I wanted to be tied up, out of control, free of responsibility. She had brought me to that knowledge and she could now use me however she wanted. I would never have the power to say no. In a sense, I let her have my soul and I never wanted it back."

"But she was going to use the tape for the play," I said.

"Exactly. And I knew I would let her, that I would get off on it, but it would ruin my friendships. It would ruin my professional life."

"And us?"

Clare stared at me as if through me, as if I were not even on her list of considerations. "So I tied her up, as she had done to me, making her consent to her death. I wish I hadn't done it," she said, focusing on me. "I'd like to go on being her slave for the rest of my life."

I've been back here in Chokoloskee now for six months. I help out my father whose arthritis nags him when he tries to bait or tie the lines. Some days he stays at home while I take a couple of businessmen out from Naples to catch a few tarpon or mangrove snappers.

We don't talk about Clare or her trunk or my brief foray into Miami and the world of people.

I've begun to think I might be content to stay right here and take over the business from my dad as he ages. My mother likes having me around to cook dinners and run her to the galleries whenever she gets a half-dozen or so watercolors together to sell.

There's a constancy I find soothing in the water, a consistency in how the fish bite the lures or fight by pulling the lines under the boat and down the channel. I am happy to deal with land that expands and contracts and changes shape with the tides and seasons in a way that follows the force of gravity, of physics.

The only thing to remember here is that gravity is not the only force.

Frances Lorraine has been a champion of women's rights since the first Civil Rights March on Washington in 1963. A writer, artist and entertainer, she is known in San Francisco's gay community for her performance in "Hot Flash Follies" and her role in Barbara Hammer's "Nitrate Kisses." Currently she volunteers at Coming Home Hospice giving love and healing massages to the dying.

Frances, as her name implies, is a great believer in freedom of expression. She adores cats, thinks old dykes are beautiful, and believes life is too short to take seriously. Ars longa!

MATILDA IN THE HIGH SIERRA

I unfasten my backpack at the waist with a groan of relief and let it slide off my shoulders. From the top of the 10,000-foot ridge the view is awesome. To the east Cathedral Peak, etched in dusky purple, strangely isolated. Behind it Tenaya Canyon and its deep, dark lake. I can see Mt. Dana, which I have climbed, and her sister mountain Gibbs. Distant ranges are shadowy, snow-capped, melting into the hazy blue clouds.

The backpack trip is a birthday present to me from my daughter Ellen and her husband Mark. Our long climb to this remote plateau began this morning when we left the trailhead in more or less single file behind Ellen and Mark, both in their early forties, carrying the heaviest loads. Then my older daughter Jane, a flatlander like me, late forties, tall and strong, followed by Ellen and Mark's son Cody, six years old, a mountain boy carrying a large pack of his own. I brought up the rear, a militant lesbian feminist hale at seventy, looking forward to our adventure and getting away from it all. I should have remembered about looking for adventure -- it is all too easy to find.

The sun was warm and the uphill trail crowded with day trippers, some of whom seemed to prefer hiking in high heels. Even though I was better equipped, I was unused to the altitude and felt as much of a novice as they looked. After a mere fifteen minutes of slogging I knew I was in trouble. It was as though a great weight were pressing me down into the mountain. The straps of my heavy pack dug into my shoulders, the belt pinched my hip bones and I couldn't move fast enough to keep up. Those coming down the trail passed me with their little postage-stamp backpacks, talking and laughing, and I hated them. At our first rest stop I encouraged everyone to drink from my water bottle, figuring an ounce down a gullet, any gullet, was an ounce off my back.

Back on the trail my right shoulder began to ache and I could feel my neck muscles bunching. All too soon I was in agony, breathing hard, sweat running into my eyes, getting further behind. Cody was dragging, too. He looked like I felt. I glared at the ill-shod feet shuffling past me and concentrated on my two big boots, willing them to take the next step, yanking on my should straps, tightening my belt. It didn't help. I felt old and incompetent. Should I apologize and go back to the car? Was I too close to death to backpack? Then I remembered what George Sand once said about old age, it wasn't sliding downhill to dissolution but climbing with surprising strides. I strode.

Following Cody around a switchback, I found the others resting comfortably beside the trail. "Take your pack off," Mark said, "and let's fix it." Oh god, music to my ears. Twenty years ago my pack might have been state of the art. But it was a soft pack, no metal braces, depending for its shape on being properly filled. I emptied the damn thing and Mark stuffed sleeping pads into the two major compartments, clothes and food bags on top. The straps were adjusted so it rested on my hips and leaned gently away from my shoulders. I took as deep breath as I could of the thin, sweet air and felt I might make it after all. Cody's pack was lightened, Mark adding to his load, and we were off.

We walked into the high country camp at May Lake in time for a lunch break beside the sparkling blue water. Two friends of Ellen and Mark joined us, a tall, quiet man who is a photographer of some note and a woman professor at Berkeley who talked and talked in a grating voice while we ate. I wished silently that she would disappear. Noisy people pollute my wilderness. One by one we sidled away to the restrooms, the last latrines we would see. From now on it would be dig a hole, burn the toilet paper, fill the hole then dig a different hole the next day. At last we got away, walked around the lake and left civilization behind, not to see another human being for five whole days.

Now the serious climb began. No trail this time. It was follow our leaders, trusting to their formidable knowledge of the topography. It wasn't a long climb in time but it was intense in effort. Rocks became boulders, trees grew bent and twisted, there were big patches of snow to cross and streams to be forded. And everywhere there were fragile alpine wildflowers, none taller than six inches, tiny perfect shapes in brilliant primary colors. It was already August but still spring in the high country.

As we climbed higher and higher, the air cooled, the light changed, clouds shifted, mountains unfolded and glorious new vistas opened up. Not that I had much time to appreciate the views since it required most of my concentration to find the best footholds and to look up and down at the same time. Every crest revealed a higher one and each time Mark would say, "It's not far now." The sun was westering before we reached the final crest, our campsite, and all the effort was worth it.

We stand on our plateau and savor the view. There are more mountains in all directions than I have ever seen. We survey the campsite and, under an arbor of white-barked pine trees bent by the wind, find a flatish area perfect for our tents and smooth-topped boulders for tables and chairs. There are snow banks on the far side which drops down precipitously to a lovely green valley dotted with small lakes of an intense cerulean blue. Huge snowfields streaked with pink -- a kind of algae -- are weirdly beautiful. One of us remembers tonight is full moon. All five of us turn our heads to the west to gauge the progress of the sun.

"There's Mount Diablo", says Mark, pointing. From here? I find it hard to believe but I don't argue, he is invariably right. I do believe we are going to have a colorful sunset though, judging by the thick band of pollution blurring the horizon.

We make camp, pitching tents, unfurling down bags to plump, unpacking food and pots and utensils, locating our water source, all the important things that have to be done before I can take off my hiking boots. Eventually I am able to sit down and loosen the rawhide laces, freeing two pale, fragile feet from their ancient leather prisons. Leaving my socks on, I ease into soft slippers and wriggle my toes with pleasure. As the heat from the sun leaves and the temperature drops, we all change from shorts and shirts to long pants and sweaters.

No campfires are allowed at this elevation, so we cook over a small burner connected to a bottle of white gas. The food tastes heavenly. Dishes are scrubbed with pine needles and rinsed in the snow. Chores done, we stretch out on the big flat sun-warmed boulders to watch the sun setting while I read the first chapters of Roald Dahl's "Matilda" to

Cody -- and three fascinated adults. Cody is soon asleep in the round yellow tent.

The rest of us have after-dinner herb tea laced with brandy and gaze at the ever-changing beauty of the mountains surrounding us. Slowly the sun slides into the ocean behind the Coast Ranges still faintly visible on the horizon. The sunset is brilliant, great crimson banners fading to orange as they melt into the still blue sky. We keep turning our heads to see if the moon has risen but clouds are piling up and it seems unlikely we will see moonrise tonight. I, for one, am too tired to wait it out. I zip into the cocoon of my sleeping bag in the little pup tent Jane and I share, and fall asleep listening to the silence.

Our days pass timelessly as we succumb to nature's rhythms, rising with the sun, eating when we are hungry, going to sleep when the light is gone. Our toilette is simple, a splash of ice water, a slathering of sun screen, a quick brush of teeth and hair, and that's it. Each day we explore different parts of our world unencumbered by packs, little day trips to the south, to the north, to the west. We take turns writing or drawing or painting in the sketchbook Mark brought. We play in the snow, tell stories, read "Matilda" and lose track of time. I feel as if I have been here forever.

One day the others decide to climb an enormous geologic upheaval to the south which we name "What's The," for what's the point. I elect to go off on my own, and we agree to meet back at the campsite. After all, people can't enjoy solitude together. Slinging a canvas bag across my chest, I drop down off the ridge to the valley below and head west through the snowfields, across a stream of melted snow and over a granite dome to a green meadow. Lounging on the springy grass I see a tiny bouquet of wildflowers with reddish stems and purple-blue flowers like little trumpets growing out of a crack in a rock. Very paintable, I decide. I get my sketchbook and pocket-size watercolors out of the bag, using drinking water to mix paint.

It is quiet and peaceful, only a faint hum of insect life and the occasional bird call break the silence. I lean back against a rock and watch little white clouds float in a so blue sky. A raptor, wings outstretched, hangs motionless above me. Rocks and boulders gleam and glitter in the sunlight, polished eons ago by glaciers. High on the crest behind me I can see the little yellow tent, cheerfully discordant amid the gray and chalk and umber of the landscape.

Ambling on in a generally westward direction -- or so I believed at the time -- I climb a rocky escarpment and cross more snowfields, marking their pristine whiteness with my boot prints. Towering rocks shelter me from the chill in the wind as it blows over snow. I settle in the shade of a gnarled white pine and make quick sketches of glacial domes, trees, boulders, meadows, the indomitable wildflowers, the mountains behind me, trying to capture on paper the feeling of this place, the tranquility, the peace. What a privilege to be alone in all this beauty.

As I meander along, I lunch on trail mix and dried fruit, do some more sketching, then drowse in the languorous heat under a rocky overhang. A tiny sound startles me. I open my eyes and see a grizzled marmot standing on a rock, still as a statue, paws folded and nose aquiver. We stare at each other for a moment. I sit up and she vanishes. Since I am an intruder in her world, I move on, whistling under my breath.

When the sun is no longer overhead and the air begins to cool, I untie the flannel shirt at my waist, button the long sleeves and head back to camp. The lowering sun feels good on my back but the landscape looks like nothing I have seen before. I climb a ridge and see a snowfield unmarked by footprints. That can't be right, I think, and veer off in a different direction. At the top of the next ridge I look around -- no, I don't remember this either. Unfamiliar as the high country is to me, I know enough to keep looking behind me so I will be able to retrace my steps. I thought I had, and I did make sketches. The sketches! I pull them out of my bag and spread them around, discarding the westward views. Yes, there is Mt. Dana and her glacier, surely I can find that again. And the sun, six weeks since the summer solstice, shouldn't it be setting a little further north -- or is it south? Oh hell! Angling to the north, I set my sights on a ridge, climb it, look around and see another untrodden snowfield.

I stumble down through rocks and boulders in the half light of a canyon and up another rocky promontory, and see nothing recognizable. Sitting down on a boulder I try to quell my rising panic. The cold strikes suddenly and thoughts of hypothermia crowd my mind. The light is leaving and all too soon it will be dark. And I am well and truly lost. I suppose I could die -- I give that a thought. I am not afraid of death and from what I understand freezing is a nice, easy, sleepy way to go.

Come on, old girl, stiffen the sinews. I get up and press on as thoughts come at me from every angle. On one level I am responding to the rocky terrain and at another level I can see in the waning light a skull-like face floating before my eyes, an old woman's face, gaunt and strong-boned. It is Ruth, a woman of ninety-two whose body I have massaged at the hospice where she lies dying. She knows she is dying and her face is calm and serene. Other faces crowd hers, faces of beautiful young men who have died horribly, inexcusably, some accepting death, some fighting it to the last gurgle. On another plane I am thinking about the cat whiskers I have been saving that I won't be around to make into a paint brush. My rapidly-chilling body jerks me back to my dilemma.

Think, I tell myself. If I keep climbing in a generally eastward direction, I should see something I recognize, a shape, a mountain, a footstep in the snow. Shivering, I button up my shirt, turn up the collar and continue eastward, climbing over and around rocks and boulders, checking the view from the top of every ridge for something familiar. In the deepening gloom I stumble, slam my shin against a rock and feel a sharp jolt of pain. I massage my shin as the pain slowly subsides, then wrap a bandana around my leg for comfort, and face the fact that since I might have to spend the night out here where the temperature drops to freezing, perhaps it would be smart to look for shelter, a cave or a hollow, something, before the light goes. On the other hand, since I probably wouldn't make it through the night anyway, I might as well keep trying. That way I would get to see my little family once again.

I plod on, favoring my leg as I climb, looking for a familiar silhouette. Nothing! Then over the next ridge I see what looks like the top of Mt. Dana and my heart races -- but it isn't where it was in my sketch, too far to the north. Confidently I move south and run into an impassable pile of granite, immense and shapeless. I can hear water murmuring somewhere as I climb around and up and over the boulders and I see a snowfield with footprints -- my footprints! Forgetting the pain in my leg, I climb and climb to the top a ridge and way up ahead I can see a tiny speck of bright yellow -- the little round tent in our campsite. At the same time I hear voices calling me. I holler back, clambering down the rocks and run through the snowfield, slipping and sliding, across the creek, up and up the rocks, sweating, skinning my hands, gasping for breath. I look up and see Mark coming down to help me. I wave him away, shouting that I want to make it all the way on my own.

I reach the campground and flop on the ground, sweaty and proud of myself, laughing aloud, and look up at the dear faces of my next of kin -- as I momentarily thought of them -- feeling life flowing in my body, and I love them all so much. I am also happy to hear I haven't missed dinner. As they cook something delicious, I tell them about getting lost and how I was afraid I might have to spend the night somewhere out there, cold and alone. Cody looks worried and comes over to hold my hand. Mark hugs me, says I did all the right things, and that he will make an outdoors woman out of me yet. My daughters look at me, then at each other. They don't say anything but I know what they are thinking -- something along the lines of what will our ditzy mother do next. I decide not to waste energy trying to justify what happened. It reminds me of when I was married.

When everything is cleaned up and put away, it is time for "Matilda," and I have fun doing the voice of Miss Trunchbull, the big dyke who frightens the tiny children. Cody goes to bed, we have tea and cookies and talk of this and that, everything except my close brush with death. The sky is remarkably free of clouds except low on the eastern horizon where they bunch up on the craggy peaks, and it seems possible we will see the moon. The sun goes down in splendor and the smog is a pale lavender when a gibbous orb peeks out from behind Cloud's Rest. Moonrise! Brilliant white light turns the rocks and the snow to silver.

On the morning of our last day we decide to go back to the valley. I am careful to keep everyone in sight and don't wander off by myself. Although Jane seems to have forgiven me for frightening her, Ellen avoids me. We lunch in a shady grove and I lie back and watch the others as they ski down the snowfields without skis. I marvel at the balance my grandson possesses. He will be hell on a ski slope in about six years, I figure.

By mid-afternoon clouds are piling up ominously and Mark says we should head back to camp and fix dinner in case we have a storm, not uncommon in the high country. Just as we finish eating, we see the first big drops of rain splatter on the rocks leaving coin-shaped blotches. Quickly we clean our dishes, put the supplies in tents or under plastic, hang the food bags, brush our teeth and don our rain gear, all the while watching the ragged black clouds streaming overhead.

All at once the storm breaks. Great flashes of lightning are immediately followed by thunderclaps which reverberate in the mountains and boom-boom-boom from every direction. The rain falls in sheets but as if we were in the eye of a hurricane, only a few sprinkles fall on us. The eastern ranges disappear behind heavy curtains of rain, clouds from the north race eastward, swaths of rain blot out the western horizon. Lightning blazes, thunder slams and roils, and we stand on our plateau in the center of the maelstrom, watching untrammeled nature's awesome spectacle. Cody is frightened by the thunder so I tell him about the Crees and Grandfather Thunder. He laughs.

The pine trees whistle in the wind and the tents billow. Some guylines break loose and we race around bumping into each other as we grab rocks to pound the anchors back in the ground. Stimulated by the electrically-charged air, we prance and strut about with wet faces, singing and laughing like fools, while the storm blows itself away. Cody jumps up and down hollering, "Grandpa, grandpa" back at the thunder. Ellen puts her arms around me and we laugh and hug and there are tears on her damp face.

The storm abates and everything is all right again. The sky is covered with clouds and it is too dark to read, so we get inside our blowing tents hoping to anchor them with our bodies. And we sleep, lulled by the song of the wind in the pines.

In the morning the sky is a calm blue and the sunshine benevolent. After breakfast, I read the last three chapters of "Matilda" to Cody while the others break camp. We all do garbage inspection, picking up every scrap of trash, and leave the area untouched by our presence except for footprints soon to be obliterated by the wind. We have just enough food left for lunch on our way out. Our leaders' careful planning pays off.

Going downhill is easier at first. Jane puts my nearly empty pack inside hers and the pull of gravity plus no pack gives me new freedom. However, after an hour or so my knees turn to mush and every time I step down I wonder if my legs will hold me. But with plenty of rest stops my rubbery legs make it to May Lake and people and the trek down the trail to the car. As we drive back down the mountains, grubby, smelly and tired, I luxuriate in fantasies of hot water and bathtubs and sweet-smelling soap.

The next morning I kiss them all goodbye and thank Ellen and Mark for a wonderful birthday present. Then for me it is back to sea level and cement and noise and throngs of people, most of whom will never have my experience and will never know the incredible beauty and peace of the wilderness.

If it is true that our souls never really disappear from the universe, I hope mine will be climbing mountains for all eternity -- whatever that is. Hanging around monumental piles of rock for an eon or two would give me exquisite pleasure. And I would never get lost. How could I?

Mikaya Heart is a Scottish dyke who now lives in northern California, on a very beautiful piece of land. She has led an adventurous life and greatly enjoys writing about it. She builds houses, fixes cars, creates gardens and orchards, keeps horses, cats and a dog, and raises trout in her old concrete swimming pool. She embraces her own magnificence and encourages all women to embrace theirs. She feels the most important things in life are to speak from your heart and live as your soul desires. She doesn't tolerate bullshit. Women are sometimes intimidated by her but if they bother to go beyond her tough exterior, they soon find out what a smush she is.

ON THE RUN

I don't know what it was that woke me: the restlessness of the horses, or the smell of smoke, or just some inner awareness of danger approaching. I lay in my sleeping bag wavering foggily between sleep and wakefulness, Lena beside me snoring gently. Gradually the meaning of the smell of smoke impinged on my consciousness and I sat up abruptly, sniffing the air.

"Lena, wake up!" I shook her urgently. "There's a fire somewhere nearby. Wake up!" I scrambled out of my sleeping bag and began to pull on my clothes, struggling with them in the darkness.

"What's the matter? For God's sake, Sal, it's the middle of the night!" Lena was never happy to be woken out of her precious sleep.

"We need to get ready to move out of here. There's a fire, and it may be moving this way. Get your clothes on."

"Where's the fire?" she grumbled. "Can you SEE it?"

"Lena! Wake UP! No, I can't see it! If I could see it, I'd be yelling at you!" I was really exasperated with her. I tried to be patient. "We're in the middle of a forest. Forest fires move really fast. We may not be in its path, but if we are, we may be in danger. So we need to get ready to move."

"Well, where's the flashlight? How are we going to be able to go anywhere when we can't see?"

I ignored her grumbling, and handed her a flashlight, silently cursing the moon, which was just sliding out of sight over the treetops. Lena was right -- it would be very hard to find our way in the dark, on terrain that was unfamiliar. I looked at my watch. 12:40. Three or four hours till dawn.

I began to stuff the saddle bags with our cooking equipment, holding the flashlight in my teeth. The smell of smoke was alarmingly strong. I was shakey and I kept dropping things. A gust of wind brought an extra strong whiff of burning, and I suddenly realised that there was a stiff breeze, which meant the fire could be moving very fast. Maybe we shouldn't be bothering to pack the non-essential stuff. I dropped the saucepan I was holding and flashed the light around to locate the saddles. As I did so, I saw an orange glow in the sky above the trees that surrounded our camp.

"Lena! We have to move it! Look at the sky!"

Lena was standing, pulling on her pants. "Hm. It could be a long way off, there's no need to panic."

"There's a strong breeze, that fire could be moving very fast. And it's downhill from us, fires always move uphill."

"OK, OK...why don't you get the horses saddled up?"

I moved off, found the saddles and carried them over to the horses, tethered to trees nearby. Abe was anxious, I could tell by the way he held his head high and flicked his ears to and fro. "It's OK, boy, it's OK. We're gonna get out of here, don't you worry." I scratched behind his ears with one hand, and ran the other along his back. Then I threw the saddle over him and tightened the girth. He sidestepped away from me, the way he always does, and I sternly told him, "Ho!" I slipped his bridle on over his halter, but left him tied.

Then I turned to Kinny. As I put the saddle over her, Lena came up and took my arm. "Sal, look!"

The urgency in her voice alarmed me and I turned at once. In the distance below us, you could just see the tips of flames licking at the orange tinted sky. I drew in my breath sharply. "Damn!"

We looked at each other, our faces no more than blurs in the darkness. Lena spoke first. "Finish saddling Kinny. We can leave the food, it would take too long to pack it." We had it tied up in a tree 100 yards away, in case of bears. "It won't take a minute to throw the saddle bags on Jade, and then I guess we'll just follow the top of the ridge as best we can. I'm going to take a quick look at the map."

Moving as fast as I could without light, I got Kinny saddled up and tied the hurriedly packed bags onto Jade, leaving half our equipment where it was, on the ground, hoping I'd got everything that was essential. By the time I was ready, Lena was already mounted on Kinny. I let Jade loose, she would stay with us. I hoisted myself up on Abe, and followed the bouncing light that was all I could see of my partner.

When I caught up with her, she said, "There's no path marked on the map, but there's probably some kind of trail along the ridge, and we should hit the Eel River in five or six miles. I figure we'll be safe once we cross the river."

"If we can get there..." I knew our flashlights couldn't last. "If only we could've gone back to the trail in the valley..."

"Too dangerous. We might be OK once we got to it because we could move faster, but we'd have to go back towards the fire to get to it."

She was right, we had no choice. At the top of the ridge we paused to look back. From here you could see the full extent of the raging flames, stretching for about a mile behind us, from the valley floor up both hills. I was awestruck at the immensity of it, at the overwhelming power of the fire. Beside me, I heard Lena swearing softly. Abe shifted uneasily underneath me, and Kinny nickered. I turned Abe and we moved off at a trot. Now at least there was no need for the flashlight -- the fire cast an eerie orange glow all around us. Still the going was difficult, barely any path could be made out, and branches hung low. I crouched over Abe's neck and let him lead the way. We came to an open area, and Jade took off, galloping past me, saddle bags bouncing on her sides. Abe and Kinny picked up the pace and we soared over the ground. I couldn't see where we were going and that scared me, but I was more scared of the fire that was chasing us. The smoke was thick in the air now. I glanced back briefly and could immediately tell it had gained on us. I didn't need to urge Abe onwards, he was already at full pelt.

The open ground gave way to scrub and stunted trees, and we were forced to slow down. We could hear Jade crashing through the undergrowth ahead of us. Lena and Kinny caught up with me.

"Sal, we need to get hold of Jade. We can't risk having her loose."

"Why not? She's probably better at picking a path than we are."

"Well, maybe, and maybe not. Supposing she panics and heads back towards the fire?"

I ducked my head under a low branch, and steered Abe away from a tree trunk to prevent him crushing my leg.

"Let's leave her for now."

We carried on, and came to a downward slope, where we had to make the horses walk, both because of the steepness and because it was darker now that the light of the fire wasn't shining on us. At the bottom of the slope lay a meadow and I heard Jade whinnying to the other horses. As we emerged from the brush, Jade came running towards and around us -- I could just make out the shape of her as she kicked her heels up in the air, and stopped a few yards away, nickering gently. I dismounted from Abe, and walked over to her. She let me take her rope and I stroked her head. She was wet with sweat, and shaking nervously, her head high.

Ahead of me, Lena called, "You got her?"

"Yeah, she's pretty freaked out."

"So's Kinny, she really wants to run."

I got back on Abe who was waiting patiently, like the gem he is, and set off at a canter, leading Jade. As I caught up with Lena, the horses speeded up, and we settled into a gallop. I was thankful for the speed, it made me feel safer. Then disaster struck. In front of me in the darkness, I saw Kinny fall, and Lena shoot over her head. I tried to pull Abe to a stop and nearly came off myself, as he swerved around Kinny who was getting back on her feet, and Jade continued to gallop onwards, nearly wrenching my arm out of its socket. Normally she was easy to lead, but now... I let go of the lead rope, and pulled Abe's head around so that he turned back towards Lena, and slowed down. I jumped off before he came to a full stop, and grabbed hold of Kinny's reins so that she couldn't take off after Jade.

"Are you OK?" I called to Lena. I could just make her out in the darkness. To my relief she was picking herself up.

"I think so," she said as she limped towards me. "I hope Kinny's OK. She must've put her foot in a hole."

I fished the flashlight out of my pocket and watched Kinny as Lena walked her in a circle.

"Shit, she's limping on her left hind leg."

"Damn!" Kinny turned her head anxiously towards Lena as she bent to examine the injured foot. "Well, I dunno what she did but I don't think I should ride her. It's obviously hurting her."

"Fuck! What are we going to do?" The flames were out of sight for now but the glow was very bright and the wind was still strong against my hot face. I was close to tears of frustration. "Lena, do you hear that noise?" There was a steady roaring sound. We both listened for a moment. "I think that's the fire. It's very close."

"Come on!" Lena set off at a run, leading Kinny.

"Don't you want to ride on Abe with me?"

"No, it's safer this way. You'd probably be better walking too," she called back over her shoulder.

She was right, especially now that we were back in thick brush. I dismounted and followed her. We carried on like that for half a mile or so. I was sweating and shaking but now we could see the flames again, shooting upwards into the darkness, jumping from treetop to treetop, and I was scared enough that my adrenalin kept me going. We came to another clearing. Once again Jade was waiting anxiously. This time I didn't try to grab her.

"How about it now, Sal?" Lena panted, looping Kinny's lead rope around the saddle with the reins.

"Come on," I said, and climbed onto Abe. Lena got up behind.

"Thank the goddess for a big horse," she said as she put her arms around me and tangled her fingers in his mane. I gave him his head and we shot forwards after the rapidly fading shapes of the other two horses.

We travelled for another mile or so like this, still following the top of the ridge, but then the trees became thick again, and Kinny lagged behind, her leg obviously causing her pain. We both got off to walk. Abe was very skittery.

"The river must be close now," Lena said, and sure enough we were starting to go downhill. As we came around a bend and into a small clearing, the flames were clearly visible only a few hundred yards to our left. The crashing of falling trees and the crackling of the consuming flames were loud and constant now. I felt my heart thumping in my chest.

"Sal, we have to go to the right!"

"Let's get hold of Jade, she's going to be nuts!"

She grabbed hold of Kinny's reins and the two of them ran ahead. I winced at Kinny's limp.

We could hear Jade whinnying wildly ahead of us, and soon she came crashing back through the undergrowth to find us. Lena grabbed hold of her lead rope. She tossed her head and pulled back, but we paused long enough to calm her with quiet words and then the five of us set off at a dead run, now moving more to our right. I don't know if we were even following a deer trail at that point, but somehow we found a way through the undergrowth. Branches snapped at my cheeks, my head pounded in rhythm with my feet hitting the ground, and the smokey air rasped in my throat. Abruptly the ground became very much steeper and rockier. We had reached the cliff that dropped down to the river.

There was no need for a flashlight now. We could see the river below us in the orange glow. It seemed like a long way.

"Christ, Lena, what now? It's far too steep!"

"We need to go further to our right." She sounded so self-assured. We struggled back up to where the ground levelled a little, and moved onwards again at a trot. The flames were closer than ever, shooting upwards in great roaring orange swords as they devoured tree after tree. It would have been beautiful if it hadn't been so terrifying. The sounds, the crackling and whooshing and the occasional bang as something exploded from the heat, were no longer distant; they drowned out Lena's voice as she called something back to me. My eyes were stinging in the smoke and I swear I could feel the heat of the flames. The horses were nearly frantic, their heads high and nostrils heaving.

But the way was downhill, and there was little brush, so we made good headway, though I slipped and fell on my butt several times, and Abe got ahead of me, and nearly dragged me along. Then Lena stopped abruptly and we nearly ran into Jade's and Kinny's rear-ends.

"Goddamn, Lena, what's the matter?"

In an even voice, she said, "We're trapped, Sal. We have to go over the cliff."

Sure enough, a couple of hundred yards ahead and below us the flames were at the cliff's edge, flickering along the sparse grass between rocks and flaring up in bonfires wherever there was a manzanita bush. I stood transfixed in horror, my chest heaving.

"Come on, Sal, move! Help me get the saddles and bridles off!"

I snapped to attention, and undid the girth on Abe's saddle. We tossed the gear down the slope towards the river; after all we might be able to pick them up later. Then I helped Lena remove Jade's load, and it too followed the saddles.

For one long precious moment we stood looking at each other, framed in the flickering orange light. Lena's eyes were narrow and stern, her hair, wet with sweat, plastered over her forehead, as she looked up at me, searching my face as though she was memorising it. I reached out my hand and brushed her cheek. She smiled. "OK, my love, this is it."

Nothing more was said. I took Jade's rope, and Lena hesitated, but then let me take her; once partway down the slope Jade would go on by herself, whilst Lena would have to go more slowly and carefully because of Kinny's bad leg.

I led the way. The cliff didn't really have an edge -- it just got steeper. Some semblance of a path wound down and I hugged it close. Jade was breathing down my neck, Abe close behind her. We crept downwards, placing our feet carefully. The horses seemed calmer now. I wondered if they understood that I was taking them to the river.

We came to a rocky outcrop and crept around the edge of it, slipping and sliding. I grabbed a manzanita bush to steady myself and managed to pause on a tiny ledge. The horses crowded along, pushing at me. Pebbles from Lena's descent rattled and rolled down around me. I could see the river gleaming below, and felt a great sense of relief -- it flowed slow and deep. If we had to jump we might avoid landing on rocks.

I had to move on, there was no room to stop. There was also nowhere to go. I stepped out onto the slope, and began to slide, grabbing at rocks and bushes, but trying not to let go of the lead ropes, afraid the horses would never choose to follow me on this insane route. There was a jerk as Jade balked, then I caught myself on a shrub. Next thing I knew Jade was sliding past me, sitting back on her heels like something out of a cartoon. Somehow I managed to let go of her lead rope. She gave a frightened bellow, like a cow, and disappeared from sight. Reassuringly quickly I heard a splash, and then within moments I saw her emerge on the far bank, shaking the water off her coat. I closed my eyes in relief and joy -- if Jade could make it, we all could.

I heard a whoop and looked up to see Lena perched on a rock above me with a huge grin on her face. I grinned back. She gave me the thumbs up sign. It was Abe's turn now. I got my footing and tugged on his lead rope. He wasn't moving. I pulled as hard as I could without overbalancing, but he just put his head up and dug his feet in. He could tell there was nowhere to go. I considered letting myself slide down, presuming all my weight would budge him -- but supposing he slid over me on the way down?

"Lena!"

"Yes?"

"I can't budge Abe. You're going to have to get behind him."

"OK."

There was more scrambling and then I heard Lena's voice from behind Abe.

"OK, Sal, are you ready? I'm going to hit him."

I braced myself and pulled hard on his rope as I heard her cursing and yelling at him. He tossed his head and whinnied. I winced at his pain and confusion and tried to communicate to him that we were only doing what was necessary. Then he half reared up and stepped out onto the slope, following Jade's path. I let go of the rope and waited in dread. Abe was bigger and less nimble than Jade -- he might not make it so easily.

The splash came and I craned my neck to see. An age passed and then at last I saw him wading out of the water. I closed my eyes and sent a prayer of thanks to the river that was saving our lives. A sob caught in my throat. There was more scrambling behind me and I heard Lena's voice.

"Here, take Kinny's lead rope."

As I reached out to grab it, I heard a whoosh and saw a manzanita bush only a few feet above us burst into flames. The heat and the brightness were enough for Kinny. She slid down past me, and in a few seconds I watched her clamber out, to be greeted by welcome whinnies from the other two horses.

Now it was my turn. I looked up at Lena. Her crouched form was framed by the flames of the burning bush. She was grinning.

"See you on the other side of the river, Sal."

I closed my eyes, took a deep breath, and stepped out. Immediately I fell on my butt and slid downwards at what felt like alarming speed. My butt was raw, then I was flying through the air and I heard myself scream. Just in time I remembered to close my mouth, then I hit the water.

The cold knocked all the breath out of me and I struck desperately for the surface, sure I would drown. Then my head was out in sweet smokey air. I gulped it down. My thrashing arm hit rock, and I remembered I had to swim for shore. The current wasn't strong, a few strokes took me to the beach. I scrambled out onto the pebbles and lay there gasping.

I heard a scream above me and turned just in time to see Lena hit the water. Seconds later she was lying beside me. I rolled towards her and we lay in each other's arms, panting and sobbing and laughing.

Finally I sat up and looked around us. Dawn was breaking, and I could see where the river broke into foaming rapids only twenty yards downstream. I imagined being impaled on those rocks.

"Christ, Lena, we were lucky!"

Just then something blew warm air down on my dripping wet head and I turned to see the three horses right behind us. They'd come to find us.

Pat Pomerleau, after many years spent building her life in the hills of Mendocino County, California, is continuing to build her life in Santa Rosa, California ... aided, somewhat, by electricity, a new and magical force in her life that seems to spring from a switch on the wall! She is also aided by her chosen companion, El Sparkito, a bilingual dog who is teaching her Spanish. If offered a milk bone, she will sit up and say: "!HOLA!"

I SEE AMERICA PASSING * ADVENTURES OF A TRANSVESTITE FLAGPERSON ALONG THE GREAT HIGHWAY OF LIFE

Hiya. My name is Faye. I'm a transvestite flagperson on a highway job near here. Highway One Oh One just south of a little town named Willits. It's a pretty fascinating job -- and educational too! The people I see!

Of course, I hope they think they see someone special too when they see me! I mean, I don't do this transvestite thing for nuthin'. But I don't primarily do it for other people either, you know. It's part of a spiritual quest for me. Been going on a long time.

I first got into it back in the late fifties when I was selling vacuum cleaners down in San Francisco. My partner at that time was a Swedish angel who, you could say, had fallen off the top of a Christmas tree one day and then she picked herself up, and -- recognizing that she needed to make a buck or two, started selling vacuum cleaners on commission. She was a tiny little fragile thing and we both agreed she needed a strong person to help lug all that equipment around. So, I'm pretty tall and big and I went down to the Helping Heart Thrift Store in the Mission and got a man's three piece suit for $3.00, and a tie and some shoes. And then we went out as a man and wife team selling those vacuum cleaners. Later on, I began to find that I was getting close to realizing my essential being, as a woman dressed in men's clothing. Now, I don't mean to say that my feelings are those of a man, as far as I can tell, that is. Least ways, I hope not, considering... But I'm a flagperson, not a philosopher, though I do write a poem now and then. Anyhow, I do like the clothes!

And I like being calm and kind inside these clothes. I just do the fake beard and moustache and cod piece because I like to tease and confound, and it pleases my complicated Piscean nature. I like to blow peoples' minds by being gentle and tender inside these rough clothes. And I get a kick out of trying to "pass." I've lived up here on Shimmins Ridge, just outside of Willits, for some seventeen years. Long enough to see a lot of things pass, and pass by. My life has settled down a lot and now I wear my clothes and I do my job and I see what I see, passing me on that long hard road. And at night, after work, I write it all down.

Today I saw a really old hippie in a multi colored 1962 VW van with American flag curtains. It had a VW bug welded to the top for a sleeping loft. I've seen that guy before. He keeps passing by.

I saw thirty Winnebagos towing silver Honda Civics and I saw a Palomino mare driving a Ford 250. She was towing a spiffy 4 compartment horse trailer filled with people. They were playing cribbage and drinking Coors. I thought it was politically incorrect and out of respect for the mare, resisted a temptation to flag them to a stop and keep them waiting for a while. The Palomino had a Mercedes Sosa tape going full blast. I blew her a kiss.

I see America passing.

This morning my cousin Mavis from Covelo drove by, on a grocery run to Ukiah, or so I supposed. She had one of her earless French goats in the back seat of the car. She grinned at me and gave me the finger.

A pink T-Bird with porthole windows came by and a young guy with a fake handlebar moustache was driving it. He asked for my phone number. Then there was a woman in a pith helmet. She tossed an apple to me. I made a one handed catch and managed to keep the

S L O W
                sign upright.

At twelve noon we shut down and I sat in the shade of a pile of culvert pipe and ate the apple and the lunch I had brought and then I wrote three short poems with a soft lead pencil on the inside of my lunch bucket. Later on, a backhoe ran over my bucket. Busted my thermos and squashed the poems. I kept trying to remember them all afternoon and I wrote some parts of them on the inside of my right arm.

About three o'clock I saw one "U. S. Out of Central America" bumper sticker and I counted eleven NRA decals before the day was over.

It's America. I see it passing.

A Dominican Sister whizzed by on a skateboard. She was towed by three Rastafarian Brothers in a blue 1967 Mustang with a chopped top. The Sister waved and tossed me an orange she dug out of an Italian string bag that was attached to her waist with a loop of wooden beads that looked like they'd come off one of those fancy car seat cushions that sort of like to come apart, you know? They were headed up to the Eel for the reggae festival, I suppose. "Holy Shit!" I said, and I rolled up my sleeve and started another poem.

I saw a dozen cars with cats in them. I saw a Chevy pickup with five Border Collies chained to the spare tire.

In the late afternoon a white Dodge van crept past. It was so hot the asphalt was melting under my boots. There were three blond tennis players in the back of the van and they were all naked. The one in the middle had snakes tattooed around her ankles. I didn't notice who was driving.

I see America passing. I see it all.

When I got home tonight I heard my partner Ophelia on the phone. "FAYEeee!", she screeched at me when I came in banging the screen door behind me. "It's yer cousin Mavis. Says she's had a cow... No, wait. It's a goat. Deliverin' a goat and broke down out on the Orr Springs Road. Wants to know can you go down and get her. Thinks maybe something's wrong with the transmission. Says to bring a couple a come-alongs and a chain saw."

So I grumbled and threw some stuff in the back of the pickup. Then I threw in a hydraulic jack, jumper cables, a crow bar and a set of plugs. Mavis never does anything half way. If she says she's blown the tranny then she's probably got that car two thirds the way up a big fir tree. And the goat too.

On the way down to the Orr Springs turnoff I caught up with a long backup of cars on the highway. Someone flipped a car over on Ridgewood again. I got out and helped direct traffic until the CHP showed up. I saw Dolly Parton go by in a maroon LTD. What a heck of a flagperson Dolly would make!

After Dolly went by there wasn't much else to see. But everyday I see America passing. All of the time. I do. I see it all.

It's late now. I've been trying to reconstruct my smashed poems. Gotta get up at five in the morning. I'll put on my beard and my moustache. My cod piece. All the rest of it. And then I'll go out there.

Wonder what kind of different people I'll see tomorrow. Maybe my cousin Mavis will come by again. I guess she didn't have time to pick up her groceries today. And anyway, there's still parts of her car she needs to collect out there on the Orr Springs Road. And the goat.

Whatever.

I know I'll see America passing.

I'll see it all.

*Jane Futcher: I live in Novato, California, with my lover, Erin,
a home birth midwife endowed with a wonderful sense of humor. (She
needs it, to survive life with an emotionally and financially
unpredictable writer.) To support my writing habit, I teach English as
a Second Language. I also do massage. For fun (ha!) I'm an editor
and co-founder of* The Slant, *Marin County's lesbian\gay\bisexual
monthly newspaper. My two novels,* Crush *and* Promise Not to Tell,
are still in print, and my two other novels -- Don't Catch Me, I'm
Falling *and* Come Home with Me Tonight *-- have been rejected by
some of the nation's most discriminating editors.*

WEDNESDAY AFTERNOONS

Not every seven-year-old girl can transform herself into a
handsome, sexy, True Romance Comic Book hero, but I could, and
did, in 1954, during my second grade year at the Canterbury School in
Baltimore, Maryland. Canterbury is an expensive little school that uses
its well-heeled students as guinea pigs in developing home instruction
programs for the children of missionaries, sea captains, and CIA agents
living in remote regions of the world. At the time I didn't to know that
I was a tool of the U.S. espionage establishment; I was just a pale little
girl with Dutch-bobbed hair who was engaged to marry her second
grade teacher.

I know what you are thinking. A seven-year-old cannot have an
affair with a twenty-five-year-old woman. But I did. We were mad for
each other. When we made love, we were consenting adults. And, oh,
how we made love.

Miss Perry was not like Canterbury's other female teachers --
strict, cold, and elderly. She was a siren, the school's Marilyn Monroe.
She wore her platinum hair in a pageboy, had wide red lips, and a pin-
up body. An elegant string of pearls caressed the creamy curve of her
neck, and beneath her skinsoft cashmere sweaters lay an inviting
cleavage. Her voice was so low that as she called out the "puh's and
tuh's and thuh's" in phonics drills, chills climbed the spines of her
seven-year-old devotees.

Liza Van Slyck and I fell in love with Miss Perry within moments of entering her classroom. By mid-October, in Miss Perry's presence, Liza and I had become one person -- one single, dreamy, good-looking suitor who would rescue Miss Perry on a dazzling white stallion and take her away from the drab halls of the Canterbury School.

On Wednesday afternoons, the school released us at one instead of the usual 4:30. On this particular Wednesday, Liza and I lingered near our lockers hoping to give Miss Perry the note that we had composed during recess. It was a basic seven-year-old's love note informing her of our profound devotion and proposing that we marry her immediately.

We were breathless when Miss Perry appeared at the door, briefcase in hand, her red lips parted in a come-hither smile. "Hello, girls," she said huskily.

"Hi, Miss Perry," we answered in unison, gripping our bookbags.

"Give her the note," I whispered to Liza. But Liza panicked. She shoved it in her pocket. "Give it to her," I hissed. We were running out of time, had come to the end of the long hall and were descending the polished tile stairs into the lobby.

At the front door Miss Perry astonished us by asking, "Can I give you girls a lift somewhere?"

At age seven, home was the only place we were ever allowed to go after school. "No, thank you," Liza said, pulling me back. "We've got dancing class this afternoon. Mummy's waiting for us, Jenny." I looked up. Sure enough, Mrs. Van Slyck's gray Dodge was double-parked near the portico. As I turned and grimly followed Liza to her mother's car, my heart remained steadfastly with Miss Perry.

"Sure," I said, squaring my shoulders. "I'd love a ride, Miss Perry." I cared nothing about Mrs. Van S. or dancing class. "Tell your mom Miss Perry is driving me home," I yelled to Liza.

"My car's just down the street, dear," Miss Perry said, taking my hand and leaning so close I could smell her Chanel No. 5.

As Liza stared at us in disbelief, Miss Perry inserted the key into her two-toned, blue and cream Oldsmobile convertible. The door opened and her perfume drifted through my nostrils. And that's when it

156   *Wednesday Afternoons - Jane Futcher*

happened. I changed. Just like that. Suddenly, I was Jim, a playboy in a navy blue blazer, red paisley tie, tan slacks and polished Weejuns. I glanced at myself in the rear view mirror and was stunned to see that I looked like a cross between my two favorite movie stars -- Roy Rogers and Pat Boone. Miss Perry slid over to the passenger side of the car. Her fingers touched my palm as she handed me the keys, her brown eyes gazing at me tenderly. "Would you mind driving, Jimmy?"

Jimmy? I almost corrected her, but when I felt the warm tingling in my legs, I stopped. "Right," I said, pushing the key into the ignition. I hoped the woman of my dreams would not realize that I'd never driven a car before. Lucky for me, the Olds was an automatic and far easier to steer than the red sports car I pedaled around the sidewalks near home.

"Where to, Miss Perry?" I said, in Jim Remington's cheerful baritone. The car was rolling smoothly down the tree-lined street.

"Call me Eugenie." Her bone-white fingers rested lightly on my knee. I managed the turn onto Overhill, and then, near University, felt such a surge of happiness, of euphoria, that I extended my right arm around Miss Perry's shoulder as I'd seen Sterling Hayden do with Marilyn Monroe in *The Asphalt Jungle*.

"Alone at last," crooned Miss Perry. Her words turned my stomach to pink cotton candy. My body lifted like a balloon. Miss Perry moved closer, kicked off her heels and curled her legs up under her.

"Gosh," I said. We were passing my parents' house. My mother was standing in the front yard pruning the prickleberry hedge. I started to duck, but I needn't have worried. Mother didn't see me behind Jim Remington's flashy smile and Miss Perry's shiny car. Thank God she couldn't stop Miss Perry's red fingernails from moving up along my legs, as they were doing now.

"I'd like to...be alone with you, Jim," she said hoarsely.

"Me too," I gulped. But where? The roof of the garages in the alley behind my house was one of my favorite hiding places, but I couldn't visualize Miss Perry climbing up the rusty, sagging drainpipe in her skirt and high heels. The soda fountain at Delvale's Ice Cream would be swarming with kids from school.

"How about the country club?" I said in my new playboy voice. Why not? That's where I was supposed to be today, learning ballroom dancing in my blue velvet dress and patent leather shoes.

Miss Perry's eyes smoked and her cashmere sweater rubbed against my shoulder. "Pull over now, Jimmy," she begged. "I can't wait."

I swerved into the parking lot of St. John's Episcopal Church, where I was enrolled in Mrs. Sadler's Sunday school class. I prayed that Reverend Bennett was visiting the sick today, and that Mrs. Sadler was at home memorizing the 23rd Psalm.

"I've looked forward to this moment for a long time," Miss Perry whispered, her fingers undoing my necktie, her breath warm on my ear. She was a dream, eager and encouraging, not cold and cautious like so many of the sweethearts in True Romance comics. I glanced over at the church. Damn. There was Mr. Bennett in his robes, clutching a cross as he closed the red Gothic chapel doors. But, gosh, I was a grown man. What could he do to me? I squeezed Miss Perry's bell-shaped waist.

"Oooo," she whispered, kissing my neck.

I hoped she didn't see my goosebumps or feel my right leg twitch where her hand pressed against me. I wished for one quick moment that Liza were here with us, could feel Miss Perry's breasts so close and smell her sweet perfume. This is what we'd both dreamed of doing since we'd met her. Liza would never believe that I was now slipping my hand beneath Miss Perry's sweater. I paused, afraid that she might slap me, like the girls in the comic books so often did, but she just smiled, leaned forward, and helped me unfasten her bra.

"Oh, gosh." I could feel her smooth stomach against my palm. When our lips met, she ignited, drew my hands to her breasts and pressed my fingers against them, gently at first, then a little harder.

"You're so nice, Jimmy," she whispered. "So sexy."

"I love you, Miss Perry," I said dizzily. "I'm in love with you."

"You feel good." Miss Perry spoke in a voice from cinemas and sunsets and carousels. "Will you bite my nipples?"

"Bite them?" I said, alarmed. The boys in True Romance never bit girls' bosoms.

"Please, darling." She lay back on the seat and lifted her sweater. The sight of her perfect body made me gasp. She drew my mouth to her breasts. "My love, my sweet captain," she sang.

Oh, those words. I'd always wanted to be a captain or a lieutenant or even just a corporal. Trembling, I closed my lips around her nipples. She sighed in the key of angels. She was clinging to me, sliding beneath me, pulling me closer. Christmas tree lights blinked in my legs. Cole Porter songs hummed in my ears as her knees made celestial vibrations between my legs.

"Marry me, Miss Perry," I cried. She had unbuttoned my shirt, was tracing circles on my neck with the tips of her fingers.

"Yes, Jimmy," she moaned, arching backwards. "Forever, my darling!" Her eyes opened wide, and for a moment I thought she was going to throw up. But no, she seemed very happy, was hugging me and laughing now. "Oh, I love you so," she sang, "My precious Jimmy. I never want this day to end."

"It doesn't have to," I whispered, leaning down to take her breast in my mouth again. But someone coughed, and a fist knocked against the window. Still electric with love, Miss Perry and I bolted up and rearranged ourselves. I rolled down the window. Reverend Bennett's soulful eyes moved from Miss Perry to me. He did not seem to see his daughter's second grade teacher and Jenny Paine, her classmate. He saw two lost lovers, inflamed with lust.

"I hope you're using condoms," he sighed.

"Yes, sir," I said, in my smoothest baritone, making a mental note to ask my sister what a condom was when I got home. "I'm Jim Remington. We're looking for the Cold Spring Country Club."

"This isn't it," Reverend Bennett shrugged, pointing towards Charles Street. "The club's about half a mile down, on your left. The entrance is between the hedges, by the golf course. You can't miss it."

"Thank you, Reverend," I said, adjusting my tie.

"Praise the Lord," he replied.

"Praise the Lord," giggled Miss Perry.

We drove slowly up the long club drive, past the fifteenth green and the sixteenth tee, stuck behind Mrs. Van Slyck's carpool of second graders. Liza turned and stared, astounded by the sight of us, but did not wave. Miss Perry and I played it safe and waited in the parking lot in front of the white clapboard clubhouse while the children's carpools unloaded -- the girls in smock dresses, the boys in navy blue blazers and shorts.

"How 'bout a drink?" I said, holding the club door for Miss Perry, then guiding her into the bar with my hand lightly on her waist. Liza would never find us in here; kids weren't allowed in the bar.

"As long as it's with you, Jim," she whispered, her breath hot in my ear, "I'll go anywhere." My stomach tumbled and I raised my hand a little higher, close to her bra.

Miss Perry's leg brushed mine as we nestled into the cushioned leather booth. Above us, the saxophone, bass and piano combo played a foxtrot for the little white children. How glad I was to be Jim Remington, powerful and handsome, gazing into my girl's endless brown eyes, and not Jenny Paine, dancing upstairs, frozen into a frightened smile, a boy's sweaty hand dragging the sash of my dress.

"Afternoon, Mr. Remington," said Henry, the bartender, bowing slightly and ready to take our order. "What'll it be?"

I leaned back dreamily. "We'll have two dry martinis, Henry."
I scribbled my name on the tab, and, when Henry returned, raised my glass and gazed into Miss Perry's dilated pupils.

"To us," I said, repeating the toast I'd heard my parents make at cocktail time. I drew the glass to my lips and swallowed. "Whoa!" I coughed. I felt like I'd slugged a tank of gasoline.

"What's wrong?" Miss Perry took my hand. "You alright, Jimmy?"

"Fine." I stifled a gag. "Must be the olive." As I wiped my mouth with a napkin, I felt myself relax; a smile of comprehension lit my face. No wonder my parents drank so much. Alcohol made you forget to feel shy. "We'll do this again, Eugenie," I said confidently, using her name for the first time.

"Of course, we will, my darling," she answered, her hand finding mine beneath the table. Outside, the green golf course winked, welcoming us to the world of pleasure, power and romance.

I barely slept that night, thinking, remembering, and took so long deciding on my blue plaid smock dress for school the next morning that I missed the carpool and my mother had to drive me. My heart pounded as I curtsied to Mr. Dillard, the principal, and tiptoed down the silent halls of Canterbury. I hung my jacket in my locker and entered the classroom. Twenty-five faces stared up at me.

"Morning, Jenny," Miss Perry said coolly, writing something in her attendance book and handing me my spelling test.

"Morning," I blushed. There were red marks all over the paper. I'd gotten a "D."

"May I see you for a moment at recess, Jenny," Miss Perry announced in a neutral voice.

"You're in trouble," Liza whispered.

When the bell rang, I waited by Miss Perry's desk, face ashen, knees wobbling, while Billy Whitby took forever packing up the silly robin's nest he'd brought for show and tell. I wanted to punch him for using so much of my time with Miss Perry. Finally, when he was gone, Miss Perry did something I had never seen her do at recess -- she closed the door and delivered the news.

"Jimmy, darling," she whispered, sitting down and extending her arms. "Talk to me."

Heart soaring, I climbed onto her lap.

"I can't stop thinking about you, Jimmy," she began, stroking my hair, her warm breath racing through me.

"Me too you." The pressure of her knees between my legs made it hard to speak.

"I was afraid," she said, her fingers trembling on my waist, "that you'd be...mad at me today."

"Mad?" Melting was more like it. "I love you, Miss Perry. I'd like us to be married."

"Married? You and me?" Tears of happiness glistened in her eyes. "When, Jimmy?"

"In the Spring," I offered. "When the daffodils and dogwood burst. We'll have picnics and take long walks. I'll throw a reception at the club."

"That would make me very happy," she whispered. "Meantime," she said solemnly. "You'd better stay after school on Wednesdays. Your spelling is atrocious."

"Oh?" I said. My hands tightened on her voluptuous waist. When our lips met, her mouth opened slightly and I was breathing the same delicious air that had come from inside her. "I'd love that." I floated up towards the clock on the wall.

"You need tutoring," Eugenie said dreamily. "But you're a genius in every other way."

I felt my genius rising up in me now, filling my chest with love as I slid my grandmother's sapphire engagement ring onto Miss Perry's ring finger. And why not? My mother never wore it.

"Oh, Jimmy." Miss Perry kissed each of my small little knuckles. "What a Springtime it will be."

What a Springtime it was. Wednesdays will always be sacred to me.

Sid Ziara is a Scorpio dyke from San Francisco who used to be in a girl gang that would steal from the rich (men) and give to the poor (us) and beat up offensive males. She is now recovering from this life of crime and only beats up offensive males and girls she really likes (or vice versa).

TENSION RELEASE

It was late Christmas Eve and I was greasy in the parking lot of Grand Auto. I was trying to get my '72 Chevy van running well enough to make it five hundred miles to my parent's house in San Diego. The duct tape holding a belt together had broken (for the third time) so I'd finally decided to get a new one. Mark, behind the counter, said I could take several sizes out to see which one fit, as long as I left my I.D. with the girl at the register. Two of the six fit. I put one on the engine, one behind my front seat with other spare parts, and returned the other four, piling them on the counter.

"Darn, none of them fit," I said, motioning to the pile. I thanked them for their unintentional generosity and casually collected my I.D. As I strode innocently towards the door, the tight ball in my stomach (the only part of my body and mind which occasionally houses my mother) screamed and twisted in moral outrage, trying desperately to alert store personnel. The rest of me, however, was in full cooperation with the plan and was quite content to have the ball if the alternative was having a job. Making it smoothly to my van, I hopped in and roared across town for a very quick stop at my favorite gas station (the only one in San Francisco that doesn't make you pay in advance). I was on my way.

Burneece crawled into her cubby hole in the back to lay on our five hundred dollar comforter and three hundred dollar Egyptian cotton sheets. She liked to sleep when I drove because the van scared and comforted her; it had been our home since she was a puppy. Reaching into my deep hidden coat pocket I pulled out an organic mango for me and a gourmet organic dog treat for her. We'd done the usual routine in the pet store ... Burneece distracts the sales clerk with her bulging sad eyes, a few tricks and a bark no one could resist trying to decipher. Meanwhile, I score lunch.

The December rains had started two weeks earlier, so I snapped Annie Anxiety into the boom box to keep my driving slow.

That ball in my stomach clicked up to high speed at the first engine clank. By the time it was clank clanking regularly, I knew I wasn't getting farther than the next rest stop for the night. This didn't feel so bad; I usually slept deeper at rest stops than in the alleys of the Mission District because the truckers' engines roaring constantly all night drown out inconsistent, startling noises. But I wasn't at all happy about the state of the van. I popped the hood as I drank a bottle of Mylanta and took three deep calming breaths (which always seemed to work until I was done taking them.) Burneece sighed at this familiar experience and hopped out of the van to charm other motorists out of chicken legs. Her eyes could convince anyone that she was sad, abused, and starving to death, in spite of her fat little sausage body standing only six inches further back.

In our romantic days of chases and escapes, my van and I had built a mutual trust. Now this had disintegrated into constant accusations and abuse on my part, while my van trembled and shook, no longer able to follow through on its promises of running powerfully forever; sure that it was a worthless piece of shit destined to go nowhere.

Luckily this time it turned out it was only a bolt that had shaken loose, and I always had plenty of wire to hold things together.

I decided to call my mom and let her know Burneece and I wouldn't be there until the next morning, so I grabbed three or four calling card numbers and headed towards the phone. The rest stop was crowded because of the holidays and the line for the phone was ten long. "Fuck," I thought and plopped down on the waiting bench with them all, preparing myself for the stares, whispers, muffled laughs and the ever popular, "Did that hurt?" (always said with a squinched up face that would never be pierced, though very probably lifted.) There are occasionally times when the breeders don't respond with at least one of these four clever and original behaviors; but walking past them is always quicker than sitting and waiting with them. At least when I get tired of all the attention, I can upset them by smiling and winking at their kids.

After twenty minutes and nine pairs of acid washed jeans, the last one walked over with that bizarre gait, that seems to say "I'll be nice no matter what!", to make her call. As she clucked away I noticed

Tension Release - Sid Ziara

a trucker drag his legs up to the phone. He hung his thumbs on his belt buckle in original trucker style. I knew what he was about to do. Burneece looked at me, then him, and went to hide in the van. Unless it's another dog stealing my attention, she doesn't get the same enjoyment out of fighting that I do.

Sure enough, as soon as the woman said, "Bye, love ya!" and hung up, the trucker grabbed the phone and started poking the numbers.

"I AM NEXT," I said in a loud voice.

He mumbled without turning around nor slowing his poking, "...gotta call dispatch..." The words dripped off his chin like tobacco spit. I was already storming towards his U.S. of A. back.

"I SAID I'M NEXT!" I clicked the receiver down and yanked the phone out of his hand (which, like his other one, was frozen into a permanent C shape, from, I guess, the belt buckle thing.)

His eyes started popping out like a squeezed hampster, his jaw dropped crooked, and one hand unlatched from belt to latch onto baseball cap bill. His dumbfounded shock lifted. "Waaggaaamufaa!"

I squinched up my face in a tight little smile. "You have to wait in line like everybody else," I said in exactly his mother's tone of voice.

"Ohsabladdahsoosafadda!!!" trembled out of his nearly exploding head. I could tell the trembling was hard for him, not because it made him drool and stammer, but because his body wasn't used to moving that much. Just then, Carl dragged his legs towards us. "Carl! Theesgaaadaaaasala!!!"

"Naaaa!" Carl was shocked. He latched one hand on his hat bill and one on his belt buckle and said, "Looks like someone otta keek her ass!"

Always delighted by a challenge, I hung up the receiver, took two steps towards them and said, "Oh yeah? Which one of you FAGGOTS is gonna try?"

"Awwwgawwfuuuuuukuka!!!" they said in unison, moving their legs like chickens scratching for bugs.

"Huh, FAGGOTS?? Put your money where your mouth is, FAGGOTS!" This was what we referred to in my self defense class as "escalating a fight."

The men's need to put me in my place grew as quickly as the crowd. Children gasped; someone got out their camcorder.

The art of fighting is simple. There are two kinds of men. You learn to pick out the bluffers who take a free ride on other men's violence and quickly cut their losses at the first sign of resistance. And you become prepared for the kamakazies who would rather die than swallow an insult from some pussy licking cunt. (Those in the latter category lack the part of the brain that can compute the concept of a woman kicking a man's ass.) When you're escalating a fight, you know that if your opponent doesn't bite by the peak of the tension, then they're bluffers. It's over -- you've won.

At this point the tension was so thick I could barely make myself hold off. (It's always my dilemma in jerking off too. I seldom have the self control to keep myself pre-come peaking. I just slip over the edge, my hand pretending not to notice until it's too late.) So I just pretended not to notice my mouth gathering a huge ball of spit. Then, giving myself over to the flood of pleasure, the spit flew from my mouth with all the splendor I imagine flying holds. The crowd held its breath as it twisted through the air...balling...stretching...tumbling. Heads and eyes followed it like a tennis serve. SLAP! Right across Carl's face. Drip. I smiled huge, my eyes nearly popping out of my head too, but for a different reason. Carl and Carl stammered and scratched the ground but with their eyes lowered like their mumbles. (Curiously, men never wipe spit off their faces.)

I turned and started to punch in one of the calling card numbers. The second one worked and as I talked to my mom, the crowd and the Carls began to slink back to their vehicles. I noticed that the ball in my stomach was gone.

Tension Release - Sid Ziara

Jen Johnson: When someone isn't around to read me a bedtime story, I write my own. Women have traditionally been taught to surround sex with shame. The time has come for women to take back our stolen sexuality - who knows? It could be fun ...

KELT BITCH

She knew me as a shy and frightened girl of sixteen, fresh out of the closet and new to the streets. You learn fast, and I was a quick learner. My white-blonde hair was buzzed down to an inch all the way around my head. I was cold and I was pale and I was alone in the extreme. Here came the Irish woman with her accent and her expensive perfume to save me from myself.

She picked me up from the street the way that one picks up a discarded coin. She spent her free time polishing my rough edges, paying attention to me only to admire or admonish. I never questioned her reasons for taking me in- she wasn't the type of woman that expected to be questioned about anything.

I knew enough to stay out of her way, most of the time, her temper volatile and swift. I shied from her touch, and she seemed to accept that for the first few months. Patience was not her virtue, however, and eventually, her libido conquered her better judgement.

She was slightly taller than I, sturdier than she appeared and full of herself. Her eyes were as green as I was, but she told me that she was going to change that. I didn't understand everything she threw at me, but I adored her and I belonged to her; who was I to truly think? I lowered my eyes when she looked at me, but I often watched her while she slept. I was in awe of her dark past and her lust for anything carnal. I suppose that I began to want her, but I'd never wanted anyone before her, and didn't recognize what the pounding heart, sleepless nights, and plagued dreams were leading up to. I'd have died for her, and she had me say so, more than once; she loved the sound of it.

She put her hands on my face and forced me to look at her. I fought that, a little, and for that, she backhanded me hard across the face. She bowed her face closer to mine, our lips touching. This, my first kiss, was and always will be, a fantasy that came true. Her lips were soft and her tongue forced open my mouth, explored every part of me. She pulled my head back with a gloved hand, making me stare at the ceiling. Her teeth made short work of the cross that hung dully from my neck; it clattered softly to the floor, taking my last remnants of the old religion with it - she was my god and her body, my temple.

She made me cry out as she cannibalized my throat, leaving purple bruises in her wake. She held my hands behind me and asked if I'd been a naughty boy. I felt my heart in my mouth as I struggled with an answer, hating the reference. It was unnecessary, because she already knew the answer. She knew that I'd never been with anyone, and the thought did something to her. She could take something forever that no one else would ever touch. She ripped at my shirt to free my breasts, and seemed surprised at their size. My clothes formed a ring around us as she threw first one item aside, then the next. I thought that the entire world could listen to my heart trying to break out of my chest. I struggled to calm it, just a bit. She slapped my breasts and threw me on the floor, suddenly angry. She took off her belt.

"Don't you fucking keep anything from me, you little whore," she growled through bared teeth. "I can do things to you that you couldn't imagine in your fucking nightmares."

I believed her, because she never lied, and I was as afraid of her as I was in love with her. I lay on the hard wood floor and I barely breathed. "Lie on your stomach and put your hands like this," she said, roughly positioning my hands behind my head. She knelt beside me and ran her tongue along the side of my face, catching a tear. She seemed to like the fact that I was crying. Her voice was softer but no less cruel. "You can make the noise. I want to hear you make some noise. This is for keeping what's mine, from me. This is what dirty little girls get for holding back..." She dragged the belt across the small of my back gently enough to cause gooseflesh all over my body. All I thought of was her. I was learning all the little facts of sex that my mother never taught me. As I said, I'm a fast learner.

The first lash smacked against my ass and I yelped, more from surprise than from pain. Three more fell, a rain of them followed. In my mind, it hurt more during the brief seconds that she rested or checked on how I was faring. It hurt during the seconds between the blows. She fell into a rhythm, and I joined her, there. I'd found a secret place in myself, driven there by the leather. The sound of it biting into me was as powerful as the welts on my ass and thighs. I began to numb to the pain, and my breathing slowed, my eyes half-closed. "Are you there, yet, love?" A voice was whispering to me. I think that I tried to say yes. I wanted to beg her not to stop, but couldn't find the words. My mind was floating and my body shook, weakly.

She pulled me up slowly to look at me. My tear-stained face, the bruises on my neck, swelling on my lip from one of her more savage kisses... She ran her hands through my hair and fingered my earrings. For a moment, I feared that she would pull them out, one by one. The way that I still felt, intoxicated by the pain, I'd have let her. She licked my lips and tugged on them with her sharp white teeth. She let her hands travel the length of my body, drawing her short nails along my new welts, making me cry out. She smiled as she slid one finger into my cunt and smeared my own wetness on my lips. She sucked on them until there wasn't a trace of it left, then did it again.

I arched my hips toward her advances, but she stopped and pushed me down onto my back, kneeling over me. She took off her silk shirt and short skirt, and I saw before me my first true woman. She was magnificent. She pressed her body against mine, breast against breast, mouth to mouth. She began to rub her cunt against mine, and I moaned in the lurch. She brought out feelings and desires I never knew I'd had. But the recent memory of her within me so briefly kept coming back, leaving me with a need to be filled. She came before me, but continued her sensual movements until she brought me to the brink. She reached behind her and produced a white dildo and a tube of Elbow Grease. She strapped on a harness, and fitted the dick inside, smiling as it pressed against her clit. She greased it up, then rubbed some onto me, and I groaned at her touch.

"This may hurt, for a minute, love," she said seriously. I knew what she meant from hearing about it from my friends. I didn't care, I wanted her. I wanted to please her. She took a glass vial from beside her and uncapped it. "You'll feel better after this," she promised, sticking it under my nose. "Breathe." I inhaled, and the room spun. She entered me, slow and steady, and I felt the burning between my thighs. After it subsided it was replaced by something else. She slid in and out of me, and I cried her name, begged her not to stop. She became more aggressive, pinching my nipples and slapping me as she fucked me. I came for the first time, and I've never come like that again. She forced her tongue into my mouth and I kissed her back as fiercely as she kissed me. My hands, unbound, cupped her ass and forced her to fuck me harder. She banged into me over and over, and I bit at her throat and chin until she cried out, too. Now I knew what she liked, and I knew how to send her out of her mind.

She pulled out of me, and I took the dildo off her roughly, throwing it aside. The harness followed. I knelt and she followed, I pulled her to me and she allowed it. I bit and sucked on her nipples until she was sore and tried to pull away, and I had my hand between her legs, her pussy dripping wet. She pushed against my hand, and I had two fingers inside of her. She wanted more. She took my hand, and we fucked for hours. I fucked her until my arm was numb and she fell into my embrace, spent and shaking. I held her, wanting her again, but too sore to even contemplate it.

It wasn't long after that that I left, and to this day, she claims that nothing ever happened between us. I saw her, the other day, five years after the fact. She didn't recognize me with my long hair and my leathers. She didn't recognize the girl she baptized into this way of life. I cruised her in a sex bar, and she couldn't place my face. She welcomed my advances, though, and I kept the secret a secret as I took her downstairs...

Adrian McKinty was born and grew up in Carrickfergus, Northern Ireland. After majoring in politics and philosophy at University College, London, and Oxford University, Adrian currently lives and works in New York City.

DIVINATION

A six foot five preacher with wild black hair was holding up a glass jar, containing what looked like a foetus. Purple veins stood out on his forehead and his nose was blue with the drink. The profanities he screamed at the whores were ignored by everybody except the curious, and even they didn't linger. An emaciated old woman was throwing sticks of fire in the air and catching them, juggling ineptly and singeing her hands. Crack heads cruised past in BMWs, pointing lugers at each other and yelling things you couldn't hear over their hundred watt speakers. The army and the cops couldn't give a shit, small fry didn't interest them, and what was possession nowadays: six months to a year, not worth anybody's time. In any case they were busy escorting an ambulance all the way through the west end of the city; hijackings for drugs were all too common and it was policy to stamp them out, at least until the headline writers got bored of the story and it moved out of public view.

Time clicked and it was the same old shit. Murphy was slipping pineal gland extract into her coffee and hoping for something interesting to happen. Two guys had tried to pick her up, but she blew them off without a fuss, no point in causing any trouble. And if she was going to Mace anybody tonight it would be that goddamned preacher, whom she could hear even through the plate glass. It was just frustrating - maybe tonight was the night to get an early one. Go home, take some downers, put on a movie, take it easy. She picked up the camera and toyed with the zoom, accidentally catching the code on the cash register. Now there's a thought, she laughed. She fingered the Mace can in her jacket pocket. No, it wouldn't do, sure she was bored, but that would just be plain stupidity. She looked at the cook, he was a big ex tv wrestler who used to play the bad guy in the ring. In real life he was no pushover either, he'd have a couple of cannons under the counter, that was for sure. Shit, he'd probably even like getting Maced in the face, probably happened so many times, he'd built up an immunity to it. She laughed again and sipped her coffee, stashing the camera carefully back into the shoulder bag.

It was 11.45 and the only thing that had happened was some guy in rags getting thrown out for hugging his coffee for an hour and a half. You couldn't blame him, it was getting cold outside. He went quietly, probably happened every Saturday night, like a ritual. The cook and the wino both had their roles to play and they played them placidly, without threats or humiliation on either side.

Outside she saw the wino try to take a swipe at the preacher who was still there despite the cold. The preacher, infuriated, put down his foetus jar and chased him down the road. Like rats, two kids came out of the shadows, picked up the jar and ran off with it. She smiled, the whole thing was so slickly done that it could have been staged.

At about midnight the juggler and the now visual-aid-less preacher went home. She gazed at her black and white image in the security camera. She looked terrible. She felt wired to the moon. Even if she did go home now she wouldn't get off to sleep until four. She ordered another coffee, read the menu for the nth time and waited for the phone to ring. I'll give it another hour and then scram, she thought. Her call came through just as the coffee arrived.

"They want to speak to you personally, Murphy."

"Put them through," she replied.

"I don't like this 'Murphy' stuff, how'd they get to know your name?"

"Christ, I don't know, just put them through."

"It's getting too sordid, too personal, it's like they're trying to impress you or something, I think that -"

"For chrissake will you just put them through before they ring off." Feedback crackled down the line before a different male voice came on: "Is that you, Murphy?"

"It's me."

"We got another present for you, what do you think it is?"

"Dunno."

"Always the yapper, Murphy."

"Get on with it."

"You in the diner?'

"Yeah."

"No cops?"

"No cops."

"Hey man, if there are cops, if this is a cross, it won't be us that's stroked, we'll cut your tits off and nail your kid."

"Get on with it before I burst into tears, big man."

"OK, well, you know the 'Dam' ..."

"Yeah?"

"Front bar, one minute."

"Why them?"

"It's full of fags."

"And they forgot to pay?" she said but the phone was dead.

Shit, one minute: she'd have to run. She thought for a second about calling up the bar, warning them, but it would take a minute for someone to answer the phone, there was no point. She was glad she was wearing her Reeboks and not her slip-ons. She cut through a garage and ran down Well Street which was full of sheltered housing for nurses. They'll be needed in a minute, she thought.

She got there with about five seconds to spare. She barely got the camera rolling when the attack happened. It was three men in a Porsche. Looked like Uzis but you couldn't tell. Fire streaked from the muzzles, obscuring their faces. The night was shattered by the sound of gunfire. A bouncer outside tried to shout a warning but he was silenced by the Uzis dancing over his chest. The frosted glass caved in on the people sitting in the snug. She heard screams from inside. Just then someone threw something from a second car, a Ford which she hadn't noticed before. It was a drogue bomb. She knew what was going to happen next, the question was, should she put her fingers in her ears and stop filming, or risk it and get what would be a terrific shot. She took the risk. The whole front of the bar flashed in white light. The shock wave put in the windscreen of the Porsche. Murphy ducked out of the way of flying glass which was spraying fifty feet in all directions like big deadly crystal spears. The window of the shop behind her collapsed and she felt herself falling into it. She could feel blood trickling down from her ears. She couldn't hear anything but a ringing in her head. Both cars drove off. Glass had blown the tires on the Ford but safety was only about a mile away: they'd make it.

The ringing noise changed key and became recognisable as the sound of a hundred burglar alarms going off in the square mile round the bar. The 'Dam' and the building beside it were now an inferno, there wasn't the ghost of a chance of anyone getting out of there unless they made it out the back way. To keep herself from cracking she pretended that the screaming she heard was yet another alarm, but she knew exactly what it was.

Only when the cops and the troops and the other tv guys showed up did she stop filming and check herself for wounds. She had a bad cut on her arm and blood on her face from something. She was the only one the paramedics could do anything about. Before she even got in an ambulance, she was grabbed by a detective.

"What did you see, miss?" She told him everything, except of course, the tip-off.

"Who do you think did it, officer?" she asked innocently.

"I don't know, could be part of an internal gang feud we've had reports of ... anyway we'd like you to make a statement just as soon as you get outta hospital." Fat chance, she thought, and plugged herself into a drip.

"You got any coke?" she asked the paramedic.

"We do not!" he replied trying to sound shocked. He looked about eighteen, had blue razor burn all up the side of his face. She put on her best smile.

"Sure you do, like for the crack heads with the d.t.s or something. Hey, if you give me some I'll put you on the news." She produced her credentials from the pocket of her jeans. "Come on, man," she continued, "you can write it up as a medical emergency, patient was a danger to herself and others ... that kinda thing."

"What channel do you work for?"

"Cable eight."

"OK, will you interview me about the bomb?"

"Sure," she said, waiting for the needle.

She checked herself out at six am, and slept till one. It had been a real bitch of a night. She played the answer phone while the coffee made itself. There was only one call and it was from Harry.

"We got the tape. Christ its terrific. I'm sure it's the best yet. We've sold it to all the nationals and even to the press for stills and of course we scooped the bastards on the breakfast news. You done well Murphy, I'll make sure you get a cut, I love ya."

"I'm sure you do," she said to the phone.

Suddenly she felt very alone. Sarah had taken herself off somewhere with her school friends and Louise...God knows where she

Divination - Adrian McKinty

was, she hadn't even left a note. Well, screw her, she thought, I got the scoop of the year last night. Harry would be true to his word, she would get a cut and a good one too. She found the morning paper unread on the kitchen table. One of her stills was on page two, they'd even credited her. Hey, this was big time. She could get to the mainland on this one if she played it right. Get a nice house in the country, get the kid to a better school and Louise could suit herself: stay or go, it was a matter of indifference to Murphy. At least so she tried to tell herself.

In the shower she noticed some big ugly bruises on her thigh. She'd no idea where they'd come from. Maybe in the bomb last night. Everything else was fine except for the ringing in her ears which she knew from past experience would be with her for a day or two. Maybe I should put in for compensation, she thought but then dismissed it from her mind. It would be small change compared to the bonus she'd be getting, and an awful lot of hassle.

She called for pizza and sat down in front of the tv. On the 24 news channel they showed one minute of her footage every half hour with a voiced over report. If she'd been more together last night she could have done the report herself and got world wide coverage. What an angle that would have been. Still what she'd done was good enough, this was definitely a break. The report said that they had pulled eight bodies out of the rubble. It was a miracle it wasn't more. Over forty seriously injured. And of course the bigger the body count the more significant the pictures would become. She tried to feel elated but it wasn't happening. She rummaged around for the hash cookies but Louise must have taken them with her, the bitch. It would have to be cigarettes and she was trying to give up, damn.

She smoked a couple that Sarah must have made up because they were laced with weed. Sarah was only fifteen and that was still too young for this sort of shit, it led to other things, heavier stuff. She would have a word with that young lady when she came in. A couple of joints put her in the mood for a bath and wouldn't you know it, the phone rang when she was just in.

She came out in her kimono towelling off her crew cut. That was the plus of having no hair - it was damn easy to dry. She played back the message on the answer phone. "Hey mom. It's me. Look I won't be coming home tonight, there's a party at Rick's, by the way heard you made out good last night, does this mean the Jeep is finally mine?"

Murphy growled at the answer phone, who was Rick and who said
Sarah could go out late on a Sunday night? She had school tomorrow.
She was just wondering how she could find out where Rick lived when
the phone rang, startling her.

"Yeah, who is it?"

"Why don't you put on the screen so we can get a look at ya,"
said a harsh guttural voice.

"Who is this?" she demanded indignantly.

"Hey baby, is that the way to talk to your prime source?"

"How did you get this number?" she said, trying to keep cool.

"You should know that we're not amateurs," sneered the voice.

"You're monsters, you killed eight innocent people."

"As if you care, Murphy. You got your story and a big fat pay
check, am I right?" She didn't reply. "In any case nobody is innocent,
Murphy, nobody."

"Shit, where did you hear that one, the 'children's guide to
ethics'?"

"Don't come the smart mouth with us, Murphy, you need us. By
the way how's your kid today?"

"If you so much as look at my kid you'll be one sorry fucker."

"Relax, Murphy, we don't want your kid, we want to give you
some information."

"Talk."

"This is gonna be the big one, Murphy. Tonight at ten, be at the
Crown. Believe me if, you tell anybody..."

"I'll be there." When she put the phone down she realised that
she was trembling. Oh God those guys really scare the shit out of me,
she thought. She lit a cigarette and took a long cool draught. Where
was Louise when you needed her. Those crazies had murdered eight
people and tonight was going to be even bigger. Maybe she should call
the cops, try and get this thing stopped. No, that would be nuts and
they might try to get Sarah, yeah they'd get her, and the cops wouldn't
be able to do anything anyway. This comforted her a little, she was
doing the right thing. It didn't stop her feeling like a ghoul, like an
ambulance chasing attorney. That's all you need now, she told herself,
a crisis of confidence...come on Murphy, snap out of it. She stood up
and made a fist at her reflection. "It's nothing to do with you Murphy,
you're just the witness. Come on girl."

It was ten thirty pm and nothing had happened yet. The bar was full, being the only Sunday night establishment in this part of town. It was decked in mock Victorian gaudiness, with polished brass and oak panelling. It was still lit by gas lamps, she didn't know how they'd got through the planning laws on that. It was a youngish crowd, wealthy, noisy and getting progressively hammered. She was well into her fourth tequila and mescaline to make time fly. Mescaline was hard to come by. She'd grown peyote in her hot house for a couple of years: Lophophora Williamsii. It looked like any other small cactus; round, and divided into sections, like a button. She used it very rarely. It was a secret, not even Louise knew what it was. The mescaline in the buttons went well with tequila as long as you didn't overdo it. She was bored though. The crazies were late again and sooner or later some jerk was bound to come over and hit on her. She took out her pocket tv and flipped through the channels.

By eleven thirty still no call had come on her portable phone. The bar was lively now, almost full to capacity. She sat in the corner near the window at a two seat table away from the noise and smoke. No-one had tried to pick her up, but then she did look like shit, they probably think I'm a lush, she thought. And they could be right, there were after all eight shots of tequila and seven pieces of peyote all playing different tunes in her stomach. She looked at the static channel on the tv and then out into the street through the bar window. Nobody was about, nothing was moving, but then it was cold out there, what could you expect. She shivered and began to feel uneasy. The waiting period was longer than it had ever been, was there something wrong, she wondered. Nah, just the frights... but then again. She didn't know why, but she had felt bad karma about the whole business tonight. She'd felt it before she left, before the mescaline, so it wasn't a bad trip, just a...just a feeling in the gut that something wasn't right. She'd even brought her .22, little more than a pop gun but it was better than Mace. She always felt more secure when she had it with her; she was an excellent shot at twenty five feet. She patted the gun in her jacket pocket and began to feel a little better. "Jesus, Murphy, you got to learn to be less of a paranoia head," she told herself smiling. She caught the eye of a waitress and ordered another tequila, determined to make this her last. She chewed the last two pieces of peyote button, wincing at the taste as they went down. Soon she felt her stomach churning. The peyote did that to you if you took as much as she had.

She went into the bathroom and threw up into the porcelain sink, then washed her mouth out under the faucet."Oh God," she said.

She went back into the bar and ordered a beer. At midnight her call came through. Just like the night before, she thought.

"Hey, Murphy, are you lookin' sexy tonight'?" It was the same guy as before.

"Where do you get all these numbers from, this phone is confidential," she asked, playing for a little time to compose herself.

"You ask too many questions now. I like the old Murphy better, no chat, just lis-ten--ing."

"OK, I'm listening, so tell me."

"How many in the bar Murphy?"

"I don't know, fifty maybe."

"Look out of the window." She wiped the condensation off the plate glass and peered out into the street, holding the phone tight as if for protection. "You see that yellow van?" the voice continued.

"Yeah." she said nervously.

"That's us, hey, flash the lights, Frank." The dull bulbs on the van winked at her slyly like a cheap come on.

"Hey Murphy, I guess this is goodbye," the voice sneered,"we're hitting the Crown tonight, in about two seconds to be exact."

Laughter crackled on the phone line for a sweet second and then it died. The side door of the van shuddered and then slid open to reveal two men with RPG 7 rocket launchers, old models, she knew, but effective. "Oh shit." she managed to say before she saw the two weapons flash. The rockets punched holes in the glass and exploded at the back of the bar. The serenity of the impact was in its unexpected quietness. A milli second after the weapons discharged the interior of the bar, stools, glasses, people and all, became transformed into an amorphous, magnificent and terrible whiteness. She felt the back of her head splinter and dissolve into the unsullied white of the room: and it was lonely there, cold. Strange that, feeling cold as she drowned in fire. God and she'd never felt quite so abandoned by her luck, it was a twist of recognition, a leap like the punch line of a joke. Ripped so suddenly from the womb of her drug haze into sharp reality and pain, so much pain. Christ, how could there be so much pain. Fuck. But it only lasted a moment. Shrapnel severed her spinal column just below the shoulder, the flames engulfed her and burned out the inside of her skull like white phosphorous burning in water. She embraced the white fire like a lover, ending the pain, ending everything. Plasma wiped out forty years of memories, forty years of experience, forty years of rich, bold life in an instant of uncreation. And unlike birth, death took her without even giving her a breath to scream with. And the cries of fifty other souls were lost in the vaporisation of her own.

Louise shuddered as a chill caught her through the window. She pulled her sweater tighter, putting her hands beneath her arms. Murphy had left the windows open again. Jesus, how much air did a person need. Louise was irritated, it was getting close to midnight and Murphy still wasn't home. This would be the second night running, didn't she have any consideration for anyone else, didn't she realise that people would be worrying about her. People, well, ok, though she hated to admit it, Louise did worry about her a lot. Murphy was irresponsible. "You're irresponsible, Murphy." Louise shouted at the open window. Even her daughter was more responsible than she was. All she had to do was pick up the phone, it only took a phone call, one lousy phone call.
Cursing, Louise closed the window and sat down on the couch. She flipped on the tv and snarled at it until she hit the weather channel, it always had the most accurate clock. And there it was counting away her life, a life spent waiting and worrying. She checked the channel time against her own watch, she was five minutes slow, cheap piece of junk. That meant it was seven minutes to twelve. "Damn her," she said aloud. "I suppose I'm going to have to do the calling again. It's always me calling her. Shit on a stick." She seized the phone angrily and turned off the tv. She stared at her reflection in the screen. "You're such a wimp, Louise," she said and forced herself to put the phone down again. She smiled at the distorted reflection in the tube. She was a well preserved forty five. Her black hair was only partly gray and her dark eyes still shone with lively intelligence. She turned on the screen again and her face vanished to be replaced by that of Gerry Lewis.
"Oh shit," she muttered, hitting the off switch. "I suppose I'm going to have to do it."
She dialled the number on Murphy's portable phone. It didn't connect the first time. Swearing, she dialled again. This time it was making a strange high pitched noise. Like feedback. "Bloody hell!" she yelled in frustration. "I'll try one more time!" This time she got through and it rang and rang, tantalising and endless. Louise said aloud that she

would be damned if she was going to put the phone down until she got an answer. For some disturbing reason she regretted this choice of words as soon as she spoke them.

Murphy looked at the phone screaming in her lap like a frightened child. It lay there looking strange and unfamiliar. For a moment she failed to recognise what it was at all. She looked at her hands, they were white with fear. She was shaking. What the hell was happening, wasn't she dead? Am I not dead, she almost said aloud. What the hell am I doing here, listening to the phone ring. People around her were beginning to stare, willing her to answer the phone, too polite to yell at her but nevertheless exerting cold moral pressure. She felt that the whole bar had gone silent while everyone looked at her, demanding that she answer her screeching portable. The pitch on the phone grew sharper the longer you left it. Glasses tinkled in the background, people coughed significantly, it was like a bizarre John Cage symphony. She could bear it no longer. She picked it up. It was Louise.

"Hello, Murphy?" she asked anxiously.

"Yeah," Murphy replied, not entirely convinced she was giving the correct answer.

"Jesus, Murphy, I've been worried sick, why didn't you call?" Louise said angrily.

"Oh Louise, I've just had the worst trip ever, absolutely the worst, a total negative death trip, shit," Murphy said sounding exhausted.

"Calm down, Murphy, what were you on?" Louise said, concern conquering her anger.

"Peyote buttons."

"What is that exactly?"

"You know the little cactus plants I've got in the hothouse..."

"Yeah, it's that?"

"Yeah, it's mescaline and I haven't taken it for a while. I was mixing it with tequila and Christ, it's screwed me completely. I had this terrible...I'd died, and we were all wiped, God, it was the worst, I don't think I can drive, can you come in for me?"

"Just when exactly did you have this trip?" Louise asked thoughtfully.

"About five minutes ago, why?"

"Nothing I suppose, its just that, I dunno, I had this weird feeling too about five minutes ago, I was really spooked. I thought it was a draught from the window. What was that stuff you were on again?"

Murphy felt the veins in her temples start to pulse faster. She could almost feel the adrenalin oozing into her system. Fight or flight, the adrenalin was telling her, her subconscious was telling her. Her body suddenly felt alive, charged, wired like no drug could wire you. She was in the presence of danger, her body knew that, her conscious brain just hadn't caught on yet. "It was peyote." she said in answer to Louise's question.

"And where did you hear about it, is it safe, is-"

"I had friends in New Mexico. Some of the Native Peoples, the, eh... oh I don't know, I think it's the Navaho, they take it in religious ceremonies," she replied, feeling she was very close now to finding out something important, close to finding out why she was suddenly very afraid. She looked into her bag checking that her .22 was there. In another second it would all fit into place. She squirmed with impatience. The bar was back to normal, laughing people, so unaware that life was hanging by a thread...if she could only...

"What do they use it for?" Louise asked, a set up question if ever there was one. A question Louise couldn't possibly have thought to ask, it made everything too clear, gave the game away. At least the answer would. The puppet masters blundered in their clumsiness. Murphy didn't believe in such things, nevertheless she found herself waiting for the answer that would resolve everything. "They use it," she said painstakingly slowly, "for divination."

She paused for a second as the thought sunk in. A ludicrous, cliched, obvious thought but nevertheless she knew it was so. "Oh shit," she managed to say.

"What is it?" Louise asked sounding worried again.

"Oh my god, 'for divination'...what time is it?" Murphy asked calmly.

"About two minutes to twelve, why, what's going on?"

"I've got a couple of minutes then." Murphy said to no one in particular, dropping the phone onto the floor. She peered through the window of the bar, in time to see a yellow van pull up outside.

Divination. Murphy almost laughed - it was ridiculous. The bar was never going to be cleared in five minutes, not a hope in hell. She could get out, she could even film the attack. Make it into the big league of memorable videotape: the napalmed village in Nam, the pin point bridge destruction in Iraq, Waco, and her tape. She would join the catalogue of infamy, and make her career. But, it was not to be, she knew what had to be done.

Murphy ran out of the bar and into the shadows behind the broken street lights. Oil floated in puddles on the asphalt, a cat scurried out of her way. The dead smell of the street drunks' urine assailed her nostrils. She caught her breath and walked undisturbed to the back of the van. Smiling like a perfume saleswoman she knocked on the door. In the far distance she heard the City Hall begin its midnight chorus. There was a momentary shuffling, before the door opened cautiously. It was a weaselly little man holding a portable phone. Curiously just what she was expecting.

"Fuck off bitch, do your whoring somewhere else," said another man behind the weasel, a man with a beard sitting on something covered with tarpaulin, something long and angular. Neither man recognised her from the tv, stupid as well as murderous. Mind you both men were as high as kites. No sense in delaying. Murphy pulled out the .22 and squeezed one off into the bearded man's face. Almost contingently a hole appeared below his left eye and blood poured from the wound like water from a stand pipe. He sat there too shocked to yell. She didn't feel like she was killing anyone, she was too detached for that. It was like being in an arcade. The other man froze, his mouth agape. It was too tempting a target. She aimed into the yellow broken teeth and pulled the trigger. He must have dodged for when she opened her eyes he was still alive. The bullet had caught him in the neck, she was being smeared with gurgling arterial bleeding. The man looked questioningly at her, hands clutched desperately around his throat. Another bullet would he a waste, he'd be dead in less than a minute, she'd seen it before at road accidents. Besides there was still the driver to take care of, she had to conserve her ammo. She turned on her heel and walked slowly round the side of the van. She moved back onto the pavement keeping the gun trained on the cab with both hands. If he tried to drive off ,she'd blow out the tires.

Circumspectly she angled round till she was facing the cab itself. She felt a stab of panic, the driver was nowhere to be seen and there had to be a driver, there had to be one more. The one that flashed the lights, the -- a bullet caught her on the shoulder spinning her round and onto the pavement. It had come from the back of the van. The bastard had climbed there from the cab. He was a big meataxe, with a zapata moustache and an army peaked cap. He had some sort of shiny automatic. He looked terrified, trigger happy. The rest of his shots were wild, drilling neat holes into the brickwork behind her. If you're nervous an automatic is not the weapon for you, she thought as she pumped four .22 bullets into his shoulder, neck and forehead by a process of corrective shooting. He collapsed onto the road falling onto his face. His neck cracked and then all was silent except for an almost comforting spluttering of blood from inside the van. Her shoulder burned from the wound, Jesus, if this was another trip it was a really bad one. She put down her empty gun and rolled over onto the recovery position. Still, she thought, the shots were bound to bring the cavalry. It would be her second trip in an ambulance in two nights.

Before they could arrive a wild eyed giant of a man in a flapping black raincoat showed up. She recognised him as the preacher from the night before. She tried to crawl away but couldn't move. His stone blue eyes smiled menacingly, as he slowly unclenched his fists and extended his pallid, nicotine stained fingers towards her.

"I'll help you say your prayers, little sister," he said, kneeling down beside her, his hands reaching for her throat.

"I'm a heathen," she replied, fumbling in her bag for the can of Mace and knowing it wasn't there.

Aspen. *I've been writing all my life: poetry, stories, articles, novels. I've taught creative writing and done some editing. I am a columnist for Disability Arts Magazine, UK, and a contributor on lesbian, feminist and disability issues to a variety of journals, using a variety of names. My poems have been read on radio and T.V. and have been used in theatre productions. The best rewards are hearing when lesbians like my work.*

THE END

Kalomi hadn't sent a message for three days. Sula took the kettle off the hook, where it sizzled gently over the fire.

"Three days," she said in an anguished voice. She poured boiling water onto herbs in a cup. The cave was lit orange by the fire. Sula cuddled into the bedclothes, inhaling the tangy smell from her cup. "I get so tense I can't do anything." Not that there was much to do except collect firewood, water and food.

Kalomi had gone south to a stronghold with Jay, to fetch metal tools and cloth. She sent her birds back with messages of love and Sula returned them. But now there had been nothing for three days. What had happened?

Sula was aching but she was being self-indulgent. She knew Kalomi was in danger and had no time to think as she sharpened her wits against the mountains and the hunters.

"You should never do this," Sula said to herself. "You should have gone with her." She had started her bleeding, however, and knew she would be a risk. There was no room for poor judgement or weakness. She washed some clothes with the rest of the hot water.

"Why am I this close to the edge?" She started humming to calm herself. The night outside was desperately blue. The bird could have been shot. Tears came to Sula's eyes as she imagined Kirsta shot down and bleeding. Kalomi would grieve.

Sula's eyelids hung heavy. She was sweating in front of the fire and her cotton clothes were damp. She went outside and enjoyed the warm fresh air on her body. The pine trees, dark in the night sky, were swaying in the wind. Sula began to sway with them. "I'm frightened,

Kalomi," she whispered. She clung to a tree. The rough bark scraped her arms, its sharp smell filled her nose and head.

She heard a small sound behind her as the dogs rushed down the trail, wagging their tails.

"It's all right, Sula. It's me. Ashleen."

Sula ran to meet her friend. "How did you get here?"

"I walked. I couldn't stand it any longer, Jay's been gone a week and I've had no messages. I've come to see if you've any news?"

Sula's heart sank. "Nothing for three days." This meant one of two things - either Jay's birds were also dead or sick, or the two women were in trouble.

Sula took Ashleen inside the cave and gave her a drink. Ashleen's feet were sore from the walk and needed bathing. Her bones and muscles were painful from disease. Sula could only guess what it had cost her friend to come.

Ashleen slept from exhaustion but Sula stayed awake and prepared herself to leave. Kalomi was in L-zone and Sula knew the implications. L-zone was adjacent to P-zone and was frequently traversed by scouts. She mustn't get frightened, she must stay practical. She had the dogs - they would be able to track Kalomi anywhere and would afford protection. She would have to go alone because of Ashleen's feet.

When everything was ready, she woke Ashleen. "They could be injured. I have to go and look for them. You stay and wait for the birds. I'm taking two of the dogs."

Ashleen looked resigned. She watched Sula pick her way down the track.

Covering her trail, Sula watched the dogs sniffing the ground. They had trained the dogs to follow their personal scents. She was unsurprised when they turned north. She let them pull her up the hillside and down to the river beyond. Kalomi would have used the river to dispel her scent.

The river was shallow. Sula took one dog across. Standing in the water she told them to 'find'. Both dogs roamed up and down the banks until the eager barking of Karil the older bitch told Sula she had found Kalomi's scent 600 metres north on the same bank.

She kept her sharp eyes open for signs but Kalomi had left no traces. Excited snuffling by a river cave lead Sula to think Kalomi met Jay there. The trail of two women should be easier for Sula to find and

Jay might make mistakes, having left a northern stronghold to live in the wilderness with her lover only a year ago. However Sula found no evidence they had been in the cave.

When dawn broke Sula was ten miles from home, heading east. Their journeys always required obscurity. If found by scouts they would be tortured for information. If found by hunters the information would be of no interest but their selves would be unlikely to escape. But this path seemed particularly obtuse. A brief shock of doubt flashed - had Kalomi and Jay fallen in love? Had they been unable to face the wreckage their feelings would cause and left on the pretext of fetching goods?

Sula shamed herself with doubts: in these last years she had come to know Kalomi's every quality. There had been no room for hiding or sentimentality: every woman's last characteristic had to be examined and accepted for survival. To leave without arrangements would be the height of selfishness, and though Kalomi could be impatient and vain, selfishness was not one of her faults.

Having decided Kalomi's elopement with Jay was unlikely Sula put it out of her mind. Energy could not be wasted on worry. She walked until noon, marvelling at her lover's skill. Over twenty miles she had only found one sign of their presence: a broken green branch on the slope to a river. Even that had been left deliberately to mislead, for the dogs could find no trail on either bank. Kalomi had doubled back to a point where she had jumped into a side stream and walked up it for half a mile. Sula smiled. Kalomi was too damn clever. The false trail cost her two hours.

She took one of the birds from the wicker frame on her back and fastened a message on its leg for Ashleen. She used the runic code developed by the Brains and still not cracked by the Others. The bird would fly to the cave and then return to its mate when Ashleen released it. Sula expected it back before the end of her sleep.

She woke with the gentle nuzzling of Karil. The dogs had been trained not to bark at the approach of Others but to alert the women without noise. Sula watched the dogs sniffing the air in the direction of the danger and noticed the wind was blowing from the source. This was good - the Others were probably a long way off. The bird had returned and was scratting about the earth. She took its message: All well, no news. She picked up the bird and put it with its companion in the wicker frame with some seed.

186

Noiselessly she packed up, giving thanks that Kalomi's trail was in the opposite direction to the danger. Had it not been so she would have lost hours or perhaps days waiting for the Others to move on, and her lover's trail would be scrambled and difficult to pick up.

She was soon troubled by another false trail. After the dogs found no scent for a mile up and down a ravine, she doubled back to look for a jump off.

She backed up two miles and searched three streams. The dogs could find nothing. Sula went back to the ravine. Baffled, she searched for more of Kalomi's tricks, looking upwards into the trees. She was cursing her lover when she noticed two scrape marks half way up a pine tree. The tree had obviously been chosen because its shaggy bark hid marks like these. Sula crossed the fast river with difficulty, the dogs swimming. On the other side she found a tree with similar marks. They had crossed by rope and continued crossing the treetops. She sent the dogs out in a fan. The trail resumed on the ground 300 metres from the river.

Sula was able to track well into the night. When the moon reached its zenith she found Kirsta's body. The bird had been shot and its message taken. The obvious trail of a hunter joined Kalomi's and continued for a mile. Sula noted the broken twigs, footmarks, charred wood, and dung piles with contempt. She had no fear that such a crass operator could follow Kalomi for long. She judged the hunter's trail to be a week old.

At a point where the dogs indicated Kalomi's trail went two ways, Sula chose the carefully concealed zig-zag and ignored the false route taken by the hunter. At sun up Sula stopped, exhausted. She released a bird to Ashleen and slept.

Waking in early afternoon Sula spent five minutes in prayer. She felt close to Kalomi yet much too far away. The dogs were eager to set off. She checked her compass: at last they were heading south.

By evening Kalomi's trail was leading into the P-zone. Sula felt apprehensive. Had Kalomi a pick-up in the P-zone? Such ventures were the most dangerous of all.

Sula tasted salt in the air. She realised she had not seen the sea for ten years. Excitement mingled with apprehension. She judged she was near the border of L and P-zones. Security would be tighter. She went extremely carefully. She was amazed to reach the sea without trouble. She had never known it so quiet.

Kalomi's trail led to a sandy beach and stopped. If Kalomi had taken a boat how could Sula possibly follow? She would have to return to the cave and wait or travel to a stronghold to ask for information.

She searched for a safe place to sleep. At the end of the bay small cliffs hollowed into partial caves. Climbing above high tide mark she arranged herself as comfortably as she could and sent a bird to Ashleen. She hoped when the bird returned it would bear some message of comfort.

Sula was woken at noon by a woman. Blinking in the sunlight she saw her two dogs sleeping soundly and realised they'd been drugged. The bird she'd sent to Ashleen had been fastened back into the cage.

"You have no sickness. What are you doing here?" the woman asked.

Sula regarded the old woman, who looked tough and clever. She saw a dagger in her hand and noticed its keen edge. She decided a fight wasn't in order. "Where am I?"

"You're ten miles south of P-zone. Tell me why you're here."

Sula considered her questioner. "You're alone?"

The woman laughed. "My man was one of the first to try the new wonder drug. He thought he was Casanova until he started to wither. He was one of the first to die. I'm better off without him. He was a nuisance. They all want a bit more than they've got. They can't understand women don't care. It's a damn pity we didn't realise sperm carries it."

"You escaped the sickness?"

"Does a man who thinks he's twenty bother with an old woman? Quite a few of us old ones escaped."

"I think my lover came this way. Did you see her?"

"I see everybody who comes here."

"Patrols?"

"Patrols, pah! Full of it, all of them."

Sula considered her words. "I've trailed my lover for days. Did she take a boat?"

"I took three women. I've no quarrel with Wicca. They paid me well."

"Can you take me to the same place?"

"For what?"

Sula rummaged in her pack.

"You've nothing I want. I've already looked."

Sula narrowed her eyes. She considered leaving a dog.

"I'll tell you what you can give me when we've eaten. I've food cooking."

Sula didn't like the woman's tone. She wondered how long the dogs would sleep. When they woke they would track her wherever this woman made her go.

The woman took her to a hut well back in the trees. At the side was a boat in good shape. Sula's stomach weakened at the smell of food wafting from the hut.

"You're a good size," the old woman commented, giving Sula a bowl of thick soup. "It's like manna to see a woman so big." For a moment Sula wondered if the woman wanted sex as the narrow eyes scanned her body with open admiration. "Those bitches in P-zone hardly have flesh left on their bones."

"Is it so bad?"

"Don't come that talk with me. You know you'll be glad when it's over and they're all gone. I know what you call them."

Sula struggled with her emotions, her repulsion at humans dying slowly, relentlessly. Inside she knew it was the truth. She longed for it to be over. The Others were dangerous but their power was waning. She hardly dared think of the future. So many women like her had been killed.

"Poor fools," the old woman went on, "eating poison to make their dicks bigger. I bet you dykes wish you'd invented the drug?" Her eyes opened as if a new thought struck her. "Perhaps you did, eh?"

Sula looked disgusted but said nothing.

"I wish I had," the old woman laughed coarsely. "There'll be some left for reproduction I daresay."

Sula heard the dogs outside.

"I've already made friends with them," the woman said, letting them in. "That grey bird has a message. Read it."

Sula opened the paper and read silently. All well, no news. She tried to keep her face neutral before the old woman's scrutiny.

"I've boiled you some water. You need a wash."

Sula lusted to be clean. "I must go after my lover. She could be in danger."

"If she's met danger, she'll be dead. Don't fool yourself."

Tears came to Sula's eyes and anxiety washed over her. The woman softened. "I'll take you when the tide rises. It'll be three hours. I told you there'd be something in return..." The woman surveyed Sula's body lingering on her arms.

"I cannot have sex without love."

The woman looked startled then roared with laughter. "You think I want your body, splendid though it is? I've been my own lover since I married. I doubt anyone could better me. I don't need that."

"What do you need?" Sula demanded. "Tell me!"

"I want a tooth pulled."

The dogs were reluctant to board the boat. The sea was calm however and the passage easy. The woman set her down at the mouth of a dry river bed ten miles south.

"I keep my wits sharp trying to crack that damn code of yours," she shouted as she rowed away.

Sula smiled. She was grateful the woman hadn't asked her to betray the code. She would have memorized the runic marks, no doubt.

The tooth extraction had made Sula sick to her stomach and the only way to dispel it was to walk and think of nothing but finding Kalomi. She picked her way over the boulders in the river bed. She walked two or three miles and then stopped when she saw the dogs listening. The wind was blowing hard in her face. Behind it she could barely detect voices. A brief lull made her realise they were close. The river bed twisted and turned. The voices grew louder.

Sula ran up the bank least exposed to view, calling the dogs to heel. She realised there was no time to make it to the copse of hawthorn ahead. She reached a gorse bush and ordered the dogs down. As she was about to lie flat she saw a band of five young men turn the corner. One looked almost directly at her. She froze. Even the slightest movement could betray her.

"Still!" she hissed between her teeth. Karil was well-trained but Croona was young and unpractised. The men came closer. Sula was hardly covered by the bush. If she moved she would be instantly visible. She saw flasks at their belts. They were shouting, probably drunk. It was hard to tell if they were sick. They walked fairly well but the lassitude came in the later stages. Two had rifles. They were

no doubt looking for food animals. One of Sula's birds crooned softly.
They were not easy to train into silence. A boy with a rifle swung
round. She did not move a muscle. She kept her eyes averted,
watching him from her side vision. He took a shot at two birds passing
overhead, but missed. One of the others cuffed him for wasting shot.

"You had a better aim with piss," one laughed. "Now you need a
splint for it."

Sula watched them round the next twist in the river, and relaxed.
"Stay," she warned the two dogs. She listened until she was sure their
voices followed the path of the river. It was easier with the wind
ahead. She must let them go further before she set off.

She tracked Kalomi into a forest. The wind from the north was
growing in power. She could smell rain in the air. Rain would cool the
stifling heat but also make the dogs' work difficult. Sula walked
sullenly, afraid of the clouds bursting, watching the sky.

It was because she was so preoccupied she did not pick up the
sounds of a camp above the wind. The dogs were confused and gave
their warning late. Sula saw torches through the trees. She squatted
down. She knew any camp would have scouts around it. Her nerves
tingled, her muscles tensed. She was already too close. The dogs
were quiet but still a risk. Sula's mind became crystal sharp as she ran
through her options.

Through the noise of the storm she could hear revelling.
Drunken camp dwellers might be easy to skirt but the scouts would be
sober. Sula was amazed she had not been caught. The old woman had
told her the weakening of the Others was escalating. Every day they
became more careless, more crazed. They were still dangerous
however. The psychs said jealousy was the cause of their violence and
sexual attacks but Sula thought the knowledge of their eventual demise
had eliminated what moral codes they had left. What they did was
their version of fun.

Sula reflected, as she lay with her dogs, that the Others had
become easier and easier to dodge. More women were moving out of
the strongholds to live in the wilderness, though some had always gone
it alone. She and Kalomi had been out four years. Most of the Others
were clustered in the old cities with the women who had chosen to stay
with them. Riots for new treatment were common but nothing worked.
The tests on rats and chimpanzees had suggested the drug was safe.
Now alcohol was all they had left.

The wind lessened. The shouting, singing voices threaded through the trees to Sula's ears. These were not the voices of Others. These were women's voices. Sula raised her head and listened carefully. Karil and Croona, their ears alert, nuzzled a warning too late. Sula turned to see a woman with a gun, her skill obviously unsullied by drink. Her skin bore the unmistakable patches of sickness.

"You are Wicca?" the woman asked, holding her gun towards Sula and the dogs. Karil and Croona snarled. "Quieten those dogs or I'll kill them."

Sula instructed the dogs to lie down and be quiet. "The dogs are trained to defend me from Others. They are no danger to you."

The woman sat down, still pointing her firearm. Sula noticed the difficulty she had with her joints. The woman was very sick despite her weapon. If she could keep her talking and take her by surprise, she would have no difficulty getting away.

"What are you doing here?"

"Tracking my lover who may be injured."

The woman sighed. The strain of bearing the gun was tiring her. The barrel nosed imperceptibly towards the floor. For such a woman to be a guard seemed inconceivable. Things must be worse than she thought.

"What is your camp?" Sula asked.

The woman laughed. "Women who have come out here to die."

"You're from the city?" Sula watched the nozzle of the gun reach the floor.

The woman looked overwhelmingly tired. "Yes. We made our decision to stay with the Others. Now we wish to die without them." The woman looked at her gun and laid it down. "It's to protect us from Others."

"Why did you stay?"

"My son. He needed me."

Sula found Kalomi's trail easier to follow as she neared the stronghold. The strongholds could not be hidden and were no longer attacked. Sula was surprised how many Wicca were in the forest. They were searching for traps and dismantling them. They said many Wicca had been injured recently. The traps seemed to have been set out of spite, since the hunters were not returning to extract their prey, beast or woman. Other women were filling in pit-traps. She asked after the three travellers. She was told so many were passing through it was impossible to identify her lover. Sula marvelled at the change. She sent word to Ashleen while she slept feeling safer than ever before. The bird returned, the message the same: All well, no news.

Sula was surprised by the slack security at the outer and all three inner gates of the stronghold. There was a feeling of subdued rejoicing. She was questioned by a small woman who said some Wicca had come in from the wilderness and suggested Sula search the apartments.

Sula spent a morning looking for Kalomi before it was suggested she try the hospital. On the third ward she found Kalomi and Jay, their legs plastered and strapped up.

Kalomi couldn't believe her eyes. Then a soft gleam of pride settled in them. "What are you doing here, dreamer?"

"Looking for you. I wouldn't have bothered if I'd known you were just lying around."

Kalomi laughed and hugged Sula. "We fell down a pit-trap."

"We had no word."

Kalomi's eyes clouded. "We sent four birds. None came back. They say the hunters are shooting everything."

"Their last fling," commented Jay. "How's Ashleen?"

Sula told her Ashleen had walked to the cave and sent bird messages regularly saying all was well. Jay sank into her pillows.

"Two travellers have been sent to the cave to give news. You shouldn't have followed me, dreamer. You could've been killed."

"It was easier than I imagined, apart from your stupid tricks."

Kalomi laughed. "I like to keep you guessing."

"And that witch at the bay made me pull her tooth."

Kalomi and Jay shook with laughter. "She wanted us to do that but Lila bought her off with a compass."

"Lila?"

Kalomi indicated the next bed. A woman with bandages around her head and ribs waved her hand. "We picked her up from P-zone. She'd been doing undercover. She was badly hurt by the fall into the pit-trap. She doesn't know how to land."

A muffled growling came from beneath the bandages.

"Peace, sister. When you come out it could be all over."

The End - Aspen

193

"Is it true?" Sula whispered.
"Yes," Kalomi said. "It's the end."
"No," Sula said. "The beginning."

M. E. Schoolfield is a woman alive and well and living in the Midwest. A lover of rhythm and words, she is a published poet, lyricist and author. Her life experience has run the gamut from flipping burgers to going "undercover" with the homeless for studies on the structurally unemployed. Her daily routine revolves around work, friends, family, facilitating and participating in support groups and "ah-choo" no cats!!! She would like to thank Ms. V for her encouragement and support during the evolution of "The Promise."

THE PROMISE

The year was 1982. The middle of a dreary December night. I stood looking out one of Cabrini Hospital's waiting room windows, watching the distant downtown lights waver in the slow trickle of a Seattle rain. The wind blew leafless tree limbs aimlessly.

"Mr. and Mrs. Kendrick, you can see your daughter now."

I turned to look at them as they rose stiffly from the couch. Their son, Paul, helped them. "Call me if it gets near," he said. They nodded and walked down the hall after the nurse.

"I wonder how much longer it'll be."

My mind walked with them around the corner and down the hall. I closed my eyes as I imagined Catie hooked up to the IV's and the monitors. I leaned against the cold glass.

A hand touched my shoulder. I turned and saw Paul standing next to me. "I wonder how much longer it'll be."

"I don't know." I replied. "She's pulled through times like this before."

At that moment Mr. Kendrick came half-running down the hall. "Paul, I think it's time. Hurry."

Again, I wasn't included in the summons. I didn't think I would be, but I'd hoped ... please God, I prayed, let her go ... let it all end. I looked out into the rain mirroring heaven's tears with my own ... remembering ...

"Hey, Catie!" I yelled waving a carrot in the air. "Have you been into my stuff?"

She came into the kitchen and looked at my writing accoutrements spread all over the table. She smiled wickedly. "Why would I do that?"

"Because you've always got to know everything and this has been misfiled."

"Don't you trust me?" She leaned over and took a bite of my carrot.

"Hey, you not only steal a look at my poetry, you're eating my carrot too!" I objected.

"How else am I to know what goes on in that brain of yours. You never tell me anything!!!"

I growled at her and refiled my poems in the accordion folder. "So, what did you think?"

"About what?"

"About the poems."

"Well, some of them I've already read."

"Oh, you've looked in here before?!?" I tied up the file. "Maybe I'll just keep this at my apartment from now on."

"And deprive me of the one great pleasure left in my life?"

I looked at her in pleased surprise. "You mean my poetry?"

"No, I mean tormenting you!!!"

Her voice echoed in my brain. "...left in my life..." I got up from the table and marched into the solarium to the desk I'd commandeered when Catie got sick. I put the file in the lower drawer and slammed it shut. Damn. Damn. Damn. I turned around, looking out to the grey mists that hovered over Lake Washington and obscured the Cascade Mountains. Where do these tears come from? I fought them down. I didn't hear Catie come up behind me.

"You wrote "Early Mountain Mists" about me, didn't you?" She spoke softly from the doorway.

The tears threatened again. I nodded mutely not daring to turn and look at her.

She went to the drawer and lifted out the file. She loosened the string, pulled out the poem and read it aloud.

How shall I tell her of my love
When the early mountain mists
Take breath from her lovely lips
To birth another day

How shall I tell her of my love
When fate's vapors rise
Casting shadows across the sun
To steal our future moments

How shall I tell her of my love
Aching in silent pain
Which fills my heart to bursting
A river flushing to the sea

How shall I tell her of my love
When the early mountain mists
Roll on the tide of destiny
To take her away from me

She took me in her arms and my tears came. She held me tightly. When I could, I swallowed the tears and turned away from her. She handed me back the poem. As I bent down to put it in the drawer, she tilted my chin so I had to look up in her eyes.

"Promise me something, Emmie."

"Anything." I answered hoarsely.

"Don't stop writing. Promise me that when I die you won't stop." Her blue eyes, once sparkling and clear, looked into mine, barely disguising pain.

"Catie..." I began but she put her fingers to my lips.

"We both know what's coming. You said it in the poem." She gathered me into her arms again. She kissed me and whispered into my ear. "I love you, baby. Promise me you'll keep writing."

"I promise," I nodded, and held her gently.

The rain pounded on the window. I didn't hear Paul calling my name. I looked up dazed when he grabbed my hand and started pulling me down the hall. "She's calling for you."

Somehow I got my legs working and I started jogging beside him, racing for the precious moments. I prayed with all my heart that I wouldn't cry. Let me smile, God. Please let me smile for Catie.

We charged breathlessly into the room. Mr. and Mrs. Kendrick were standing on either side of the bed. Catie was looking around and asking, "Where's Emmie? I want her. Where's Emmie?"

Mrs. Kendrick moved away grudgingly to make room for me. I took Catie's hand in mine and moved the bangs off her forehead like I always did.

"Emmie?"

"I'm here, Catie."

"I'm tired, Emmie."

"I know, sweetheart."

"I don't want to go." Her breathing was coming out in rasps as she fought for each breath. "I want to stay with you."

Lord let me smile. "It's all right, Catie. It'll be all right."

"Emmie..." I had to lean close to hear her. Her voice was barely above a whisper. "Don't forget..."

"I won't."

"You promise..." Her hand grabbed feebly for mine. Her eyes so beautiful and blue fluttered.

I squeezed her hand. "I promise." I took her in my arms and whispered, "I love you."

A faint smile tugged at her mouth and her face became peaceful. Her eyes closed. The lines that creased her forehead disappeared. Her hand relaxed. Her breathing became shallow. Her head rested on my shoulder. I rested my head on top of hers.

I don't know how long it was... seconds, minutes or hours. It seemed an eternity to me before the last breath came and she was gone.

It's been difficult, but I've kept my promise. Catie knew better than I what writing meant to me. Through the years that have passed like nameless ghosts since her death, my poetry has sustained me.

When I look out of the window now and see the fog lifting from the river, I wonder if she knows that I've kept my promise to her. I like to think that as the morning mists rise she knows how very much I loved her, that every poem I write is a symbol of that love, and that...

like a candle burning in the darkness
my heart rises from the ashes
to embrace the dawn
flickering with hope
fueled by yesterday's love

The Promise - M. E. Schoolfield

Sally Bellerose is a forty three year old writer, nurse, and mother. Since the age of fourteen she has worked at twenty three different jobs. She is laboring to have writing become her last, long lived means of employment.

A FAILURE TO ADJUST

I always thought of myself as a hot shit, work hard, play hard. A good friend, but don't get on my bad side. You know the type. But then somehow, something changed. I changed. I started to feel, not so gutsy, disgusted I guess. I was tired of working so hard and I didn't feel like playing at all.

It wasn't just one thing, it was everything. The three kids, four counting the husband, were driving me up the wall. The job was the pits. I wanted to just dump it all and start over, but I was forty, and that felt too old, at the time.

It was living in that second floor apartment that started it off. A four room apartment is just too damn small for five people. All the kids in one bedroom, bumping and grinding into puberty, one screaming at the other two to get out, every time they had to change a tee-shirt, which was often. That's my clearest memory of the kids at that age, screaming at one another, wading through a pile of dirty teeshirts. It's no wonder. My kids learned to holler from the best of them. They thought "Pick up this pig sty" yelled loud enough to be heard above the heavy metal playing on the stereo, was every mother's standard greeting when she came home from work.

My husband and I weren't doing so hot either. He liked me better before I was pissed off all the time. He wasn't in love with the new me. I wasn't in love with the old him. Suppertime was the worst. His idea of helping out with meals was adjusting the T.V. set before we ate.

"Annie, quit slamming those plates around. I can't hear the news."

I slammed my way through Sports and Weather, then straight into Star Trek reruns for desert.

Neither of us would leave the kids. He wouldn't leave the marriage bed. I slept on the couch. That couch didn't help out my state of mind any. It had been peed on numerous times, by my kids, other people's kids, and a Chihuahua.

The shrinking apartment, that's what started it. That, and loosing sleep, worrying about work. I work in a paper factory. Management was putting in a new wage earning system. Under this new Incentive Production Program our work gets reviewed every few months and our hourly rate goes up or down accordingly. Some smart company man thought this one up. We used to have piece work. You bind ten score of looseleaf notebook, you make $1.09. You get it the next week. Now we wait twelve weeks. What kind of crap is that and how come the union let it go by?

So I pondered these heavy questions and tossed and turned on a couch that wasn't only uncomfortable, it was just where you'd expect a couch to be, in the living room, with the T.V., and the stereo, and the kids, and the husband, and me waiting for the last person to go to bed every night.

So you see, there were reasons for my condition, my "break with reality" as Jerry calls it. Jerry's my therapist. He says "These stresses were internalized." Jerry says I "Escaped the pressures of Motherhood, adult relationships, and the burdens of my socioeconomic status by retreating to an alternative reality." What he meant was I was freaking out over a two story house. This house that I took particular interest in was no apartment block, it was a whole house, a nice house, right across the street from my best friend Sarah. The house on 10 Bridgeman Lane. At the time it felt more like the house was taking an unusual interest in me, but of course, that kind of thinking was part of my problem.

This guy Jerry, I started seeing him through the shop where I work. He's the Employee Assistance Programs Counselor. Jerry still thinks I'm nuts, better, but not quite on line yet. He doesn't say it like that. It sounds more treatable when he says it. I have an official diagnosis: Adult Adjustment Reaction. You have to have an official diagnosis so that the insurance will pay. I have failed to adjust to adult life. They've got guys like Jerry in lots of the big shops now. They're suppose to keep people glued together, functioning at maximum capacity. If you mess up on your job because of your problem, the shop's more lenient if you're seeing Jerry.

It was my friend Sarah who suggested that I start seeing Jerry. Her cousin Leo works with me. He's an alcoholic. Jerry was his

A Failure to Adjust - Sally Bellerose

counselor. "You know yourself Leo hasn't missed a days work since this Jerry guy helped him get off the booze. Maybe he can help you too."

I didn't think it was such a hot idea. I didn't want people at work to find out that all my ducks weren't in a row, but I *was* screwing up. I never missed work, but I was a bitch when I got there. I needed my job.

So, one day in July I punched out for lunch and dragged myself up to Jerry's third floor, air-conditioned office. He wasn't there, but I filled out a yellow form hanging on the door and slipped it through his mail slot. I peeked through the mail slot to see if anyone standing outside, where I was standing, could read what was on it. No sweat, dark as hell in the Employee Assistance Program's Coordinator's office.

I got an appointment notice the next week. Jerry got down to practical matters right away. I could spill my guts on company time up to one hour a week, an additional hour on my time, his schedule permitting. He gave me a three page list of community resources: the Yellow Pages of human suffering. Phone numbers for the Mental Health Center, Detox, Battered Woman's Shelter. The same list that's tacked up near the time clock. He also said "Nothing we discuss will ever be used for disciplinary action at work."

After his schpeel, Jerry asked me why I'd come. The first time I just told him I was jittery, confused. He wanted to talk about my husband and my kids, boring stuff. I wanted to talk about my house. My sweet house. My big strong sturdy house, with the pretty smooth slats and the smily windows. So I did.

Like I told Jerry, it was the house itself, the physical structure that caught my eye. What can I say? She was beautiful.

My thing with the house started in late spring. Sarah and I had kids on the same baseball team. Sarah didn't have a job. She had her kids, her husband, her house, the yard and the dog. Her husband made pretty good money. They bought a house fifteen years ago, before prices and mortgage rates made a few people richer and the rest of us wondering what the hell we were doing wrong. Their house is on the same street as the ball field, Bridgeman Lane Memorial Park. Two nights a week I'd pick her and the kids up for baseball. I would get out of work at four-thirty, run home to make sure uniforms were clean and everyone was fed, then off to Sarah's. The kids usually ran over to the baseball field as soon as we got there. Sarah was always late. She has a thing about not leaving the house until the dishes are done. I didn't want to help her with the dishes, and it depressed me to watch her, knowing that mine were home in the sink with the mashed potatoes turning into cement on the plates. So, I'd sit outside on her steps, glad to be alone for a while, staring across the street.

I admitted to Jerry up front, a certain bent toward daydreaming. But hey, I still say that this house was encouraging me. That first spring evening I wasn't even interested in that house, any house. Then, softly, so you had to pay attention just to hear it, comes flute music, floating out of the second story window, pretty, kind of sad.

Jerry says I was entering the realm of magical thinking, grasping for symbolic markers, some sign of the unusual for my mind to play with, but at this point, I knew I was just daydreaming. The house looked perfectly normal. Common, built like a box, put up cheap, after the war, like most of the houses on Bridgeman Lane, and exactly like my friend Sarah's. A front door in the middle, a picture window on one side, a smaller window on the other, with windows above each of these. Painted off-white, the house looked just like the ones I had drawn in grammar school. Well, it didn't have a picket fence, but it had a sidewalk leading up to the front door.

It was a few weeks later, a hot day in July, when I realized that something really strange was going on with the house. I was sitting on Sarah's bottom step again. The kids were always looking for odd jobs. I could see that the grass across the street needed to be cut. Then I looked at the trim around the picture window. It was getting kind of shabby. I tried to figure how much the kids would get for scraping the trim on seventeen windows and two doors. I had never seen the back of the house, but I included four back windows and a back door in my count. I looked at the picture window and thought it would be tedious because it had some fancy trim work that I hadn't noticed before. Beautiful work, intricate. I thought I might not mind painting it myself. I got up and looked at Sarah's picture window. It didn't have any special trim. I could have sworn the front windows of the houses were identical.

"Ever notice the lattice work on the picture window across the street?" I asked Sarah when she finally came out.

"What lattice work?"

"On the picture window. Was it always there?"

"There's no lattice work on the picture window. We almost bought that house." she said, trying to manage a jug of kool-aid, a bat and two lawn chairs. "Take something, will you?"

"Sure, gimme the lawn chairs. Look at the window, Sarah."

"Oh yeah, when they put that on?"

"Yesterday."

"Yesterday?"

"Well, I didn't notice it Wednesday."

"Probably been like that for months. So who cares anyway?"

I cared. Now that I was really comparing the houses, I noticed that the picture window on ten Bridgeman Lane was bigger then Sarah's too.

"Who lives across the street?" I asked the next Saturday morning.

"Two women. Marlina, nice lady, and Tina, kind of strange."

"Well, the two women have four front steps now."

"What do you mean?"

"Used to be three."

"Oh please. Are you fighting with Joe again?"

"Again?" Joe's my ex-husband. In those days we did nothing but fight.

Sarah sat down next to me. She put her arm around me and gave me a sideways hug. "Really, everything O.K?" Sarah's got good hugs. "Come on, spill it."

Since she gave me an opening and kept right on hugging me, I bitched some about Joe and the kids, then I went on a long tirade about the new Incentive Production Rates. Sarah had already heard all of this stuff, but she let me rant and rave. I was trying to point out that my paycheck has taken a turn for the worse, now that I have Incentive. Well, I guess I got pretty loud and flung out some words that Sarah found "positively vulgar". This is the point when she started talking very slowly and patiently. "Annie, I think you need help. Professional help." I paid attention to her, partly because I was scared and partly because she started rubbing my shoulders.

Sarah and I didn't talk much about the house across the street for the next few weeks. The discussions made her nervous. After I hooked up with Jerry, I kept watching the house, against his advice. I tried not to, but the damn thing kept getting more beautiful. And it was growing. Slowly, very slowly, just an inch a week, maybe, but faster than the old oak tree on the east side whose lowest branch held a bird house. The bird house was directly across from the second story window at the beginning of baseball season. Now it was a good six inches below. I started watching for traces of construction, a pile of brick, a backhoe discretely hidden in the backyard bushes. I found no evidence. Maybe they worked at night. Maybe I was insane.

I decided to take a picture of the house. I took three, actually. Sarah groaned, "Annie the house fetish. You'll never get well." None of the pictures came out, although I got some great shots of the kids in their uniforms from the same roll.

By late July, baseball season was over, but I still saw Sarah, and Jerry and the house a couple times a week. I had almost convinced myself that I had made up the whole business. No more fantasizing. I needed more rest was all. I had my back to the house on ten Bridgeman Lane when Sarah got me started again. I was telling her about a new diet. In my effort to forget the house I seemed to be eating anything that didn't move.

"Oh shit." she said.

"What?" I asked, listening for a screaming kid.

"Look at your house." Sarah leaned forward in her lawn chair. She was facing me, staring across the street.

I stood up and turned around. The picture window. Why hadn't I measured it? Why hadn't I measured the whole damn house? The picture window was now a bay window, bulging right out of the house with two smaller windows attached on either side.

"So they had a bay window put on the house, huh?" I said, trying to hide my triumph. I was about to prove that this house was jerking me around or have Sarah for company in la la land.

"Why don't we just ask them?"

"O.K." I said. Ready to march right across the street with my friend and do just that.

"I was thinking maybe you could do it." Sarah had the nerve to look me in the eye when she said this.

I wanted to strangle her. "Sure, why not? Everybody already knows I'm nuts, Sarah."

We argued on and off for the rest of the day about how crazy it would seem to Sarah's neighbors if one or both of us asked a few neighborly questions about the growth of their property. We decided a covert operation was the best course of action. I slept at Sarah's that night. Her husband had ring side seats for wrestling. We waited until her kids were in bed, hoping everyone in the neighborhood was asleep. We flipped a coin to see who would measure the house. I lost.

I crouched low, peeking through the bay window. Midnight, and there was still a light on in the kitchen. I could make out two women, sitting at a large kitchen table. That table would never fit in Sarah's kitchen, I thought. I could hear talking, but couldn't make out the words above my own labored breathing.

I decided to get the job done anyway. What the hell. What's the difference between a jail cell and a room in county hospital? How much trouble can you get into for attempted house measuring? A full moon gave me light to work by. I put myself into my work assbackwards. My butt leading the way as I bent from the waist, taking a few steps backward at a time, trying to make the tape measure behave. I wanted an accurate measure, but the tape was hooked to the house only by the little tab thing at the end. Pulling too hard would dislodge it. I worked slowly and secured it with a rock every few feet. I inched my way, until one step brought my rear end in contact with- something. My heart froze. My breathing stopped. I stared between my legs. There stood the largest human being I had ever seen. The woman carried a weapon, a long thin knife of some kind, a skewer maybe. An Amazon was about to skewer me. That wimp Sarah was suppose to be watching from across the street. Why wasn't she trying to rescue me? I fell to my knees sputtering, "I.....I......Please....I"

She offered me her right hand and pulled me to my feet. "Come on. Get up." The weapon dangled in her left hand.

She stared me up and down and played with the skewer, turning it from end to end, then holding it between two fingers like a baton. "What are you doing here?"

"That's a knitting needle." I said, realizing too late that this would not be the revelation for her that it was for me.

"You drunk?" she asked. "What's these rocks for?" She picked up a rock and snatched the tape measure from my hand. She seemed normal enough. But then, who was I to judge?

"No, I'm...I was just here to... I was measuring your house."

"Marlina, come out here," she yelled.

A light snapped on. "Where are you?"

"By the bay window."

"Are you alone? I'm not presentable."

"Get out here..... Please."

Marlina poked her head out the door. She was smiling. Marlina is usually smiling. "I make it a practice never to leave the house with my midriff bulge exposed." She tightened the straps of her halter top and extended her hand to me. "Hello."

I stared at her midriff.

"Introduce me to your friend, Tina."

Tina was actually medium height, hefty, about my size. She growled an introduction and rolled her eyes toward me. "Noise we thought was a dog peein' on our shrubs", then she shot a look at her housemate. "I'd like you to meet Marlina."

Marlina shook my hand. Tina said "Cut the shit. It's midnight. Why are you snooping around?"

"I thought, it seemed, your house...."

"Here, sit." Marlina guided me to the steps. "Don't be afraid of us."

"Be afraid." Tina said, " Talk."

I went with the truth. It was all I had. "I thought your house was growing," I squeaked out. I readied myself to put up a fight if Tina made a move toward me.

"Plain old garden variety nut. So I ain't the only one in the neighborhood. I hate competition." Tina walked back into the house. "I'm going to bed. If you can't get rid of her, wake me up."

Marlina drew the story out of me. It was easy after Tina left. She didn't seem surprised. She said Tina had a special problem herself. Tina gets upset when she's in tight places. A few months before, she had gotten so upset with her boss when he backed her in a corner behind her desk, that she decked him, right there in the accounting office. The company agreed not to press charges if Tina took an extended vacation. Tina sees a full fledged shrink. She has to pay for it herself. I'm dying to know her official diagnosis. Jerry says "Don't push." He never met Tina, but he thinks she has trust issues.

Marlina sat with me a long time. We talked about other stuff besides being nuts. She told me that she and Tina had lived together, right in this house, for over ten years. They had made some changes in the house, especially since Tina was out of work. Tina is real handy, but not good enough to put in a bay window overnight. I tried to get Marlina to tell me exactly when the window was put in. "Recently," was as specific as she got.

She thought Tina and I might be psychically simpatico, you know, we sort of clicked into each other's faulty brain waves. I lean more toward Tina's explanation. We're both common place, garden variety nuts. But I smiled and nodded at Marlina. She was being so nice to me. I felt less crazy then I had in months, or anyway, I cared less. She gave me some grape juice, then sent me home saying, "Come back and measure away in daylight if you like."

When I returned, Sarah was a basket case. She had stood, peeking out, with her hand on the phone ready to call the cops, for over two hours. She sucked up the part about Tina doing some work on the house. "Of course, of course. How could I ever have gotten drawn into this thing?" Sarah's my best friend. Sometimes she's an asshole.

I stopped talking to Sarah about the house altogether for a few months. We kind of cooled off towards each other. She was jealous that I was starting to hang around with her neighbors. Jerry wasn't so sure that it was healthy either. But who can argue with success? He could see that I was getting calmer by the week. He was starting to get caught up in the story too, I think. There were times now, when I wanted him to help me try to figure out how to tell my daughter that her new boyfriend was a useless punk without pushing her further into his hairy tattooed arms, but Jerry kept coming back to the house, and Marlina and Tina. I bet he has closet fantasies about being Tina's counselor.

Then I started having this recurring dream. I dreamed that there was a secret room in the house, up in the attic. A small room, lots of light, an overstuffed chair with big pink flowers on it. I told the dream to Tina. She was smoothing an oak board by hand at the time. She handed me a piece of sandpaper. "Like this," she said, and made even circular movements with her hand over mine. "You do it."

When I first asked her to show me carpentry she said no. She couldn't stand having somebody follow her around. Now she was showing me woodworking stuff once in awhile. I'm hoping to get her to help me build a dog house for Sarah's carpet destroying mutt, to sort of help bring my friends together.

"So what's the room for?" She didn't really seem interested, but Tina doesn't make chit chat, so I told her.

"For me. It's waiting for me. It's my room."

"Christ, the only waiting room you're ever going to see is in the shrink's office." Tina laughed. She even grinned at me. Then she was Tina again, working with no unnecessary conversation.

For the next few weeks when I came to visit, Marlina wouldn't let me past the kitchen. Tina was working on the stair wells and wanted to be left alone. Marlina and I were spending a lot of time together, shopping for winter clothes for my kids. Marlina's into kids. She's even more into clothes. She likes all of that horrible mismatched punky stuff. The kids love to shop with her.

One Tuesday after work I brought over a cranberry nut bread, Tina's favorite. She ate two pieces with us in the kitchen. She was acting funny, friendly almost. She smiled at me. Then something really weird happened.

"How's your finances?" she asked.

"Tina!" Marlina was mortified. "How rude." Marlina's a funny mix, loose about some things, but she's a tight ass when it comes to money.

Tina shrugged, "What? I just want to find out if she can pay her way."

Marlina stood and looked sternly into Tina's eyes. Her voice had an edge. It was the first time I had seen Marlina pissed. "Tina, we agreed, we won't ask for any money unless she can afford it."

"How you plan on finding out if you don't ask?" Tina laughed, leaned back and folded her arms over her broad chest. "O.K., do it your way."

Marlina gained her composure. She threw her head back, looked like a mare, I thought she might whinny, but she turned to me and straightened up, dignified, like the Pope had just walked in. "Annie, Tina has a surprise for you."

"Room's done," said Tina. Just like that. Like I was supposed to know what the hell they were talking about. I just stared at them. Marlina had to take me by the hand and walk me up to the attic before I caught on. Tina didn't even go up with us. We walked up a narrow staircase, Marlina swung open the door and there it was, the last of the afternoon sun streaming through the south window, pouring over the slats on the new wooden floor, white sheet rock walls, waiting to be painted. My room.

That was a few years ago. Life's better, but it ain't easy. I don't think it's ever going to be easy. Two of the kids still live in the apartment with Joe. That apartment is a mess. Sometimes I go over and clean it. I can't help myself. I know they should be doing their own dirty work. I miss my kids. They're getting old. The oldest one's got her own place now.

Jerry thinks moving in with Tina and Marlina was a bad move. He says living in this house "leaves too much potential for further delusional thinking." Jerry says that I "should face the problems of the modern adult world head on, work through my emotional milieu, and accept that changing roles may cause ambiguous feelings, conflicting with the value system of my cultural and socioeconomic background." But, like I said, Jerry talks about the room and the house more than I do now. He's earned his money. I've been making incentive for months. We were working on terminating, but I had an unfortunate setback.

I got into a big fight at Union Hall. I was merely trying to point out the facts. With Incentive Production if your rate is high, the company gets a two month free ride. To make matters worse if your production rate gets too high, they up the base rate, but no matter how low production rates get, the base rate never gets lowered. What really bothers me is that the rank and file vote this mess in. Afraid the company would pack up and move some place where people had more incentive. I used the F word. I was out of control. I don't want my kids using that word and there I was in a public place screaming it.

The incident got management pretty upset. They sent out a memo "Although a certain few employees are resistant to change, the Incentive Production Rate Program is a great success, a more manageable system, whereby all parties benefit, through which, we as a team can reach top efficiency and production."

I figure it's not a good time to stop seeing Jerry. We're dealing with working out anger in constructive ways. Tina thinks I should can Jerry and run for Union Steward. Joe thinks I should can the room. Marlina's worried I'm going to burn myself out running between two houses. Sarah thinks I should find a rich old man with a country estate. I listen to everybody. I sit in my room.

*Kay Lieberknecht is a vegetarian who is in love with nature. She has gone to great lengths to relocate rattlesnakes rather than kill them. A survivor of childhood sexual abuse, she is now dedicated to appreciating her life. She has self-published her poetry (*moons, leaves and other loves, *$8.50, PO Box 914, Ukiah, CA 95482). She's completely crazy over horses and is working with her partner on a book called* Wild Horses Don't Wear Clothes, *about a horse who enriched their lives recently with lessons about unconditional love and determination to be real.*

TOO YOUNG TOO KILL?

I knew what to do when you got a snakebite. You made a tourniquet out of a rag and a stick, cut an X through all punctures, sucked the poison out, and spat it away, praying you wouldn't have a sore in your mouth or an unfilled cavity. You did all this sooner than quick because I knew that you could die of a rattlesnake bite within two minutes.

So when my little sister came in from a trip out to the freezer for bread, with a complaint instead that a snake had bitten her flip-flopped foot, I was alarmed. Mother got on the phone to the emergency room and was scaring me to death with unnecessary delays in treatment. I ran about collecting razor blade, rag, and stick, and held them out to Mother-on-the-phone. "Two minutes, Mother, you have to do something within two minutes!"

About when I was screwing up my courage to do the procedure myself, Mother got off the phone and said, "Two *hours.* I'm taking Peggy to the emergency room. You please kill the snake."

Now, you may think a fourteen year old is too young to kill a rattlesnake, but I was sure I knew how. I just needed the correct implement. Ah ha! This heavy old skillet-minus-handle here will do! "No," said my older sister Carol, "you can't hang onto it to hit him or he can reach your hand to bite you."

"Then I'll throw it on him."

"But then if one hit doesn't kill him, how are you going to get back the skillet?"

"OK, how about Dad's gun," I ventured. On our way to Dad's closet, Carol and I agreed that besides having never dared to be sure where it was kept, neither of us knew how to use the gun, and it could blow a hole in the concrete anyway, for all we knew.

Looking in Dad's closet, I saw his cowboy boots. Carol objected though, "The snake could bite you on the leg!"

"They reach to my knees and he's only a skinny little thing about a foot long!"

"No, Kay, don't do it! He could strike higher than the boots!"

Boy, it was looking pretty hopeless. Let *her* think of what to use! She noticed the big pan from the bottom of the oven.

"Oh gross, Carol! I just cleaned that! And anyway, that's no better than the skillet!" Far be it from me to add that I wasn't too sure I could wield the thing at all!

So we traipsed back to the other end of the house. There on my bed was an overnight case. Carol wanted to use that; after all, it had a handle. "No Carol, that's totally disgusting! Blood all over it? No!"

Realizing neither of us liked each other's ideas, we decided to think about the task from a more objective point of view. Don't look for what's around, but think of what would satisfy the criteria -- long handled and heavy and sharp. *Ah ha*, a shovel or hoe! All right! Let's go to the garage.

"No, you can't walk through the porch, Kay. The snake could bite you!"

"Geez, then I'll go out the front door and around to the garage."

Just outside the front door, to our humble surprise, was a shovel! Now to find the snake. It must have taken five minutes to find the shovel. But the snake was coiled in front of the freezer, patiently awaiting his fate, I supposed.

Suddenly Carol squealed and slapped her head. "I didn't put gas in the car! They're going to run out of gas!" She ran to the neighbor's and asked to be taken along the route Mother would have driven. They could relay Peggy from the gas-less car and get her to the hospital.

In spite of my confidence that I knew how to kill a rattlesnake, given the correct implement, it was unnerving to whack him on the head with the back of the shovel and see him squirm. I killed him again, nearly halving him with the edge of the shovel. I thought of my little sister's life being endangered by this beast, and I killed him again. I thought of my frustration in getting the proper implement to hand, and

I killed him once more. I thought of other snake-like objects that had too many times threatened my young safety, and I killed him several more times. Just to be certain, I killed him till he was in shreds. And, still shaking with rage and fear and pride, I buried him. He wound up six inches under, in the neighbor's gravely field. I didn't want him anywhere near.

Mother called from the emergency room, "The doctor needs to know the exact shape of the snake's head, to tell what kind it was."

"Well, it was diamond-shaped, like rattlesnakes' heads are."

"He wants to know the type of markings on the snake, especially on the head."

Oh great. I went and dug up the shreds and put them in a bag to analyze over the phone. Somehow that was satisfactory. And somehow the four little bitty rattles were intact and Peggy got to keep her snake's rattles as a souvenir.

It turned out Carol had gotten only half a mile down the road when the neighbor's car got a flat. And Mother had been stopped by a policeman for speeding. He was nice enough not to ticket her, and he followed her to the hospital, which would have been a comfort to her if she had noticed her gas gauge.

Peggy got lots of shots, as well as a beautifully bruised and swollen foot. And I got a story to tell my grandkids, and anyone else that will listen.

Jessy Luanni Blackburn: I am a middle-aged Lesbian living in the rural San Joaquin Valley on land which I share with several animals. The dawn and dusk feeding rituals bring me peace and harmony. When my four children visit I love to watch them ride the horses and play with the dogs, cats, and various birds. In the past I've published under the name Jessie Lynda Lasnover but a year ago I legally changed my name to Jessy Luanni Blackburn; both to identify with my Cherokee ancestors and to separate from a childhood of abuse. I am primarily a writer but I also teach on weekdays, work in mental health on weekends, and study evenings for my Master's in English. I wrote this story many years ago for a woman named Lynn. I hope you like it.

THE COLOR OF LOVE

The cat was there on the step when they opened the door, waiting. A small cat, fluffy, with patches of various shades on a mostly white body. She was a girl cat, you could tell, you didn't have to check. Her femaleness shone from her face and manner.

One of them loved the cat right away. She picked up the cat and held her..."I love you," she said and the cat purred "I love you," back. "You're mine," she said and the cat answered, "You're mine."

The bond was established and the cat moved in.

The other one didn't much like the cat. She'd always preferred dogs. But for the sake of harmony she kept her mouth shut. "You intruder," she thought at the cat and the cat replied, "Tough shit!" and smiled and purred. Greeneyes named the cat Topaz, "because she has such pretty yellow eyes." Browneyes didn't answer. Topaz purred and gave Greeneyes a small love-bite on her wrist.

A chair with a cushion was pulled up to their dinner table for Topaz. Greeneyes fed Topaz morsels of food from her own plate. Browneyes watched as Topaz licked first one paw and then the other after her meal. Topaz stretched. She curled up on Greeneyes' lap while they sat on the couch. Browneyes read aloud from a book by Joanna Russ. Topaz licked along the inside of her wrist as Greeneyes scratched under the cat's chin. Browneyes' voice was soft as she described alien planets and strange dilemmas.When they went to bed, Topaz crawled under the covers and cuddled against Greeneyes' belly.

Browneyes hugged against Greeneyes' back, one arm draped over and caressing her lover's breast. Sometimes Browneyes' hand slipped down and stroked the cat's fur and Topaz purred.

The next morning, Greeneyes stayed home when Browneyes left for work.She had the day off and planned to write letters. Topaz jumped onto her lap while she was at the table, writing. Topaz kneaded her paws on Greeneyes' thighs. She decided to write another time.

Browneyes learned to tolerate Topaz. The cat's body was soft as she rubbed it against the woman's legs. Browneyes began to look forward to those leg rubbings. Topaz smiled.

The cat became a part of their life together, accepted and comfortable. She was an affectionate cat. Stroking Topaz was easy, she was always there, soft and seductive. At night she moved from one woman to the other; rubbing, kneading, licking, and purring. She entered into their dreams. Her yellow eyes glowed; watching as she purred and smiled her long cat smile.

They had been accustomed to going out a couple of evenings a week; to a show, dinner, or a friend's. Now they felt happiest at home, cuddling on the couch with Topaz. The cat was very content.

Friends called once in a while to ask them out. Topaz rubbed against their legs and as they stroked her, they made excuses and stayed home.

Late one night Greeneyes woke up and saw Topaz there on the bed, kneading against Browneyes' breast while she slept. Topaz was purring and watching her face. Browneyes smiled in her sleep. The cat's eyes glowed, and she bared her teeth. Greeneyes shut her eyes before Topaz could see her. She went back to sleep and dreamed of tigers.

The next day Greeneyes came home early from work. She held Topaz on her lap, stroking her and listening to Bessie Smith records. Halfway through "The Backwater Blues" she pushed the cat away. When Browneyes came home she smiled, got up and turned off the stereo."What's wrong?" asked Browneyes, "you were playing Bessie's blues and you only play Bessie when something's wrong."

Topaz growled but Greeneyes was silent. She did not return to work the next day. She wrote a lot of letters and made some phone calls. Topaz followed her from room to room, but Greeneyes wouldn't touch her.

Browneyes came and went. She brought presents for Greeneyes. A bouquet of yellow roses and daisies, a package of bagels, and a book by Rita Mae Brown. Topaz watched; silent, big yellow eyes reflecting the beginning of a feeling of betrayal.

The next morning Greeneyes got up and put on a bright red sweater. Topaz watched with her sad, unblinking gaze as her woman got some things together and left. The cat jumped on the windowsill and watched the red sweater move down the street. Topaz remained on the sill long after the red sweater was no longer in sight.

She moved to the bed, curled up on the pillow and slept until Browneyes came home. Topaz watched her walk through the apartment and waited until she had looked in every room. Topaz followed her to the couch and sat in her lap, not purring.

"She's gone," Browneyes said as she rubbed the cat's back. They went to bed and Topaz slept on the pillow by her face. Greeneyes didn't come back all that week, and Topaz slept with Browneyes. They ate almost nothing. They spent their evenings listening to Mozart concertos; flute and harp, piano and violin. One night they listened to Willie Nelson, and Topaz kneaded her paws on Browneyes' belly while they sat together.

Greeneyes came back on the eighth day.

"Hi," she said, and smiled.

"Where the hell have you been?" said Browneyes.

"I had to get away, I felt there was something wrong, I don't know...maybe it was silly. Anyway, I'm back now."

"Couldn't you have left a note or called or something? I thought you were dead somewhere."

Topaz didn't say anything. Greeneyes looked at both of them a long time and then said, "I'm sorry." The women embraced. Browneyes said, "God, I've missed you." She kissed her cheek, her neck; she touched her breast. They sank to the floor.

"I love you," said Greeneyes."

"Take off your clothes," Browneyes answered.

Topaz watched, purring loudly. She started kneading her paws against the carpet. She crawled up along Greeneyes' body until she was able to put her paws in the woman's hair. Topaz purred as she kneaded in the hair. She licked inside Greeneyes' ear and bit her earlobe with her sharp cat teeth.

Browneyes said, "I love you," and both Greeneyes and Topaz answered with a low growl. Topaz moved away from the hair and watched her women make love. She walked down to beside Browneyes' hip and pressed her soft, furry body against Browneyes and reached her paws up and over so she could knead, claws sheathed, on the small of Browneyes' back and then on her buttocks. She purred deep in her throat. When they reached orgasm, Topaz looked up, eyes bright, watching. Greeneyes thought she was forgiven.

The lovers' need for each other increased every day, and Topaz was always there, watching. She grew sleek and shiny. She seemed to get larger and her eyes became a deeper shade of gold. In contrast the women became smaller, thinner, and a little bit faded. They ate less and so did Topaz but Topaz didn't miss the food.

The cat became more and more of a participant; licking and kneading the lovers on their backs, bellies, necks and ears. Sometimes she crawled down and bit their toes as they made love. Topaz liked to sit on Greeneyes' back and swish her soft tail across the woman's back as she watched Greeneyes' face. When they changed position, Topaz would crawl right between Browneyes' legs and knead her paws against her inner thighs. Sometimes she'd bite Browneyes' leg just below her buttocks.

Topaz drove the women on. They made love until they slept, exhausted, where they lay. They stopped eating altogether. Their faces became maps of valleys and shadows. Their bodies developed ridges and hollows. Topaz rounded out, fat and glossy. Her eyes gleamed as she woke the lovers from sleep by biting softly on their nipples to arouse them. Their lives were framed in sensuality.

It took Topaz three months to kill them.

Topaz gave each woman a first, and last, kiss on the mouth and then she cleaned herself. She left through an open window.

Topaz put a lot of thought into the selection of her next lovers. She still felt a pain in her cat's heart whenever she thought of Greeneyes and remembered the way her red sweater looked as she walked away. Topaz wanted a woman she could love without fear of losing.She chose an older couple this time. One had silver hair and the other's hair was black with streaks of gray. Both were blue-eyed.

They named her "Fluffy."

Luanne Armstrong is currently living in Indonesia where she is editing an environmental magazine and writing and researching ecofeminist issues. Challenge is nothing new to her: she has lived most of her life in rural British Columbia, on an island in the area of Kootenkys, where she ran an organic farm and raised four children while saving money to go to university. Her writing and her love of the land are her greatest inspirations. "A'thyraa" is one of eleven erotic fables, all connected by a sense of timelessness, and all in some way about some aspect of lesbian sexuality. Two of the fables and a book of her poetry have already been published, and her novel, a feminist cowgirl story, is due out in 1995.

A'THYRAA

I lay in my black tent, contented. In those days, I was mostly contented. Outside, I could hear the horses tearing at the grass, the soft thud of their hooves, their determined munching. I lay on my bed, warm and soft in every bone and thought about what I might do with this new day. I might go hunting; I might work on training the new colts; I might go swimming in the afternoon. I might simply lie in my tent.

I turned and nuzzled gently into the back of the woman sleeping by my side; for a moment, I couldn't actually remember who she was, but then the mist cleared and I remembered the night before, drums and dancing and laughter over the fire, and catching her eye, the tendrils of heat and tenderness rising up and spinning the threads back and forth between us. And then the hours of kissing and soft crooning moans, and the delight rising from my toes up to my belly and on to my face and eyes.

But this morning, she would go back to her tent. Such was our way. Such was my way. Some women joined and partnered for weeks and months and years and even for lifetimes, though that was rare. I had never met anyone I wanted to share my tent with and doubted that I would. But at the gathers, I never lacked for partners. Fucking was such joy, such an endless delight and pleasure, I was quite sure the goddess came to slide between us at times to take her share.

I had always loved to share nights of delight and joy but I also looked forward to the moments when I woke alone, early in the grey dawn, and slipped outside and down to the river, to slide into the cold silky water and lie in its embrace while the sun reddened and sent slithery gold fingers down through the leaves on the trees to dance along the water ripples.

Sometimes, I left the camp to ride alone among the high peaks. I wandered for days, looking into lonely valleys and over cliff edges, or I tethered my pony and climbed for the sheer joy of testing myself against rocks and cliffs and handholds until I found myself in the high mountain gardens, full of tiny goddess-arranged delights, boulders and minuscule flowers and satin streams.

I lived as I pleased.

I took my place among the other women when it came time for hunting or riding or herding or trading. Most of the other women had children; when the time came, they would go to the men's camp and remain as they chose, until their purpose was done. Most came back; some remained with the men for several seasons. But all returned home during the time when the child was to come into this place; a child was always born to a tent full of mothers and grandmothers, waiting to welcome it with singing and wonder.

But I had never felt the urge for a child, and so, though I played with the children, and taught them riding and hunting, more often I left them to the tenderness of the other women. What I liked best was to look and wonder at the mystery of what I saw around me, its endless intricacy and complexity; I marvelled and I played, and a child, even a child beloved by many women, I knew, would take time away from this.

We didn't always stay in this place; sometimes we journeyed, over the plains, to other camps, and occasionally to the city, which was three days slow riding away or one day's fast riding. We went to the city for amusement, and to look; we traded with them, but more for their pleasure than ours. There was little we needed that we couldn't make ourselves but the city people liked our drums, our hides, our weaving and pottery. So we traded with them. It was an excuse to visit, to drink, which we did seldom on our own, to go the temple and listen to the goddess speaking, to look at art and listen to music and hear the gossip, which mostly struck us as funny or incomprehensible.

But sometimes it was serious. There had come news of some kind of fighting in the north. Fighting had never come to the plains in our memory, and we were not sure what such a thing could mean, but people in the city seemed very concerned so we listened too.

I didn't often go to the city but when I did, it was fascinating and I got very excited, listening in the market to new ideas; I was silent although I would have liked to add my voice to the discussions and arguments. But I was dark, a plains person, and I could not speak if I didn't know that I would be heard. Our people learned to listen carefully, but city people rudely interrupted each other and didn't seem to listen much at all. Sometimes I got too excited and had to ride away and calm down. I also liked to think and talk and play with words. It was a game, a bit like hunting except nothing died. But I would not have wanted to do it all the time like the city people seemed to do.

I went to the city one day with a group of women, some from my band, some not. We always dressed up for it, and rode easy in our bits of decoration, on our curly haired black ponies, joking and laughing and talking and gossiping about who we might meet this trip, about city women and city men and their ways, and what they might be like in bed, and lying hugely about our experiences and laughing at our own lies.

My own horse was one I raised as a colt; he knew me and my ways as I knew his; in the last trip to the city, I had traded for a red blanket, and on this trip, I braided hawk feathers in his mane and blue beads into my own hair and I rode most of the trip sitting backwards, partly to show off and partly for ease in talking.

When we came in sight of the city, our talking and laughing quieted, as usual, for though none of us ever admitted it, we felt the differences in the glances that city people gave us, in the difference between our plains finery, and their smooth hair and shining immaculate clothes and soft hands. We insisted to each other that we didn't feel any less than them, but sometimes it felt to us that they thought they were more than us, and they let us know. We had no way to understand or withstand such difference, since in our daily life, such behaviour was unknown to us. And we were always unused to the feeling of being shut in, of not being able to see the horizon, of being surrounded by people we did not know. Time in the city was time spent enduring this feeling. For most of our lives, those about us were our relatives or lovers or children. Approaching people with whom we had no relationship was always difficult to know how to do.

When we entered the city, we crowded together, and I rode frontways on my horse, looking straight ahead. When we got to the market, we unloaded the pack ponies and laid out our trading things and braced ourselves for the people who would come. We had learned to take care to give each other rest from the strain of meeting strange eyes and strange voices. So while some were trading, others were free to wander and to look.

This day, I rode through the streets to the gardens by the river. These gardens always fascinated me in their order; they were like the high meadow gardens in the mountains, but one is made by the Creator Goddess, and one is made by the city people. I tied the horse and looked at the patterns of colour and order. Another woman was also there, but not looking at the flowers. Instead she was intent on staring at the paper in her hands and not wishing to disturb her, I went as quietly as I could.

But she looked up and smiled a greeting. Awkwardly, I nodded my head. I did not know this woman, but now that she had greeted me, courtesy and ritual said that I should also greet her. I waited. Again she looked up and smiled and this time there was a frown in the smile, that I should still be standing before her, and not seem to know what to do next.

I waited. Since it was her place I had come into, it was her place to speak, and finally she did.

"This is a beautiful garden," she said, "and a beautiful day to enjoy it in. Have you come here before?" Her voice was clear and throaty. She wore a plain white dress; her hair was golden and braided. She had blue eyes.

"Yes," I said, "we have nothing quite like this on the plains. And it is peaceful... after the market."

"Ah," she replied, smiling kindly, "you have come to trade then."

"Yes," I agreed, and after that there seemed little more to say and she went back to her papers and I went back to the flowers, and then back to my pony. I didn't want her to be there, and I left before I wanted to.

I went back to the market, to take my turn at trading. A crowd was beginning to gather in the square. Something was going to happen and I went to watch.

220   *A'thyraa - Luanne Armstrong*

After a while, I saw her come from the park, still in her white dress, and mount the steps beside the square, and make a speech, to which everyone listened carefully, sometimes interrupting to applaud. It was a good speech, I thought. She was warning them about preparing for fighting, and about paying attention to what was going on in the world outside this small safe city; I didn't really understand all of what she was saying, and I wanted to ask her questions. But there was a crowd of people around her. I listened and watched her from a distance, and when it was over, I went back to trading.

But she came by the row of blankets where we were. She seemed still enclosed in a crowd of people, all talking and chattering and laughing and some touching her to get her to pay attention, and she was talking back, lively, her arms and hands and eyes flashing, and people listened when she spoke.

I bent my head over the blanket. I did not want that flashing attention turned my way, didn't know how to meet it. So when she stopped in front of me, I saw only her feet in sandals, and then was forced to look up and meet her smile.

"This is beautiful pottery," she said. "Did you make it?" and I shook my head, for making things is not what I do. Fucking and riding horses and hunting and travelling alone in high places is what I do. But I said nothing. She picked up several bowls, frowned over them, put them back, and finally chose one, and handed me some city money, which I took without looking at it.

And then she went on and the light went out of the day and I snarled at the other customers, until my sisters told me to leave. I sat and thought and then I rode through the city in the direction I had seen her take. I had to ask directions several times, but people seemed to know who I meant, and though they were startled by my question, still they gave me the answer I wanted.

But when I came to her house, I paused. Her house was bigger than many of the others around it. Flowers grew everywhere, and there was the sound of running water. I rode into the yard, over stones laid flat and then stopped, unable to think of what to do next. On the plains, if a door is open, one enters, and if a door is closed, one does not. Her door was closed, and yet I thought that perhaps, here, that meant nothing. Perhaps it was only a barrier I could pass through by asking.

I waited and one came to the door and asked my business. I said I had a question to ask of the woman inside, and that one, a young man, disappeared. Soon, she came to the door, still smiling, but I did not smile back.

She asked me to come inside and I did, leaving the horse in the yard to eat the flowers if he chose. I took a deep breath and stepped inside and the walls closed around me. It was much bigger inside than I had supposed. The walls went up to a high ceiling and light came in from above. There were rugs on the stone floor, and the walls were painted with pictures of birds and women and cattle and horses. Some of the pictures were of the plains, my plains, and I felt a flash of anger, that anyone should presume to picture what they could never really know.

She took me to a place beside the fireplace and motioned for me to sit down and left and came back with tea and something sweet on a platter.

"What is your question?" she asked when I had drunk the tea and eaten whatever was on the platter.

I looked away at the pictures on the wall, of women dancing with flowers and each other.

"How is it," I said finally, careful with my words and my tone, "that one who makes a speech about opening up walls and learning about other things outside the city, does not know the people who live on the plains outside these walls?"

She looked at me in surprise, and then she laughed. Her laugh was like the river water, chuckling in the reeds.

"You're right," she said. "I don't know much about your people. But I always thought that was by your choice. We in the city think of you as wild and proud and looking down on those of us who live within walls, and not wanting to talk to us. Although we live side by side and are one people, still we hardly know about one another."

I laughed a little. "When have you given us a chance," I said. "You look away, you talk to each other, you look at our rough ways and you walk on."

"Tell me then," she said, "for I would like to hear, and I have always wondered and wanted to know. I used to come by the market and marvel at the horses, for their beauty and the easy way you rode."

"I will", I said "but you must tell me as well, how to grow such flowers and why your houses are so large and how you can stand to live within walls with so many strangers, and what it is you read and what your papers say."

A'thyraa - Luanne Armstrong

We talked and talked and people came in and lit the lamps and brought food and more tea and still we talked. Finally I went out to check on my horse and found him unsaddled, fed and brushed, enclosed, and not very happy about it, in a small house attached to the big one.

So I went back. It was getting late and my sisters would be wondering but they also knew where I had gone and they would not wonder too much, but would wait for me to return and tell them the story.

A silence had fallen between us. I looked at the flickering candles and at her hands, lying in her lap where they had fallen among the folds of the white dress and I hesitated. It was she who moved first, taking my rough hands in her smooth ones, and rubbing her thumb, over the rough places and the little hollow of the palm and between fingers, while I felt my cunt loosen and shivers ran up my back and I could not look at her.

When I did, I looked at her eyes, and her lips and then I leaned to kiss her. Her lips were dry and warm, and I placed my hand onto the softness of her breast and felt her move and felt the heat between us and we kissed and kissed, each of us wondering when the other would speak. Finally she leaned away.

"I do have a bed," she said, "and you are welcome to share it, if you would like."

I laughed. "Yes," I said, and she led me to her room and she took off her white dress and I took off my leather and my blue beads and we lay on the bed together in the light from the lamps.

Her breasts were beautiful, and the nipples rose to my tongue and she fell back on the bed in need and desire, but I took my time, exploring the lift of her belly and the curved ivory of her thighs and the small spaces in the hollow of her neck. I wanted to know all of her, all the secret warm places and the taste and smells of apricots and honey and hot summer days and the sound of her breathing and sighing when my fingers slid between her legs searching for the folded hidden warmth there, and when I moved down and put my tongue where she wanted me to put it, and her fingers grabbed my hair and I heard her singing, and I felt in my own body, the tension and excitement growing until her cunt convulsed around my fingers and I held her there with my tongue and my fingers, until, gasping and sweaty and exhausted, she pushed me away, and kissed my wet face and pushed my hair off my face. I waited, content whatever happened, but she put her hands on me, and finally in me, so deep that I lost all sense of where and who I was and I only remember the goddess singing in my blood, and knew that I was lost in this woman, that between her and I there was no division, and when my body cooled, and I lay in her arms, I wept.

At that, she was alarmed, for nothing we had done called for weeping, but how could I tell her of my fear, I who feared nothing, and of the sense I had both lost and gained something indescribable. When I touched her body, it felt like my own, and she said as much to me, in wonder, and we were both silent, struck by the newness of something so familiar.

Finally we slept and when I awoke in the morning, she was there, and we spent the morning talking and lying, flesh against flesh, until we felt the singing begin again in our blood and hearts. When I held her this time, I thought that I would faint, for I shivered and the bed whirled and I went deeper and deeper into myself, to where I could hear the grandmothers talking, to where the goddess herself spread her wings like an infinite, iridescent blue butterfly, and I sprawled, open and singing and moaning on the bed while she went after me, and when I said, no more, she said, no, come on, more, just a little, and I came and came and something in me that had been clenched and protected, let go and melted and was gone.

After that, we got up and dressed and went out of that room, and down to the kitchen for food; the woman who had brought food before was nowhere in sight, but the food was there, and all the time, we talked and talked, such talking as I had always longed for and wanted, and words and ideas spilled from me and from her, and we laughed and could hardly wait for the one to say something and the other to complete it.

It was a glorious day, and finally, we went back to bed, exhausted and slept.

I stayed with her for seven days. I sent a message to my sisters to go home without me.

Each day was more wonderful and complete than any other but also each day, the walls closed in tighter and the sense of strangeness grew. After all, for all the time we spent in bed and spent talking, I didn't know her. Her ways were strange; her house was strange. People came and went and I didn't know who they were. Food appeared and disappeared. The house had a whole life I wasn't part of. She went out,

A'thyraa - Luanne Armstrong

twice, to go to meetings with people I didn't know, and though she courteously asked me if I would like to go, I didn't think she wanted me to, and I didn't go.

At the end of that time, I went to bed one night and closed my eyes and thought myself back onto the plain. It was so clear that pain stuck in my heart like a sharp splinter, like a fierce arrow. In the night, I awoke, and didn't know where I was and in the morning I told her I was leaving. She said nothing, but her eyes closed.

"Yes," she said, and turned away and said nothing more. I went to the little house and got my horse, who was wild and kicking and fretful with standing and loneliness for the others of his tribe, and I was sorry for him. When I came into the courtyard with the horse, she came and stood beside me. I put my arms around her, and held her, and in our bodies, I could feel it, the seal, the joining we had made, slowly ripping and tearing apart, like flesh tearing.

"I'll come back," I said. "Please know that I'll come back," and I laughed, a little, both with joy and sorrow, and not knowing how to live with this new feeling. "I have no choice. You are part of me, and I am part of you. I am not sure how this happened or if I chose it, or even if I want it, but it is so."

She looked at me, this proud woman of the city, who made speeches and read books and had others around to do her bidding. "I will wait," she said, "I will wait here and I will have my life, but part of me will ride out and onto those plains where I have never gone."

"You could come with me," I said, pleading, but she only said, "I will wait."

And so I got on my black horse and came back to the plains, where everything was both the same and utterly changed, and all the way home, I felt that perhaps I was a finer and better person than I had guessed, to love and be so loved, by her.

I was teased of course. And questioned. Gently. I sat at the fire, that night, smiling with happiness and remembering. It was only as the days began to lengthen in number that the foolishness of what I had done began to come into me. Our elders teach us that each person is a circle and we are connected in all directions to the world around us. I know this is so, for I have stood on the plains and seen the joining, the rays of light, go out from me to all that I loved. But now there was a torn place in me, and to fill it, I would have to leave all that I love and that makes me what I am. I waited. I slept with other women. I went riding and climbed the mountains to my favourite valley, and then one day, I slid back onto my black horse and made the journey, riding faster than I normally would, back into the city.

At first, we were shy with each other. When I first saw her, I thought, there, now I can go back to the plains and be free, and I wondered why I had ridden this long way to be with a stranger. She asked me in and had the other people bring food, and then they went away and she asked me questions about my life and what I had been doing on the plains. I told her, and asked her questions in turn, and then she took my hand and turned it over and stroked the softness there, and along my fingers and said nothing more, but only continued, stroking my hand and holding it. My heart turned over. I knew that I loved her. I saw the light woven between us.

I took her hand as well. I was relearning her body, the smell of her flesh, the smooth texture along her inner arms, the soft down on her cheek, the feel of her hair, as soft and fine in texture as a child's.

Our bodies met and greeted each other with delight, toes meeting toes and hands touching and stroking and breasts touching breasts.

We lay together on the floor for a long time, healing what had been torn, and peace came into me, and wholeness and I knew that I had missed her and would always miss her until we were like this again. She went and found pillows and blankets and we slept there, in front of the fire, like two tired children, and in the night, I touched her, and she touched me back and we held hands and then we slept again.

After that, I divided my time between the plains and the city, but I was never easy in either place. Nor would she come onto the plains with me even to visit. I asked her to come, to visit, even for a few days, but there was always some reason, some business she had in the city, which prevented her and very quickly, I stopped asking. So the travelling, and the division in my life, was mine and when I left, she wept, and I carried the memory of her weeping face home with me. When I left home, my sisters wept, and said I was out of balance and needed to go the healers and so I went back and forth, pulled in two directions, and never able to settle in either one.

I tried to live the life of the city. After a while I went with her, to visit, to meet her friends, to listen to her speak. Everyone was friendly and pleased to meet me, and seemed to greet her and my coming together with gladness but I saw the fear in their eyes and heard the strain in their voice when they asked me questions.

It was what they didn't say, what they didn't do, that left me out, so that at dinner, when all were speaking about something ordinary, the weather, or gardening, and I would venture something about the plains, there would be the briefest, the tiniest of pauses, while everyone looked at me, and then the talk went on as before, as if I had not spoken.

Or what they took for granted...astonishing amounts of food, and servants, who were well and kindly treated, but still, servants, and being among strangers, and the courtesies of behaviour among strangers, all of which were new to me, and the sense of being endlessly shut in, among walls, and streets and more streets. The more I got used to it, and accustomed to it, the more I hated it, and though I tried to tell her my feelings, it was like a fish trying to tell a bird about the air. We had no language to share for some things.

But in the evenings, as she sat on the floor, looking into the fire, I would sit and watch her and she would know I was looking. Sometimes I lay with my head in her lap, while she stroked my hair, and disassembled and reassembled my long braids, and put beads in them, and always I knew that this woman was now my heart's blood and without her, I would be lost.

After a several trips, it settled into a routine, and I would spend time with her until my longing for the plains grew too much, and then on the plains, I would stay until I missed her too much to bear, and so I went back and forth, like some demented toy on a piece of string, and the seasons wore themselves away.

We came together, each time, shy, and waiting to feel each other's presence in our bodies. We left each time, parting like souls being ripped apart, and then the pain would lessen; we would go back to our lives and routines until it was time to do it over.

She did come to visit, once. I had suggested and then asked and invited her to come. I stopped short of begging. She said she felt left out of my life on the plains...that I disappeared each time I left her, into the midst of my sisters and lovers and friends and people.

"Come and see," I said. "They will make you welcome." And wondered if I lied. What would my sisters do? They felt I spent too much time away already.

She came, but she did not come alone, nor was I alone, and in the end, it was more like a diplomatic mission than a visit, a useful mission, perhaps, but not what I had imagined. The whole time she was with us, she was charming, and asked questions designed to get my sisters to open up and talk. They thought she was wonderful. Only I, who knew her well, saw the mask and the fear and it made me sad and furious. At night, I lay awake beside her in the tent while she slept. When she left, I was sad and confused and I went alone to the river and wept. I didn't know what I was weeping for. I ached for the touch of her hands and yet I delayed visiting her in the city. After all, if I did not come, what difference would it make to her, with her busy life and her busy friends and her house and her garden and the people around who served and loved her. I didn't go. I waited and summer passed into autumn and my sisters asked no questions and still I waited.

Until one morning, I dreamt her weeping and in fear, and I left before the camp was even awake, riding through the dawn wet grass. But she did not weep when I came into her house, only later, lying beside the fire, when she turned away from my hands. "I'm afraid," she wept. "I'm afraid," and I was bitter and got up and went out into the night, away from her. I was saddling my horse to leave when she came to me, and held me and I held her. After all, there was nothing to be done. Our lives were the way we had made them. I came back into her house, with the candles lit and shining and her bed warm and inviting and knew that as long as she wanted me there, and as long as I could, I would come to her.

It was morning and we were lying in bed when we heard the rumbling. The earth shook and the wall across from her bed suddenly cracked and we could hear noise and screaming from the city.

It was the mountain to the north, the mountain I had so often climbed and loved to play on. A long expanding finger of smoke extended from its peak towards us, and the sky darkened even as we watched. A bitter hot ash-laden wind slapped our faces.

"My sisters!..." I said. They were much closer to the mountain than we were. Even as I spoke, a fine white burning ash started falling on the city. I ran out, ran to my horse, who was frantic with fear and the ash sparks on his shining hide. I rode like an insane person to the gates of the city. People were fleeing everywhere; there was noise and panic and screaming. Even as I watched, people were getting trampled. There was nothing I could do. It would take me a day to reach my sisters and if they were alive, they would be coming here, towards the city, towards the boats, towards the sea. The boats, the harbour, I thought, there might be a chance to leave that way. I stood in frantic

A'thyraa - Luanne Armstrong

indecision, knowing my place, my duty, my training, turned me towards my sisters. But my love turned me, turned me back . The sky was darker now, much darker, almost black, except in the direction of the mountain, where it glowed orange and scarlet. I rode like a fury back towards her, back towards my love in her white dress, standing on the wall of her house, straining to see me, to reach out her arms towards me, and even as I rode, I heard the noise, the groaning, the earth shrieking in the pain of birth and grieving and death, and fire came from the mountain, and covered all the land.

But we were lucky, my love and I. I reached her in time, gasping from burnt lungs in the hot ash choked air, and she slid up behind me, and we rode with death behind us, rode for the harbour and the boats rocking there.

Of course, other people had the same idea, and the harbour was pandemonium, but I was of the plains, fierce and swift and born to run and climb. I stopped for one moment and gave my horse, the friend of my youth, my willing partner for so many years, a gift of mercy. I cut his throat and left him there dying, and then I fought my way through the masses of crazed people with her at my back, and by some miracle, got us onto a boat that was just pulling away. It was covered with people. Some were even in the water, clinging to the sides, and these we helped to pull aboard.

The boat raised a sail, and we flew away, over the black water, away from our burning city, and I held her hand, my love's hand, and felt the land, my mother, and my sisters die.

And then we were alone.

Sandra Hayes: a lesbian mother\grandmother living in the Midwest, trying to read more lesbian fiction, write more lesbian fiction, and love more lesbians. I am currently working on stories about my relationship with a hearing impaired lesbian. Life is wonderful.

THE RETREAT

The house nestled into the side of a hill, overlooking the Illinois River. Rosa stood on the porch by one of the windows. Her sight drifted like the current from upriver, to the loading dock near the end of the road. She liked watching the gentle yet treacherous waters that brought paddle boats loaded with city visitors to their side of the river. The sun, warm through the glass, caressed her face, reminding her of the hands that stroked her during the night. She sighed, looking back up the river. Surely the boat would come today.

A dog interrupted her, running through the door from the house onto the porch, charging down the worn black painted floor towards Rosa. The two women who'd moved into the house some months earlier called the animal Sanky. She was a doberman, doberwoman, they explained to travel weary females who spent time at their retreat. Sanky bared her vicious teeth and snarled at Rosa.

Rosa's eyebrows furrowed. "Shut up before you wake everyone."

Growling, Sanky skidded to a halt. She was intent on protecting her masters. Saliva formed along her bared lips.

"Go away," Rosa responded to the dog's threats.

A voice called from inside the house, "Sanky! Sanky, come here!"

The dog looked at the doorway she'd rushed through, then to Rosa as if deciding what to do.

"Scat!" said Rosa, clapping her hands at the dog. Sanky backed up a step and the voice came again from inside the house. "Damn it, Sanky, come here!" Then the woman whom Rosa knew as Barb emerged from the house onto the porch, her black hair mussed from sleep. She was wearing only a short silken nightshirt. Sanky looked at her master. "What is wrong with you? Come here."

Rosa smiled as Sanky walked slowly to Barb, and taunted the skulking dog, "If you had a decent tail, you could hang it in shame."

Barb looked around to see what Sanky had been barking at. As usual, nothing. There was no-one on or near the porch. "What's wrong, girl?" She patted the dog's head. "You getting spooky in your old age?" She sat on a blue metal summer chair and sipped from the mug she was carrying. "You want to go down the river later?" she asked as she scratched Sanky's ears.

"I hope you take her somewhere and soon," said a voice behind her. Barb turned to see Elaine enter.

"I'm sorry, honey. I tried to shut her up before she woke you."

"Crazy dog." Elaine growled at Sanky who now lowered her head behind Barb's hanging arm.

"You've hurt her feelings," cooed Barb, patting the dog's buried head.

"Give me a drink of your coffee before I hurt both of you."

Rosa, still standing by the window a few feet away, watched as they shared the cup and then a kiss. Sanky growled halfheartedly as she went around the corner of the porch and up the stairs that led from one side of the porch to the second floor. She drifted past closed doors until she reached the windows that overlooked the river. There, undisturbed by the occupants of the house, she sat on a side ledge to continue her eternal vigil for the paddle driven river boats.

On the porch, Elaine pushed her lover's hand away from under her tee-shirt. "You ever get the feeling we're being watched?" she asked.

"No one's here but Sanky and she's pretty open-minded," Barb teased.

"Barb, I'm serious," the younger woman frowned. "It's just a spooky feeling that we're being watched."

"Ghosts," Barb laughed and stood up.

"That's not funny," Elaine yelled as Barb went into the house with Sanky close behind. "Not one damn bit funny!"

Elaine leaned her chin on her palm as she looked through the window to the river flowing past their property. A ferry boat loaded two cars at the crossing and pushed away from the bank to carry its passengers to the other side.

"I love mornings out here," she said when Barb returned with another cup of coffee. "It's so peaceful."

"We have those three couples coming in tonight for the weekend," Barb reminded.

Elaine sighed heavily. "I wish we could keep this place our secret."

"We agreed to the retreat for lesbians when we bought it." Barb sat her cup on the table.

"I know." Elaine sighed again.

"And besides, we need the extra money," Barb added. She stood up. "I better check those two water beds. "Gets cold at night and we don't want our guests to catch their death."

"Ha ha," growled Elaine.

"Of course I could just take you back to bed and release the grumpiness out of you." Barb pushed the blond hair from Elaine's neck and nibbled on the exposed ear. Meanwhile Sanky crept along the floor sniffing for Rosa.

"Only if you put Sanky outside." Elaine leaned back against Barb. "Look at her, sniffing the wall. I swear, she's nuts!"

"Come on Sanky." Barb opened the porch door to let her out. "Mommie's got some business to tend to."

"Business?" Elaine's eyebrows rose questioningly. "I'm business now?"

"Monkey business!" Barb grinned.

Elaine stood and pulled the tee-shirt over her head. Barb watched blond tresses webbed over brown nipples.

"You are beautiful, woman," Barb's voice spoke hoarsely as she reached to touch bare skin.

"You better stay away from there!"

"Whatever are you talking about, grandma?'

"Standing there gawking at that house like you was wishing she'd appear naked on the porch!"

Grandma's warning voice droned into Rosa's head as her sinful ways were denounced over starched white sheets clipped to a rope line. Rosa continued to watch the house not fifty feet from them, built against the bluffs and shaded by low bending trees. She'd spent many nights sleeping in her hideaway until daddy rented the place to Audry.

Audry was a student from some university in northern Illinois. She was doing summer work at a dig about a mile from the house.

Almost three weeks ago, she'd come tramping up the lane with a canvas backpack strapped to her wide shoulders, toting belongings to sustain her through the summer. She wore khaki green shorts, a white tee-shirt that did not hide her nipples, and high top walking boots with white crew socks flashing orange stripes. With her short cut brown hair, Rosa had first thought it was a man coming up the drive.

Rosa watched her daddy's red tongue flicking over his lips as he listened to Audry tell how she'd been sent down to see if he wanted to rent the little house. His eyes never left the tee-shirt that caressed her nipples to hardness. Rosa wanted to laugh out loud as Audry stomped up the concrete steps to the house. She wanted to stop her daddy's envious thoughts by telling him that Audry would never let a man's hand touch her bronze skin.

"Ever since your momma died, he's done the best he could with you."

Grandma snapped a pillowcase before hanging it over the line. Rosa held out a wooden clip without looking to see if the old woman reached for it.

"Now he had to rent that little house just so he could make payments on this land." Her sharp seventy year old voice continued on the endless rampage about how life was getting the best of her boy.

The sun felt warm on Rosa's head. At times she was sorry she'd refused to get her hair cut. Long black strands stuck to the back of her neck as her body sweated beneath her shirt and shorts. She wished to be done helping grandma so she could go to the cove and swim naked in the green tinted water.

"You prancing round here like a dog in heat, wearing next to nothing. No wonder he's gone to drink for comfort!"

"Southern comfort," Rosa couldn't resist saying.

"Some day," the old woman warned, stooping to pick up an empty basket. "Some day!"

"Soon," Rosa moaned under her breath, as she gave one last look at the empty porch of the little house, and then followed grandma up the steps to the back door. "Do you need any more help?"

"No. No!" A bony hand stabbed the air, accenting each no. "Do whatever it is you have to do. Leave an old woman to...."

The rest of the sentence was lost to Rosa as she skipped down the four concrete steps and over the grassy hill that led to a lane. There wasn't any traffic where she crossed to reach the river. Trodden weeds made a path through trees and brush until she reached a small half moon cut in the bluffs, offering privacy from watchful eyes that might cruise the waters. She quickly dropped her shorts on a log that had been sliced from its parent by lightning. Her cutoffs fell on the shirt. She'd given up wearing panties because she liked the stiff denim rubbing her.

Swimming in the river was dangerous. Undercurrents could suck a person beneath the surface and deposit a lifeless form some miles along the banks. Within the cove, the water was gentler and offered wonderful relief from the heat of the day.

She waded until the water rose to her knees, then leaned forward into it. She felt like a baby in a womb as she dove deep into the darkness and held her breath until she was forced up for air. She pointed her arms toward the sky and broke through her placenta. Treading water, she shook hair from her face, wiped water drops from her eyes. As her vision cleared, she saw Audry sitting on a large boulder.

Audry wore her familiar khaki shorts and tee-shirt. It seemed that her already brown skin had become even darker since her arrival. Rosa thought she could almost pass for color.

"How's the water?" Audry asked.

"Like an orgasm," Rosa answered as she pushed herself backwards. She enjoyed giving answers that produced shocked expressions from prudes. She drifted on her back, not caring that her breasts were exposed to the sun above. She thought about the only decent orgasm she'd ever experienced. That was when Roger Clement had taken her to a dance. They'd danced three songs with Roger rubbing her maleness against her, until he'd coaxed her into the back seat of his mother's fifty four Chevy. Then he'd fumbled with Rosa's dress, tearing buttons, slobbering over nipples that did not beg for saliva, and tried to force his hardened penis into her through her green silk panties. Thoroughly disgusted by his ejaculation between her thighs, Rosa pushed him to his knees on the floorboard. His face radiated with surprise as she removed her soaked panties and placed her feet on either side of him over the front seat. Then with both hands she guided his lips to hers. Rosa was not to be cheated.

She felt the throbbing now as tiny currents washed over her pubic hair and into swollen lips. Her nipples arched as sun rays caressed them. She turned to swim back to the bank where Audry sat.

234

"What are you doing?" she asked as she walked naked from the water.

"Found a few pieces at the dig that I'm trying to clean."

Scattered at her feet, Audry had about a dozen pieces of what Rosa thought were rocks. She held one in her hand as she scraped at flecks of dirt. Rosa waited for some response to her nudity but Audry's eyes only looked at the work she was doing.

"Then what are you going to do with them?"

"Take them back with me to study if they have some historical value. If not, I'll use them for paper weights."

"Boring," Rosa sighed. She found a place where cushiony grass grew, and stretched on her back. Heat had already dried the river from her body. She let the sun turn her skin darker. Audry worked on her rocks in silence, seeming to ignore the offered form so close to her. Rosa watched her through slitted eyelids. Audry scraped gently and fine particles drifted from the piece in her fingers. Once in a while she would lean over and soak the rock in a coffee can of water. Then she would return to her uncovering, searching for treasures from the past. Her legs were firm and muscled from many miles walked. Audry was strength.

"Are you what they call a dyke?"

Without missing a scrape, Audry laughed aloud. "Is that why you've been trying to tempt me?"

Rosa gave her an "I-don't-know-what-you're-talking-about" look. She certainly didn't have to beg for sex. At least a dozen men in the area would crawl on their knees to see her lying naked in the grass. But they were men.

Audry laughed again and it angered Rosa.

"Fuck you!" she snarled, and reached for her clothes.

Audry returned to her scraping as Rosa threw on her shirt and shorts. She didn't raise her head to watch Rosa stomp away. She dipped the rock once more in the coffee can and looked at a future paper weight.

"Thy name is temptation," she said aloud to no one.

When the night temperatures fell to ninety, Rosa slept on a cot on the south side of the house. She listened to grandma try to talk some sense into daddy about sending Rosa to a school in the city. Daddy only promised drunkenly that he'd discuss it as soon as he had some money. Grandma warned that no good would come to Rosa if she wasn't sent away.

Rosa left her cot and crept to the back door. She was careful not to let the screen slam and alert her family to the fact that she'd gone out. Her feet moved knowingly in the darkness to the edge of the bluffs that rose above the little house. No one would see her nakedness. She crouched down to watch.

A light was on in one room and even though shades were drawn, light filtered through. Once Audry walked by inside but didn't return. Rosa stood and walked down the path that led to the little house. She held her head up and moved unwaveringly, letting her arms hang at her sides. She felt like she was a sacrifice being offered to the goddess. She stepped onto the wooden porch and entered the house as silently as she'd crossed the yard.

Audry looked up from her place on the bed. She too wore nothing. Rosa noted the bronze that pigmented every pore of Audry's body. She had a book held on her stomach and papers strewn across the sheet. A small lamp on the bedstand circled her shoulders with yellow. Rosa seemed to glide to the bed, took Audry's book from her, and dropped it on the floor. She reached for the lamp and was stopped.

"Leave it on," Audry commanded.

Rosa felt sparks where Audry's fingers touched her. They entered her skin and burnt a path to her loins. She felt her sex swell as fingers traveled down her leg. It was not as a man touched. Audry's fingernails scratched a line to Rosa's knee and then moved upwards to the silken hairs between her thighs. Their eyes locked in an intense embrace. Rosa moaned as Audry slid her fingers over the place that sent a wave of fire through her body. She leaned over the sitting woman until their lips touched. Audry's moist tongue probed in Rosa's mouth. Rosa knelt on the bed, pressed her knees around Audry's hips, felt Audry's hand on her wetness.

Rosa breathed smells of earth and sweat as her mouth sucked Audry's neck and shoulders, and paused around one swollen nipple. Guttural sounds rose from her throat. She threw her head backwards, thrust her hips against Audry, felt the sparks explode and burn. Her mouth opened to release a cry she could not contain. The heat seared her flesh and she trembled uncontrollably until her legs weakened and she fell limp over Audry. A wet hand rested on her back.

236   *The Retreat - Sandra Hayes*

"I have fallen into temptation," whispered Audry into Rosa's ear.

At dawn wandering coyotes paused to watch the rising sun and darted into hidden caves to wait out the day. They slept exhausted from hunting, killing, lusting, answering calls from other wild mates. Inside the little house Rosa slept with her face buried against the fleshy part of Audry's underarm. Their legs were entangled together. A messed sheet stretched across them. Window shades barred the light from interfering with their rest.

The sun setting allowed coolness to whisper throughout the house. Rosa left her window ledge. It was time to return home. She heard voices at the back screen door and watched the two women enter with Sanky behind. The dog's ears rose up as she spotted Rosa. Instantly her lips pulled back to expose her teeth. Rosa heard the growl as she stepped off the porch.

"Sanky, stop it." Elaine tapped the dog's head. "She growls every time we're on the porch."

"I said, probably ghosts," Barb grinned. "Remember they told us about the two women who drowned down at the landing during some moonlit swim."

"How do they know it was a swim?"

"Because that's what lovers do." Barb shrugged. "I don't know."

"Why on earth they'd want to haunt this place has got me," Elaine said. "I'm almost sorry we bought it, as much work as we have to do."

"It's too bad the little house got so mildewed." Barb turned out the porch light.

"Bound to happen. The way it's so far under the bluffs, it can't get any sun to dry it out."

"I know, but we could have rented it for extra income."

Barb put her arms around Elaine and they stood in front of the multi-paned windows, watching moonlight flashing on the river. Sanky watched Rosa as she moved around the two women. She whined.

"What was that?" Barb looked behind her.

"What?"

"I'm not sure. Just a ... I don't know."

"I bet it really freezes in winter," Elaine spoke after a few more moments of watching the river.

"At least we know how to keep warm," Barb teased, turning Elaine to face her. Rosa stood for a moment on the back step, watching them kiss. Sanky growled, and Barb said, "Come on Sanky, let's go to bed."

The dog reluctantly allowed herself to be coaxed into the house as Rosa scooted towards the smaller building. She stopped on the porch and looked back to see the lights go off. A deer slipped from the brush hiding the bluffs and crept down the grassy slope towards the river. Rosa watched as it stopped at the landing and dipped its head for water.

"I warned of undercurrents," she spoke to herself. " But no, she wouldn't listen to me."

The animal lifted its head as though listening to something.

"And I couldn't lose her after all."

She turned the handle and entered. Audry looked up from her place on the bed. Rosa scanned the familiar small room then looked at Audry.

"Did you find any more paper weights at the dig?"

"A couple." Audry sat her book on the floor next to worn walking boots. "You spot any riverboats?"

"No."

Rosa glided over to the bed and stood still as Audry's hand stroked her leg.

"Have you noticed any mildew in here?"

"No," Audry answered.

"I can't understand what they're talking about."

"Do we care?' Audry smiled.

Rosa looked at the naked brown woman. Fingers searched and easily found her wetness. She sank onto the bed. "No," she whispered.

*J. **Running Scared** was born in Miami, Florida on November 26, 1955, with a Number 3 Life Path, which she is currently fulfilling, thanks to the graceful intervention of her Higher Power. She loves listening to and writing music, enjoying the solitude of sunset walks on the beach, playing with her Yorkie (Idgie Towanda), and sharing life with her most cherished Mary. She believes in many things, but above all else, she believes in Love, and hopes one day to live in a world that is free of hate.*

She has lovingly dedicated this short story to Celeste, whose Light now shines in every starry sky.

ANGELINA

"It is so true that a woman
may be in love with a woman,
and a man with a man.
It is pleasant to be sure of it, because
it is undoubtedly the same love
that we shall feel when we are
angels, when we ascend to the only fit place
for the Mignons..."
-Margaret Fuller (1838)

For Sarah, it was an exceedingly cold winter.

Outside, the winds howled in the darkness, changing mid-day into midnight. Ice, sleet, and snow invaded the Colorado landscape, metastasizing into bizarre creatures casting enormous dancing shadows against the panelled walls. Though she lit a fire in the familiar little cabin, it was no longer comforting for her to be here. She no longer sensed tranquility in the room. The fire would spark no romance. Its flames no longer matched the intense inferno that once was their desire.

She was numb. Frozen solid by choice.

Choosing survival over despair.

Choosing to exist rather than suffer the feelings.

Choosing apathy before allowing pain to destroy her.

Choosing to stay within the safety of controllable absolutes rather than chancing the surreal unknown of a surrendering heart. A heart irreparably damaged. A heart she'd buried along with Angelina.

And so she sat, alone. As inescapably lost within this tiny room as she had felt among the crowds in Times Square, with friends at the beach in Provincetown, or with her family during holiday celebrations. As lost as she had been since the moment she'd gotten the news. Even more lost than she had been before they'd met.

She cradled the horn in her lap, holding her cheek against it, moving her fingers delicately across its valves. Sitting forward, she lifted the mouthpiece to her lips, circling it with her tongue, pursing her mouth into the tininess of its opening. Playing the memory of Angelina over and over again in her mind. Angelina sitting there, eyes closed and listening. Angelina lying there, eyes open and wanting. Angelina rushing into the blizzard, throwing herself into the snow, laughing, chuckling, a fallen angel surrendering to the instantaneous joy of life. Angelina breathing, whispering, touching, arching, imploding within her arms. Angelina, playing lullabies on her horn. Playing softly, strongly, passionately for Sarah.

She cradled the horn, rocking to and fro.

She could not make it sing.

It was no longer the conduit of Angelina's soul.

It was cold and brittle and silent as death. Her grief piled around her, suffocating her. Burying her alive. She bent over the instrument, sobbing. It grew darker outside, the winds now howled with unbearable frenzy. After her tears were exhausted, she placed the horn gently onto the rug, wrapped an afghan around herself, and drifted off to sleep.

The music began faintly, growing in loudness as it seeped into her consciousness. The patterned beating of hand-made drums matched the rhythm of her heart, as she sang to the Moon above, her voice blending with the others who joined in this Winter Solstice circle ceremony. The voices and faces were all familiar. As the swirling bodies danced, she instinctively knew where each foot would land, what image each arm and hand would create against the backdrop of silhouetted forest.

She realized in that instant she had been here before.

Her voice strangled into silence. She turned around, knowing Angelina had entered the circle at this very moment. She'd held her horn, and facing the stars as she walked, entered the innermost circle, pouring her soul spirit into the instrument. They'd met in this way, that year of the Blue Moon. The sweetness and power of Angelina's playing had brought magic to the celebration. Sarah had been drawn to her as she had never been drawn to a woman before. After the celebration, it was as though she felt the bright power of the Moon pushing her forward, until she and Angelina stood facing each other. Sarah had spoken first, becoming lost in Angelina's eyes. From that moment, they'd become the beacons which forever guided her home. Years later, she stood by Angelina's bedside and watched, with shattering helplessness, those beacon lights dim into opaque lifelessness.

And so she turned away from the circle, expecting to see the glint of silver moonbeam cast by Angelina's horn. Instead, she faced the indigo of space. It was a thick, rich blackness, empty, yet full.

It surrounded her, spreading out and beyond infinitely in all directions. She was filled with profound silence. The chanting was gone. The circle had vanished. She fixed her sight on a distant shaft of bright light. It glided as if on a slide, moving in slow motion yet simultaneously arriving at her feet in an instant.

And then the Light was upon her. It filled her with energy, and complete wisdom in full consciousness. It spoke, without speaking. Sarah heard without listening.

"Sarah. I've been waiting a long time to see you. It has been nearly twenty eight years...."

The voice was gentle, lullaby-soft. Sarah stretched her arms out, touching the Light with her own energy field.

"We met many years ago, Sarah. Do you remember the time? You were much younger, filled with sorrow and anger. You came running outside into the night, screaming at my stars. You thought you had been forsaken. It was after your father had packed your things and told you to go. That first time, when you'd realized the power of womanhood, and the powerful love of two women. You asked for me to guide your path. You told me you would follow. "

Sarah stared and listened in disbelief. She remembered that time. A time she had long ago forgotten. The Moon had heard! And She had answered.

Sarah hadn't realized until now.

She heard a distant tune, the notes drifting into space. A popular tune from the fifties.

The voice continued.

"As you grew older, I was still here, watching. I saw you at the moment you lost your faith. I watched you begin throwing away little gifts of magic. As though it was easier for you to believe in pain and sorrow than it was to believe in love and joy. As though it is easier to embrace hopelessness than to believe in the possibilities. Well. You can. You must. For I am real. And I am still here. So tell me, child, what is your heart yearning for?"

Sarah gazed at the Light, as tears welled up in her eyes.

"It is time to believe in me again, child."

She heard a voice answering from deep within her. It was a strange voice. The voice of a woman emptied by sadness, lost and searching, more dead than alive. It was Sarah's voice, without Angelina. And then the voice changed. It was a woman's voice, longing to believe the child within, yearning to dare believe again that wishes could come true. And then the child spoke.

"I want just one thing. Only one thing. " She lifted her head, and looked longingly into the Light.

"Please," She felt her heart stop as she spoke her wish. "Bring her back to me."

A gale of wind burst around her. It swept Sarah up, propelling her with a mighty force. It lifted her higher and higher, the sound of song reverberating up and beyond. Rising into the stars, Sarah could barely make out the Light now fading below her. She continued rising higher into the starry sky.

Then, as suddenly as it had appeared, the gale eased into a whisper, dropping her like a delicate flake of snow onto the drifts below.

She lay there, face down, the cold dampness of it starting to freeze her nose, her face beginning to burn. She heard the crunching of footsteps running up from behind her, and that song, playing on a radio, somewhere off in the distance. This time she heard the lyrics. "Blue moon.... You saw me standing alone...without a dream in my heart... without a love of my own." Sarah felt a grin spread across her lips.

"Sarah! Sarah! Are you alright?"

Her soul tingled as the beloved voice filled her entirely. It poured into her head, resonating in the breath she took in, and coursed through her body, touching each cell, filling every corpuscle, until it released through the tips of her toes. The wave of recognition swelled and rolled back through her body, escaping through teary eyes.

Familiar hands pushed under her shoulders, and across her collar bone, lifting and rolling her over. Sarah kept her eyes closed, letting the sensations consume her. Her heart was now pounding with anticipation and fear. *What if this is not real? Oh, Goddess! What will I do if this simply isn't so?* She kept her eyes closed long enough to make one last silent wish.

"Please, Goddess. Let it be true. Oh, Goddess, please let this be real! " She opened her eyes slowly, afraid to believe, fearing she might be wrong. The light illuminated Angelina's golden hair. Her eyes were more blue and even more beautiful than Sarah had remembered. Her smile, more cherished, treasured beyond any sight Sarah had ever and would ever see.

"Geezuz. You really took a spill! Thank the Goddess I was on my way out to help with the wood! Are you O.K., darlin'?"

Sarah cried out her name, touched Angelina's face to verify it was real. "Lina! Lina! My Lina! Oh, Lina!" she sobbed.

"Oh, baby. You're really hurt! Let's get you inside and get you out of these wet clothes."

"Thank you, Goddess. Thank you Goddess. Oh, Goddess...Thank you!"

Angelina chuckled quietly at the silliness of Sarah's murmuring.

"Sarah, you're alright. You're gonna be fine. You just took a nasty spill. C'mon, hold on tight. Let's get you back into the cabin."

Wrapping her arms tightly around Angelina, Sarah promised to never ever ever let go.

The forest was dense with darkness, and the howling wind shrieked through the trees, snapping their branches, tossing icicles like tiny spears through the air. The snow swirled and shifted, caught in the frenzy.

"It was fifty-three years ago. To the day." The old woman stood ankle deep in the snow, wrapped in layers of scarves and sweaters, covered with a black moth eaten coat. Two young women held her up, bracing against the wind.

"Miss Sarah, you can't stay out here. You'll catch your death of cold."

"Fifty-three years. Right here. It happened right here. My Solstice miracle." She looked like a tiny shadow between them.

"Yes, Miss Sarah, right here. And we want you to tell us all about it, but let's get back into the jeep. The heater's running and it'll be warmer inside. You've had such a hard day. Can't we please just get back to the jeep? We've been standing out here now for too long."

"Janine's right. Let's get into the jeep and talk. We can stay here long as you'd like. We won't leave here until you're absolutely ready to go. We promise. But it's just too cold to stay out in this."

"Fifty-three years...."

Janine glared at Julie, making no effort to disguise her anger. Her expression became sympathetic as she shifted her eyes back to the old woman. Her voice was meant to be reassuring and reasonable.

"You wanted so badly to drive all the way out here. And there's nothing here but a beat up old shack. Looks like the thing's been deserted for half a century. You buried your best friend today, Miss Sarah. It's been such a long, hard day. Look, you're shivering with cold. What on earth is possessing you to stand way out here in the middle of this wilderness?"

Julie and Janine stared at the old lady, their teeth chattering. They were both very fond of her. Miss Lina and she had lived with them and their two other boarders for five years now, and they'd gotten to hear stories about so much of their life. They were both saddened by Miss Lina's death. They'd never seen two who'd been closer than those two. They expected it would be hard for Miss Sarah.

"Fifty-three years ago, I buried Angelina here. Buried her and watched her resurrection. I lost her, and she was given back to me. It happened right here. In this very place."

The old woman started shouting: "Goddess! Goddess! Can you hear me now? I haven't asked a thing from you since that winter, but I've worshipped you each year! Oh, Goddess, I'm asking you now. Are you here? Is this your wind? Send the wind! Oh, send it to me and let it lift me to the stars!"

She lifted her arms up, as if waiting to soar. "Take me, wind! I'm here!"

Janine's attention and anger shifted back to Julie. "I told you this was going to be too much for her, but you insisted on going through with it. Now let's just get her back."

Julie understood her lover's anger. It wasn't directed at her. It was just Janine's way of releasing her own helpless feelings. Julie held tightly to her dearly loved Sarah, knowing that Janine's concern was real. None of them could stay out in the weather any longer.

"Miss Sarah, calm down. Come on, let's go on now to the jeep..."

Janine and Julie turned her around and started walking her back toward the headlights.

"You see, I'd come out here to gather wood from the pile. Was a brutal winter in '92. I came out here, and I fell, and Angelina was there when I came to. She always said I must've hit my head real hard. Said it was just a bad dream and I'd blacked out. Told me how silly I was to ever think I'd lost her. Or that I could ever loose her. But I know what I know, and I know it was real. She was gone. Gone. And she brought her back to me. And I promised I'd never ever let her go again."

"Yes, Miss Sarah. We understand. Let's go back home now."

"Don't you see? I've lost her again. And it's almost time for the celebration circle. And I'm asking you, please, please, Moon Goddess. Please. Please. Let me go with her. I've lived a good and decent life. I've watched her and loved her. I polished her horns and listened to her practicing and loved every minute that I lived and breathed since you brought her back to me."

Miss Sarah began to cry. She broke from the two women and threw herself face down into the snow.

"Oh, Miss Sarah. You've had a very trying time. We're going back now."

Julie and Janine lifted her up and walked Miss Sarah back to the jeep, helping her into it.

"Now. Isn't this better, Miss Sarah?"

"Yes. Nice and toasty. Now there... " Julie turned to Janine. "Go ahead. Turn the jeep around. Let's go."

"Please Goddess. Please. Let me be with her again. Oh, please. I never asked for anything since. Not in fifty-three years. Please. Grant me my wish. Just this one last time." Miss Sarah was sobbing. "I believe in love! I believe in joy! I believe! I believe!"

The jeep headed out of the wilderness, back toward the paved road that would lead to Highway 29. They were surrounded by the thick blanket of snow now howling around them. Julie turned the radio on to try to catch a weather report.

"Blue moon...you saw me standing alone...."

The music filled the cab of the jeep, the tempo of the windshield wipers matching its steady rhythm. Miss Sarah's sobbing quieted into the sound of humming. She leaned across Julie, turned the volume up, and smiled.

"Julie. I'm worried about her. She's never acted like this before. Do you think we should take her to the hospital?"

"Look. She lost Miss Lina today. They were together for over sixty years. She needs rest. We'll get her back, and she'll be fine in the morning."

"I hope so. What a time to loose her. So close to Solstice celebration..."

The jeep approached the stop sign and rolled to a halt. The road was icy, and the snow made it impossible to see beyond nine or ten feet ahead. Janine glanced at Julie, then at Miss Sarah, as she pulled out onto the paved road. The instant she did, they were struck head on.

Janine awoke in the emergency room.

"Where's Julie?"

"Patient's awake, doctor." The nurse was bandaging her head.

"Everything's going to be fine. Just take it easy. The doctor is right over there talking to your friend right now. She's banged up pretty bad, but she's going to be fine."

"Miss Sarah.....Where's Miss Sarah?"

The nurse broke eye contact immediately and busied herself.

Janine knew by the immediate silence. Miss Sarah was gone.

It is Solstice celebration.

Sarah and Angelina are long ascended from this earth, now part of the canopy of night.

The scent of pine and winter's chill fill the air. The drums beat out steady rhythms. The women's voices chant with power and joy. The dancers lift their arms toward the ceremonial beacon. All eyes focus on the constellation in the western sky. The one shaped like a large circle, supported by an inverted cross. It is the moon sign "Ghia".

The brightest stars are Angelina's, marking the constellation at its southern most tip. Sarah's glow next to them on either side, promising guidance to all who call on the power of the Moon.

Char March: *I grew up in Central Scotland and now live in Huddersfield, Yorkshire, which I love. Primarily I am a performance poet, but I also write sketches and short stories. I have been writing and performing seriously for the last seven years. The zing and zest I get from this is one of the main factors in keeping me well, happy and alive. I have just brought out my first collection of poetry - called "ridge walking" - and have been published in a number of anthologies and magazines in Britain and America. I'm always looking for ways of living up to Maya Angelou's vision "the question is not how to survive, but how to thrive with passion, compassion, humour and style."*

THE RUNNERS

We are travelling by night. The motorway is packed with whirling lanes of cars. Their lights flicker - heavy lines of white and wobbling red - picking out the sinuous contours of the road.

"You awake again, love? I'm aching tired, could you take over soon? The car's thirsty so I'll pull in at the next station."

Gaudy neon of the petrol arena strains my eyes and the penetrating interrogation lights in the toilet are even more disturbing. A grey face stares back at me from the mirror. Eyes rimmed with crust, hair alternately flattened and spiked. I emerge from the stale smells and the night air knifes through my jumpers. Ella motions me from the pump to go and pay. I change course under the neon, my shadow rotates and lengthens.

Nothing is said. The digital display tells me the amount and the automatic relay lights up the yellow numerical eyes of the till behind the cashier's grill. Cold, my fingers fumble with the change and I glance up to see 'Diane' pulling a sneer across her lipstick. The request for chocolate freezes on my paler lips and I thrust my hands deep into my pockets and stride back across the oiled tarmac. Again the warm stuffiness of the car and its smells surround me.

I open the air vents and pull out onto the silent road, glad to take the controls of our star ship and slip back into my space fantasy. The scarlet sneer nearly grounded me.

Ella checks the scanner, it glows calm and green, and then she settles back, her hand warmly cupping the nape of my neck. The dark miles brush past my window as her breathing softly evens out.

Out of a bank of mist comes a convoy of bright lorries steaming up the long hill in the opposite lane. Decked out with dancing coloured lights and chrome on all their angles, multi-coloured streamers flying from mirrors, they wheeze and gasp loudly with gear-changes. The billow and flap of their red tarpaulins makes them appear to undulate, romp almost, up the long haul. They seem like Chinese dragons - a festive spectacle from the mist.

To my right and far below now, the shape of a city's hills are picked out by strings of wildly discarded necklaces of light. It looks sumptuous - the greedy opulence of winking colours - like huge shimmering mounds of lazy treasure.

We've turned off onto quieter roads and now onto familiar lanes. These last sixteen miles of high banks, hedges, sharp bends and crazily angled humpbacks - the well-known road home. Ours are the only lights.

The wind has picked up steadily and snatches at the car through gaps in the trees that now crowd close and thick. It's still three hours 'til dawn so we'll have at least a couple of hours rest before we have to move again. It'll be bloody hard to pull ourselves away so quickly.

A scattered cloud of moths wobbles towards us. Dancing white motes like the first large flakes of a snow flurry. Some splat into the windscreen, the others, veering into the slipstream, are swallowed by the dark.

I drive fast, but smoothly along the known way, feeling at last part of the night. Ella's hunched form beside me is picked out dimly by the glow from the dash. The hump of her shoulder. A light triangle of turned up collar against the dark of her face.

A red line of blips appear on the scanner as we start the long descent towards the river. I have to force myself not to throw the brakes full on. Instead I slow gradually, indicating to pull in beside a low banking.

Tick Fl-ick Tick Fl-ick. The rhythms of indicator and wipers. Ella pulls her hand slowly down from my neck and massages some life back into her arm. The removal of this patch of her warmth makes me shudder and I pull my scarf round. We look at each other. Ella shudders slightly too, rubs her face briskly and reaches for both pairs of binoculars. I douse the lights, but keep the engine purring.

We wait. The rain drumming on the roof - feels so like a can.

Almost together we see them - matt black and powerful, a different species altogether from the dragons we passed earlier. Even with **their** engines they are only crawling up the long hill of the main road that cuts across our route.

We watch them through the powerful binoculars. There is movement in the cab of the seventh lorry. I zoom in; the window opens and there is a swill of orange sparks on the road - the silent explosion of a cigarette butt. I turn my bino's on the cab and watch the driver's mate pull his next cigarette alight. He shifts the heavy rifle and turns to stare at me and puff bored smoke into my eyes. It clouds almost my entire field of vision. I feel the urge to cough. I lower the binoculars and the matchbox-sized lorries drone on up the hill.

Ella is craning forward with her bino's, searching the moon for features. I wrap my arms round her.

The red blips die slowly from the screen. A dogleg across this intrusive dual carriageway and then only three miles to home. I dash to the central island and tear on up the empty lanes, eager, willing us home.

For sheer joy I slip the car in and out of the cat's eyes before slowing down for the turn-off for home. The shots ring out as I see the dark figures run onto the road and I try to haul us away. The wheels squeal and lock, then bite into the gravel and I careen the car backwards, swinging it wildly to shake their aim.

Slam into first, fear tearing at our throats, and away again, back down the main road. I cut our lights and jab the switch to send our distress call. The car bucks sideways, wrenching the steering from me. We head for the banking.

It has stopped raining. The wipers squeak up the windscreen and judder back. Behind this noise I can hear a delighted chortling - the petrol tank, it's emptying itself. Squeak, chortle, judder, chortle. Gods, I can see the heavens clearly from this angle. Cassiopeia, Pleiades, Taurus, Andromeda. Squeak, chortle.

"Do you think if I can reach the bino's we could see the moon's smile, love?" I ask Ella, but as I turn to look over and see why she's not answering, there is another noise - it seems to be me, screaming.

They are crowded round the car. Some beat with flats of hands on bonnet and roof. I pull the keys from the ignition and stab the security lock. My right arm is very numb...all of me is very numb. I try not to look to my left - at Ella.

They are shaking the car - swaying it back and forth between them and chanting. Some deform their faces against my window, licking at the glass and rolling their eyes. In other words - they are enjoying themselves.

I sit inside with my dead lover and wonder what they are waiting for. For me to crack up?

It amazes me how deadly calm I am now that it has at last happened. All the warnings about each Runner's operating life I know have never sunk in. I find I am counting up for the first time how many over the average we have done together. All I feel now is a kind of release.

I am slipping into the automaton response expected of a reaction trained Runner except I'm beginning to feel a little sick with the rolling motion of the car and the crushing reality of everything. I hate death.

About six of the chanting bodies on my side of the car are blown to bits by the first explosion. Confusion breaks out and some panic - canned girl it seems is okay, but only if she plays along with what you have in mind. I'm not about to wait for them to collect themselves - as it is a sharp volley of shots smacks through Ella's window just after I've released her hand and dropped low through my door, rolling under the car, hefting another grenade into the nearest clump of legs.

I've made the gap I need. I drop two slight delay incendiaries and head for the mass of smoke caused by the last explosion.

My back is seared by the huge puffball of fire that takes Ella's body well beyond the reaches of the screaming men. I stumble over the top of the bank and throw myself forward to avoid skylining an easy target.

I hug the box to my chest and roll fast down the tussocky hill. My specs slip from my face and I feel them crunch under me. On my feet as the slope levels out - running hard, trying to guess at boulders and grass. I grab a squelching handful of peat bog and smear it all over my face, hands and neck and into the white V-shape of T-shirt on my front. Run. Peat-juice trickles with sweat between my breasts. Run.

I don't think of the 'real' reason, in terms of my indoctrination training, for destroying the car and its contents. The pain of my back and singed head has brought hot tears through the frozen core of my mind.

Behind me I hear the heavy revving of engines and then the sky overhead is lit by strong, slanting beams of light. I risk a quick, useless look round and run even harder, my feet pounding across the surface of the bog. They are trying to get the vehicles to the crest of the banking to light up their target.

Several hundred metres ahead of me small hillocks loom out of the flat bog and behind them what I think may be thin woodland. I can only just hear their shouts now above the engine noise, but the beams of light in the sky aren't levelling out - they can't get up the banking.

I run into the water without seeing its dark surface. Floundering in the cold, trying to tell the relative firmness of bog from pool.

The engines stop. I am instantly aware of the loud, sloshing noises that I'm making. I stop, still, and slowly, carefully, sit down into the water. It closes darkly up round my chest. I lean my head down to its surface, my breath makes quick fluttering marks across it.

They start shooting. Strafing the bog. Bullets hiss and splat into the water and wet peat around me. I sit still. My back feels huge, rising from the water, aching with waiting for the heavy thump of a hit. I stay still. They stop firing and the engines start up again.

****

It's hard to run with everything so wet, but Ella is running beside me now, helping me with the awkward box chained to my wrist. Flashing me a wide grin in all that blackness - "Never be afraid of the dark again, huh, white girl?" she says - same as she did after we'd been making love the first time.

I've done the three-quarter circle route as drilled and my breath is coming up in rasps - like continuous retching. The pain is bad, but the savage fight inside myself is worse. Willing myself to scream her name again and again and the training forcing my gagging silence. It keeps my legs going, my footfalls light, my breathing - though rough with tight-held anguish - as quiet as possible.

The Runners - Char March

251

But the training had always stressed that we would be able to think of nothing but the required survival and flight reactions. I am choking on Ella, on leaving her, on incinerating my lover...

I am on the road towards the cliff. The route to this safe house memorised a million times. Running on the soft verge. I managed to send the distress signal only seconds before the car went up. Central Control is staffed 24 hours - they **will** have picked it up. I keep telling myself this as I run. A mantra to keep my legs moving.

I know they won't have lights. I know I must quiet the drumming in my ears if I'm to hear the engine. I can't believe I haven't been shot...maybe I have.

I must concentrate - can I hear anything? Is there any pursuit? I keep on running. I consist of nothing but pain. Total physical and mental pain. Ella dropped away what seems like several miles ago.....I can't have gone **that** far. Do I know where I am? In the blackness, afraid of the dark without her.

I push my tongue out at full stretch from my mouth and loll my head back as another misty flurry of rain comes over. My throat and mouth are very sore and dry, but trying to catch moisture like this just makes breathing even more difficult and the root of my tongue aches like it has been twisted on its moorings.

My feet sink into the grass and my legs bend all ways under me. Ahead of me, maybe 500 metres, the road cuts through a hill. Diffuse moonlight catches on what looks like the wetness of stones in drainage channels.

The stones are rough and sharp as I scrabble at them. They yield nothing but an acrid-tasting and gritty sheen of wet to my sore tongue. No water lies under them in the ditches - only damp sand. I clutch up a handful and squeeze, hoping for a drop or two of water, but the stuff just oozes through my fist in a damp sausage, breaks off and splats back into the ditch like a soft turd. If I had enough breath I would swear at it - or maybe even laugh - why not?

I want to stay here, sunk on my knees half in the ditch, gulping in cool, dark air to heal my lungs. I look at the metal box. My arm takes up the weight of it as I get up.

Walk thirty, run thirty, concentrating on counting, on keeping my legs moving. I mouth the numbers through cracked lips - they are right after all - I can think of nothing now, nothing but these numbers.

But I must listen too, I remember this - it floats up at me from somewhere buried.   "You must listen";   "They won't have lights"; "You will only get one chance".

Every fifth set of running I stop. Quite still. I allow myself ten long gulps of air and then - quite still. Listening. No use to trust my eyes. My ears feel like they are reaching out, straining to sample the air's vibrations. It is so silent at first that I know I must be deaf and then faint, faint sounds edge in - of wind in the grass, of very distant birds. A sludge-grey dawn is starting behind me.

17, 18, 19 - I am looking forward to 30 when I get my ten gulps of air again. They step out together and grab my arms. I flail with the box. Try to shout. Knocked down onto hard road. Air forced from me. My mouth is stuffed with woolen scarf. Struggling. Pinned to the tarmac. I feel the chain on my wrist tighten and then go slack; they have taken the box.

Then my head is lifted by a strange apparition; a young woman with starched hair. Her face, macabre in the muted light, is heavy with blusher, eye-shadow and lipstick. She stares at me hard and signs, "Other one - where?" My head shakes mechanically while my mind tries to unravel what has just happened. There is a long pause. Both of them stare hard at me and then the other - another perfectly painted doll - pulls the scarf from my mouth and pours sweet, cold liquid into my parched throat. I vomit weakly and I am sucked into oblivion.

My knees are up under my chin. My left arm and shoulder feel very dead. My head thunders with pain and it takes some time before any other signals get through. It is totally dark. I would try and touch my eyeballs to see if they're still there, it's so dark I can't believe they are, but I can't move anything.

I am in a short coffin. My feet - freezing blocks of pins and needles hanging from trapped legs - wobble a bit now and then, I don't seem to be telling them to, they just do it. This is my first clue.

My whole body being dragged into one end of the coffin and then into the other gives me my second. My head hurts so much I don't hear the quiet purr of the engine for quite a while. By then however I am certain I am travelling in a vehicle. Where? Who with? I have no clues on these.

Ella cradles my head gently in her lap. The curtains are drawn on the sunshine, but it still finds its way into our room. Colours from the curtains' patterns sidelight Ella's face as she leans forward to put a fresh, cold flannel on my forehead. My head heaves with thick pulses of pain. "A real live Black Florence Nightingale - turn out that bloody lantern will you?" I manage to slur. Concern and held-in laughter creases up her eyes and I love her. "My name's Mary Seacole actually - why use a blacked-up white reference when you've got the genuine article?"

Much later, when evening blues and deep greys are calm behind the curtains, we sip hot chamomile tea and sit close under the blankets. My head feels cleansed, light-weight. The clamour of roosting birds has settled and no longer beats like pain against me.

I reach over to refill Ella's cherry-red cup with the pale yellow heat of the tea. Instead she shakes her head and takes the small teapot from me and places it, with her cup, on the windowsill by her shoulder.

"I need to pee," I say, but we slide together under the covers, her hands lifting my shirt and my lips brushing along her neck.

I feel us stop, which makes me realise I haven't been conscious for a while. How many migraines did Ella come through with me? There are voices. I must concentrate. Male voices - sounding amused. I hear the vehicle doors open and the sounds move away. They return a while later - I have no sense of time left. The vehicle rocks as bodies get back in. Doors slam, there's a couple of slaps on the vehicle and we move off slowly.

My head collapses into pain again after concentrating so hard to pick up this meagre information. We are travelling fast now and it slops from side to side, spilling pain in all directions as the burns on my back and head are ground into the coffin.

Again we stop and this time there is quiet. Then doors open and there are low, female voices. Very close. Sliding noises as if heavy things are being moved. The lid of the coffin is lifted, the light is too much - I can't see anything but the torch beam.

"Turn it away from her!" I see the two women's faces again, their scarlet cupids' bows still look completely out of place.

I lie on my side on the big bed, while Alex cleans up my burns and Cathy wipes the last of the peat and the lipstick imprints off my face. I look up at her own dishevelled face. "I don't know how you got through that road-block - those blokcs should have spotted you a mile off - dykes never can get false eyelashes on straight," I say, and then make enough room to start crying.

Kirsten Backstrom makes her home in Portland, Oregon, with her partner and four cats. After living from one crisis to the next for many years, her biggest adventure these days is to consider herself relatively settled. She cultivates a low thrill threshold, and finds plenty of excitement in quiet adventures like scrubbing the sink, digging an herb bed, walking to the library, brushing cats and making popcorn. She takes on different jobs at different times to support herself: bookstore work, basketmaking, editing, teaching, yard work, housekeeping, etc. But her two central, full-time commitments are to writing and to relationship, and she is discovering how both of those tend to mature and develop in astonishing ways when given enough time and care. Her fiction, essays, and poetry have appeared in several journals and anthologies, and she is currently working on a novel and collection of stories.

COMING TO GRIEF, GOING FROM THERE

The church was white, upright, square and plain, but it was a sanctuary for Jodi. She remembered the services as something that she and her mother had shared. It wasn't like a regular church; people weren't passing judgements. The patchwork sermons were offered by visiting ministers, poets, musicians, and even a rabbi once. Anyone was welcome; anything might happen. Jodi and her mother would sit close together, close enough to keep warm. The windows were tall and drafty on all sides; the white walls were brilliant and cold as snow in the sun. And the voice of the pipe organ sounded shivery and hollow, echoing up to the high plaster ceiling. Jodi and her mother would share a hymnal. As a small child, Jodi had liked to sing really loud, to make an echo of her own. By following her mother's quieter voice, she'd kept on key.

Jodi's mother used to wear the same best dress every Sunday; it was her chance to look like someone other than a waitress. Nobody noticed how the flower pattern had faded after so many washings. Anywhere else, someone would have noticed. But among Unitarians even rumpled weekend clothes would have been all right. Jodi always wore a skirt to please her mother, but she was allowed to change into pants as soon as the service was over. Then, while the grownups drank coffee, all the kids would play hide and seek in the church basement, squealing as they raced down the long hallway, ducking in and out of the many rooms.

As a teenager, Jodi had joined the choir. The congregation was painfully serious about music, but the choir was notorious for its awfulness. All those independent tempos, determined ascending strains, grappling harmonies. Being a fine steady alto, Jodi was given the soprano solos. But it was fun, anyway. She'd felt comfortable among those people. She'd felt at home.

Now, Mrs. Bailey the church organist remembered her well enough to lend her the key. Mrs. Bailey imagined that Jodi might like to play the pipe organ for a few hours alone in the echoing empty church.

It was cold in the church. It had always been cold. Jodi remembered how she used to fidget on the polished icy hardwood of the pew as the cold seeped through her wool skirt and itchy tights. But now, she felt the cold differently. On the surface of her skin, the cold kept her alert; she needed to be alert. But if it penetrated deeper, it was danger. Cold alarmed her whole body when she felt it reaching for her core. She headed downstairs to see if she could get the furnace going.

It was late November already, but the church had little money for fuel and the furnace had not been started up yet. The monstrous tank with its dusty tubular tentacles squatted in the cloakroom, where it used to frighten Jodi and generations of other children. It frightened Jodi differently now. It seemed to exude dull cold, and a smell of stale oil. She knew she couldn't risk starting it up. Suppose she burned the church down? So she went to the deep cardboard lost-and-found box instead and dug up a stained down vest and a couple of ratty sweaters she could wear over the several layers she was already wearing.

Next, she untied the knotted lengths of twine and clothesline that held her battered pack together. She emptied the contents of the pack on the cement floor. Assorted plastic bags contained her toothbrush and paste, aspirins and stomach tablets, tampons and toilet paper, some food. Her stuff still looked more like camping supplies than like the survival gear of someone homeless. There was a small bundle of dirty clothes: two pairs of socks and underpants, a t-shirt, a jersey, a flannel shirt. She was wearing everything else. The clothes were worn thin, but only the socks had holes in them so far.

Jodi rolled up her sleeves, ran the utility sink full of hot water, scrubbed the clothes with powdered hand-soap and hung them over the cold radiators hoping they'd dry by morning. She would need clean, decent clothes tomorrow. The scrubbing warmed her a bit, and calmed her. It was already very dark outside, and the wind was coming up so the rain spattered against the windows. She couldn't allow herself to be hypnotized by the lulling, shushing rhythms of wind and rain. She had to keep moving.

Certain ways of doing things had become automatic to Jodi by now. Things to keep herself occupied until panic subsided. She'd learned that panic welled up and receded, welled up and receded, continuously, so she could pace her life to its pattern. It wasn't a panic over anything specific, but more of an absence, an absolute vacuum that could suck her down if she allowed it to open inside her.

Her solid fears about survival were not as bad as panic; in fact, they kept her sane, they gave her a catalyst to keep going. For the sake of survival, she tried to keep her thoughts practical, her actions mechanical. Whenever she had access to water, for example, she'd automatically wash her hands and face, brush her teeth, and fill her plastic water bottle, following a particular routine. She did those familiar things now, slowly, meticulously. After that, she'd stake out a place to sleep and make it as comfortable as she possibly could. Now, she chose the vinyl couch in the big open room where they used to have after-church coffee. She spread her sleeping bag, placed a standing lamp within reach, unpacked the paperback book she'd been reading and rereading since July, removed her shoes and put on the extra pair of socks she'd saved for slippers.

She found the kitchen locked, so she made instant coffee with hot tap water from the utility sink. After drinking it, she went to the bathroom, then washed her cup and brushed her teeth again. But, inevitably, the panic surged up and fell back and surged up higher. It was different, it was worse, to be in such a once-safe place, taking sanctuary where it hadn't been offered.

It was almost a boast, the way she often told people that she'd lived in over thirty places in the past year and a half. She looked younger than twenty-six, and people worried about her. Where do you live, honey? They asked because they wanted a reassurance so they could stop worrying. I'm staying with friends in Cambridge. Mattapan.

Chelsea. I've got a room at the Y. I'm house-sitting, subletting, going camping. And then, inevitably, she'd add the bit about the over-thirty-places she'd lived. All this time, she'd thought of herself as having dozens of homes. Home for a month, a week, a couple of days. Only recently she'd been staying at the shelter. Only recently she'd spent some nights in an abandoned building. One night in a doorway. Only recently she'd thought of herself as homeless. And people weren't asking, anymore, because they were afraid they'd hear that she had no place to go.

She was at the end of her possibilities now. She couldn't go further. She'd spent her eight-dollar (used to be ten) emergency money on the commuter train south to her hometown. She hadn't hitched a ride because the panic had welled up and held her, telling her she would die if she stuck out her thumb and turned herself over to a stranger.

She'd decided to take this last step, to take the train to her hometown, before it became impossible. Before the panic showed in the hollows of her cheeks, before her clothes began to stiffen and her eyes to unfocus. Before she looked too much like a starved dirty runaway to be recognizable even to her mother. Coming back had to look like her choice. It had to look like she wasn't desperate. It had to look like she'd decided to give in. She had to seem to be coming to her senses.

When she ran into Deb Bailey at the train station, she practiced acting like a regular person. It wasn't hard to lie, because Deb politely helped her to avoid uncomfortable truths. Deb was coming home from her job in the city. Deb was staying with her parents, back in the old home town, while her divorce went through. Scrupulously, Deb avoided noticing the army surplus backpack, the twenty-pounds too thin, the shakes, the mostly clean but chopped-too-short hair. It's great to see you, Jodi. What have you been up to?

Jodi lied, carefully, keeping every word from being one too many. I've been camping, with friends. On retreat. (Suggesting religion? Suggesting that she had something normal and hectic to retreat *from*?) I thought I'd visit my mother on my way back to the city. Deb didn't ask where she lived and what she did in the city, why she'd arrived on the outbound train, how she expected to just drop in on her mother after six or seven years away. Deb would have known that Jodi and her mother were not on speaking terms. Deb and Jodi had gone to school together, and Deb always knew everything about everyone.

Deb knew all about Jodi. She knew how Jodi's mother used to come home from the restaurant late with a doggy-bag of leftovers for their dinner. She knew how Jodi's father had been chronically unemployed, until the job that killed him. She probably wondered why a family like Jodi's would ever want to live in a town like this. Where they didn't belong.

At the train station, of course, Deb didn't talk about past history. But Jodi imagined her thinking about it. How nobody ever saw Jodi cry, even once, after her father fell down an elevator shaft when she was fourteen. She didn't even miss a day of school. She went right out and found work bagging groceries, while her mother took a second waitressing job. Then her mother remarried within a year. Probably Deb wasn't thinking about any of this; Jodi thought about it. Her mother had married a shoe salesmen. Jodi left home right after graduation, to make things easier for them without her. Deb knew all about this, but she wouldn't be thinking about it.

Deb came from a good family. Mr. Bailey owned a realty business, and he served on the Board of Selectmen term after term. Deb's mother raised two girls and two boys, volunteered on the school playground, played the organ at the Unitarian Church. But Deb and Jodi had been friends. They even used to kiss, sometimes, practicing for the boys.

Deb wasn't the worst person in the world to run into. Tactfully, she invited Jodi home for dinner and (with a slight, embarrassed tightening of the lips) offered a shower. They left the train station together and rode home in Deb's little yellow two-seater. Jodi held her pack in her lap.

Later, clean and warm and half-terrified, Jodi sat at the table with the Baileys. She ate every bite of her steak and mashed potatoes, gravy and green peas, canned peaches and whipped topping, oatmeal cookies. She drank three glasses of milk, slowly, to settle her stomach with the meal. She managed to keep her hands from shaking too badly as she ate. But she understood that she'd made a mistake when she took an extra slice of bread and butter after the others had already finished dessert.

The first thing she'd loved about Liz was the way Liz didn't mind making mistakes, breaking rules, having nothing to lose. She made the most of every possibility, even though her possibilities seemed so limited. Jodi was 21 when they met, and Liz was around 40. You'd expect the older one to be settled and predictable, the younger one to be wilder, more willing to take risks. But Liz was living on moment-to-moment impulse, and Jodi was the one who had to learn flexibility.

Jodi was working on a hospital cleaning crew, nights. It was the kind of work you'd expect. Not the worst work a person could do, but bad. Anyway, Jodi was a musician, too, and an instrument-maker. She was learning to build guitars, hammer dulcimers, maybe someday even violins. She'd met this old man who was teaching her. She was a member of the food co-op and the Clamshell Alliance, and she lived in a house with a bunch of college students. The night job kept her alive, and she was capable of all kinds of small compromises and big commitments.

Liz was always awake when she came into that hospital room at three in the morning. Liz, who'd just lost a breast to cancer, whose wide grin was lopsided and up-to-no-good, whose condition had not stabilized after the operation. Liz waited up for Jodi. And Jodi looked forward to Liz, sometimes all day long. They'd talk. And Jodi helped Liz to break the rules. When you're already dying, Liz explained, you might as well live dangerously.

Liz was explicit about her cravings. She wanted two slices of soft white bread, spread thickly with margarine and sprinkled with sugar (don't be stingy with the sugar). Jodi was horrified. If you ate things like that, your teeth would fall out and you'd get hugely fat and end up shuffling around in house slippers before you were forty. But Liz was over forty, skeleton-thin, and lucky to get out of bed long enough to get into slippers. So, Jodi brought the sugar-bread, and even some for herself (though she put honey on hers). Another night, Liz asked for chocolate bars with peanut butter sandwiched between them. Jodi brought the chocolate and the whole jar, and they ate peanut butter by the tablespoonful together.

After that, Jodi came up with treats to surprise Liz: marshmallow taffy (pinched squishy between the fingers), potato chips and onion-soup dip, a can of butter cream frosting. And Liz didn't die. Not then. She got better. And when she came out of the hospital, Jodi moved in with her. They were lovers. They loved each other.

The way she loved Liz, Jodi had everything to lose. Other times, she'd been terribly lovestruck by women (unrequited and perfect, like it was supposed to be); she'd been to bed with a woman once (an unsuccessful experiment), and with a couple of men (both <u>very</u> unsuccessful experiments). But with Liz it was a bigger risk, a real risk. Liz tried to make her understand this, but Jodi didn't want to know. Even if the cancer went away completely, Liz said, even if they had fifty years together, eventually they would lose each other. Liz couldn't help knowing this, because Liz had known what it was like to be dying. Liz had been living with it. But Jodi hadn't, Jodi couldn't. Jodi was building a big, endless life with Liz.

When they'd barely met, she was already imagining their home together, though this was a crazy thing to imagine at the time. A hospital graveyard shift isn't supposed to inspire romantic thoughts. And Liz was supposed to be dying. Nevertheless, Jodi had these wild, inappropriate fantasies about lingering over breakfast with Liz, every day, in their own kitchen, surrounded by the hovering fragrance of toast and coffee. It was a very bright kitchen, very warm and difficult to leave. Jodi imagined Liz across the table, pressing her finger into the toast crumbs on her plate to pick them up, licking her finger, licking her butter knife. Jodi imagined the winter-naked maple branches waving outside the window, behind Liz's shoulder. This was a very detailed daydream. Jodi would startle herself out of it to find Liz propped up in the hospital bed, smiling like she was having a daydream of her own, and hers included Jodi, too.

Liz had more immediate daydreams; she told them to Jodi and made them happen. She imagined every moment as she wanted it to be, then felt it fully. She wanted Jodi to sit on the edge of her bed and talk to her. She wanted to listen to Jodi's plans, and tell Jodi about the quiet that could be so frightening late at night. She wanted to smooth the hair off Jodi's forehead, and when that touch made them both breathless, she wanted to let herself love Jodi.

When Jodi offered to rub Liz's neck, she wasn't offering because Liz was a patient, and Liz didn't take the offer as if it had come from some nurse's aid. They touched each other slowly, until they were both sure what they meant by it. And Jodi kissed Liz first, because she wanted Liz to know it wasn't pity, and she wanted to put everything she felt into that kiss. And it *was* one of those great kisses: unbelievably urgent and careful at the same time. Liz knew it wasn't pity; she didn't consider herself pitiful. Liz took Jodi seriously. When Liz came out of the hospital and asked Jodi to live with her, it was serious. She cared about every moment they spent together. And Jodi believed they were safe in those moments, beyond those moments.

They lived in Chelsea, down the block from just about everyone that Liz had ever known. Liz had brothers, sisters, cousins, nephews, nieces, aunts and uncles. Her parents were both dead. Both dead of cancer, a long time ago. Liz owned a diner, with her brother Mike. Liz and Mike did all the cooking themselves, while Jodi waited tables along with Mike's wife and daughter. Nobody talked about the relationship between Jodi and Liz. They just took Jodi into the family. Liz didn't look for any more acknowledgement than that.

But Jodi brought Liz home to her own mother and step-father, looking for acknowledgement. Expecting it. Her mother must have known about Jodi. It couldn't have come as a surprise. But it did. Or, at least, her parents acted as though they'd been taken by surprise. They didn't expect to have to confront it. If they thought about it, they must have thought they'd be able to talk her out of it at some point, when she tried to tell them. But when she told them, it was already done. Here was this woman, living with their daughter.

Her step-father wouldn't stay in the same room with "dykes". He went straight to the kitchen for a drink, and they could hear him muttering imprecations from there. Meanwhile, Jodi's mother sat in a tight white silence, shrugged at Jodi's insistence, said she needed time. Jodi gave her time.

Liz drove on the way home. She kept catching Jodi, gently, in her glance. There was Liz, breathing carefully, driving so carefully, being so carefully quiet that Jodi felt dizzied by all that care. Jodi wanted to make a joke of the whole thing. My step-dad's been a bigot all his life. He always told me he'd disown me if I married a Catholic. Liz laughed out loud. There was silence. Then Liz asking softly, What about your mother? My mother. My mother was always pretty open-minded. Shrug. Pause. Jodi couldn't say, couldn't ask, How could she give up on me?

Two years later, when Liz was back in the hospital losing the other breast, Jodi wrote a note to her mother. It was the kind of risk that Liz always advised, having nothing to lose. She wrote and told her mother all about the coffeeshop where she'd done a gig, singing songs she'd written herself, playing a guitar she'd made, with Liz right up front applauding and grinning that lopsided grin. How they'd asked her to come back, because she was good. And she had some commissions to make instruments, and Mike had let her set up a workshop in his house. She wrote that she always thought her mother and Liz would get along great if they got to know each other. She wrote that Liz was in the hospital. That Liz was in the hospital dying. That Jodi was going to lose her. That Jodi was afraid. That Jodi missed her mother, wondered if they could talk, wished they hadn't given up on each other so easily. That Jodi loved her. There was no answer.

Liz lost the other breast, came home from the hospital, started chemotherapy again, lost all her hair, threw up whatever she ate, started to pray, even went to confession. Loving Jodi was not one of the things she confessed. Liz never questioned loving Jodi, never made a sin of it, never repented or apologized to anyone. She reassured Jodi that she thought she could live through this. Thought she, herself, could live through this? Thought Jodi could live through this? Liz kept living this way, dying, while Jodi waited and Jodi couldn't eat or sleep.

In a little while, Liz stopped living through it and started just surviving in the midst of it. She wouldn't go back into the hospital. She wouldn't take her medicine or go in for treatments any more. She sat across the breakfast table with Jodi every morning, to satisfy the daydream they both needed. Neither of them eating. The trees lost their leaves outside.

Finally, Liz began to lie awake crying with Jodi at night, sometimes all night. She was too weak to sob properly and would lie on her back with the tears running into her ears. One of those nights she died in the middle of crying. Jodi, beside her, not expecting it. Jodi, feeling the silence, the sudden seeping cold, the death.

Not long after the funeral, Mike asked Jodi, cautiously, stiffly, to move her workshop. He was thinking of renting the space to a cabinetmaker. She couldn't work anymore, anyway, not with her hands shaking like they did. She couldn't keep food on her stomach, had the shits every day, though they told her at the clinic there was nothing physically wrong. She lost weight so fast, got weaker. She didn't cry, now that Liz was gone. But she looked like grief, and her hands shook, and Mike told her he couldn't have her waiting tables in the diner any more. He let her wash dishes for a little while, then laid her off. She couldn't pay the rent on Liz's apartment, and her name wasn't officially on the lease, so she lost that, too. Liz had left half of the diner to Jodi, but Mike never mentioned it, changed the subject when she asked. It was his diner, Liz had been his sister, what could she expect? Then, she didn't have a job and couldn't get another one. She had friends for a while, all Liz's relatives and friends, but she used them up. This was over a year ago. For a year now, she'd had no one. She'd lived in over thirty places. For a year, she'd lived like this.

Now, the Baileys probably realized she couldn't go to her mother looking like some kind of street person. So, they fed her, helped her clean up, probably would have offered her a place to sleep except that they were all pretending she had a home to go to and no reason not to go there.

Her step-father had died. They told her this in the context of conversation, pretending not to notice that she didn't know. Two years ago now. Heart attack. He was a nice guy, your step-father. It was hard on your mother. We see your mother almost every week, Thursday nights, when we treat ourselves to supper out at Beveridge's, at the mall. We always sit at one of her tables. She's always so friendly. But she seems to take things hard. She looks tired. She doesn't talk so much anymore. Keeps to herself. We never see her at church. Jodi nodded, concentrated on chewing and swallowing neatly with her lips pressed together.

Deb changed the subject, then, to give her parents a break. She brought up music, and they all talked about that. They got Jodi to describe the instruments she made (lost or sold after the funeral, but she didn't say that, of course). The curved, thin slices of wood, layered and shaped around a hollow. The music that moved inside the emptiness. The Baileys avoided looking at the tremor in Jodi's hands as she described that delicate work.

They didn't offer after-dinner drinks, though they were the kind of people who probably usually enjoyed a glass of brandy in the evening, especially with company. Jodi understood that they would assume alcohol was behind her shakes, people always did. There wasn't anything she could say to deny it. Anyway, alcohol was a simpler explanation than grief, illness, hunger, fear. And they'd probably think that Alcoholic was a better identity than Lesbian or Vagrant.

Jodi might have taken to drink, if her stomach would have taken it. But instead of drinking, she'd found ways of pacing herself through the days, from one routine to the next. She'd learned to keep doing something, anything, every moment. And so, it was automatic to spread butter on another slice of bread. To swallow the memory of Liz and her sugar-bread, to look up and notice that the Baileys had finished eating. She gulped the bread and stood quickly to help Deb and Mrs. Bailey clear the table. The stack of plates rattled as she carried them to the kitchen, and she concentrated on holding them steady, on keeping her dinner down. Behind her, Mr. Bailey retired from the dining room to the living room and turned on the TV.

When Mrs. Bailey wouldn't let her do the dishes, Jodi had a moment of panic. There was a dishwasher, of course. But Jodi managed to get busy scraping and rinsing plates while Deb made coffee and Mrs. Bailey put the leftovers in plastic containers. Why don't you take some of these cookies to your mother? Mrs. Bailey wrapped the cookies carefully in clingy plastic.

The kitchen conversation lingered around Deb's divorce for a while, then circled back to music, to the church organ and its antique pipes. Did Jodi still sing? Jodi didn't answer whether she sang or not, but said instead that she'd learned to play a lot of different instruments. Piano and organ, too, yes. Jodi told how her mother had made her take piano lessons when she was small (saving the money from tips), and she liked it and taught herself synthesizer and organ later when she was hanging around with other musicians. She didn't get access to an organ very often, though, or a piano either for that matter. There was a piano in the next room, and Jodi regretted her words suddenly fearing that Mrs. Bailey would invite her to play. But Mrs. Bailey thought of the church organ instead. Said that Jodi should try it, really. A pipe organ is so different from those little electric ones. And the acoustics in the church are marvelous, you remember. You used to sing with the choir, didn't you? Mrs. Bailey looked wistful, said sometimes she went to the church alone during the week, just to play the organ. It's not just to practice, she confessed, it's really a passion of mine, the resonance in the empty church, the solitude.

Jodi could hear it, she could feel it, the swelling, haunting resonance of the church organ. She lost the rhythm of her tasks and stood gaping at Mrs. Bailey, falling into the pause, swallowed by the dizzying emptiness that opened between one long thought and the next. Mrs. Bailey got suddenly nervous, restless, busy. She talked more quickly, and perhaps it was the awkwardness of the moment that led her to offer the key. She hurried to fetch it from the drawer in the hall table. She said, here, no, it's all right. Why don't you try the organ yourself? You'll be in town for a few days, won't you? Just leave the key in our mailbox when you're done. I won't need it till next Sunday. And as long as you turn out all the lights, I'm sure no one would mind. After all, you're a member of our little congregation, in a way. Really, it's no problem. Take it, from one music lover to another.

She couldn't just sit there on the crackley vinyl couch, listening to the rain spatter the windows. She couldn't go to sleep yet, in spite of being exhausted. The rushing gusts of rain were coming harder, more often, with the waves of panic. She couldn't let the panic attach itself to memory, attach itself to now. Jodi was having a hard time breathing. There were the usual spasms in her gut and shivers in her stomach, as though she were starving in spite of that big meal. She folded herself forward, leaning over her knees with her arms around herself, opening her eyes wide because when they were closed she saw things. She saw Liz smiling in the hospital, with crumbs on her cheek and a milk moustache on her upper lip. So Jodi opened her eyes and stared at the gray painted cement floor. It was dirty. She stood up, and went looking for a push broom, or something.

There was no broom near the utility sink where it should have been. She found a locked janitorial closet, and had to give up the idea of cleaning. Instead, she decided to explore, to see what else had changed.

Flicking on fluorescent lights as she went, Jodi peered into each of the small rooms along the hallway. One was a nursery, with a sandbox in it. She remembered being one of the bigger kids who kept the littler kids from throwing sand, but she couldn't remember being one of the littler kids. There was a choir practice room with the same out-of-tune upright piano they'd had forever, and metal folding chairs stacked against the walls. There were several locked rooms. She remembered what a great place this had been to play hide-and-seek, but there hadn't been locked doors in those days. There'd been a room full of art supplies (smelling of peppermint glue, and chalk, and poster paint), there'd been a big comfortable office with overstuffed chairs and a heavy desk. But she couldn't know whether those things were still there.

The church key was the big old-fashioned kind, and she could feel its weight and coldness in her pants pocket. Mrs. Bailey had loaned it to her, trusting that she would want to play the organ. Mrs.

Bailey hadn't intended for Jodi to spend the night here. Or maybe she had. Either way, somehow, Jodi felt that she was supposed to play the organ, to fulfill an obligation.

She climbed the narrow back stairs, avoiding the wide flight at the front of the church where the echoes were harsh and forbidding. She felt her way to the top of the stairwell, then found the panel of light switches and switched all the lights on. This was the room where the choir used to wait, thrilling with anxiety, before their solemn parade into the church on special occasions. It was a storage area cluttered with folding chairs, music stands, boxes of extra hymnals. Someone's half-cup of cold coffee had been left beside the spread-open Sunday funnies on a card table. There was a dark plush curtain instead of one wall. Jodi went through the curtain, and came into the church behind the altar.

The buzzing undercurrent of white noise from the fluorescent lights was punctuated by rhythmic gusts of rain against the windows. Jodi remembered that there had been a lot of debate about installing such bright lights; some said they made the church feel like a supermarket. It certainly was stark. Cold, too-- Jodi could see her breath. The tall windows on all sides were black, mirroring the interior as though each window opened onto another empty room.

Jodi crossed to the organ, and the bench made a terrible screeching echoing noise when she pulled it out. She intended to sit down, but the panic was there. If she sat down now, it might be like sitting on the couch downstairs and feeling everything slow to the center of her heartbeat, to the bottom of her belly, spiralling down to nothing. But standing could be just as bad. She had to keep moving.

She took a few steps away from the organ, then looked up and saw herself reflected back, wavery in the black glass. A kid, just a skinny, scared kid. No, she wasn't. She walked to the window because she saw something else. Before she realized what she recognized, her heart started stuttering and sobbing in her chest. At first she didn't know why. She didn't know what she was seeing in that expression, in the window. And then she knew part of it, not everything, but one thing.

It was Liz, with nothing to lose. Liz, with a face like this. It was the end of everything, but there was Liz. This was what Jodi couldn't face. This. Imagining, this, now. What if we were here together? Even with nowhere to go, even exhausted by our lives, just surviving. Liz was back there, only a few steps behind Jodi, maybe reading the funnies, or flipping through the hymnals looking for something to laugh about. And then she'd come through there, reading from the hymnal in a grand dramatic voice, throwing the curtain aside. And Jodi would be standing here feeling sorry for herself, and Liz would see. Would come over and smooth the hair off Jodi's forehead. You shouldn't have cut it so short, honey. The cold can get at your neck that way. Come on and show me how to play the organ. Don't look like you just lost your best friend, Jodi, sweetheart. I'm right here. Let's rock this old church, make some noise or something. Something.

Nothing. And she couldn't think about this, couldn't let this happen. She was starting to cry, and if she started it could kill her. It did kill her, losing Liz. Everything afterward had collapsed. And the grief was too much. She held her face still, held her breath, stopped herself. Picked up the sheet music that someone had spilled from the organ and left scattered on the floor; she folded it neatly, set it on the bench.

And when she sat down at the organ and thought about herself, it wasn't Liz she recognized in that reflection. It was another face, another expression. When her step-father was storming in the kitchen, and Liz moving slowly backward toward the front door, and Jodi explaining and insisting and expecting, her mother was just sitting there. Her mother, with the flat emptiness in her face. Jodi hadn't known what to read into that emptiness. She could only read condemnation, because the expression was like nothing she'd ever seen before.

Now, she could see. She recognized that expression. She recognized the emptiness, the end, the limit of what was possible. Her husband in the next room with his ultimatum, her daughter already going, already gone. No time to ask what was being asked of her. Not able to risk feeling what she felt. Only a boundary that was the edge of her world, the limits of her life, the extent of it. Her husband on one side of that boundary, her daughter on the other. It had been coming to this for so long. Her daughter crossing too quickly, too predictably, out of her life.

Still, Jodi couldn't know. She could only see it from where she was sitting now. She could only imagine. When her mother hadn't answered that letter, it hadn't been condemnation, only a silence in the absence of hope. There was this hard glass surrounding the possible, reflecting everything back on itself. And the imagination, the grief, could be too great to face once everything essential was gone.

Jodi could imagine her mother folding and refolding the letter. Finding a place for it in the shoe box where she kept mementos and loose buttons. Then putting the shoe box back on the closet shelf and deciding to organize the closet. Putting the shoes in pairs, hanging all the coats in the same direction. Jodi could imagine her mother making herself some supper (no husband, anymore, to make supper for). Taking off her coat and her waitress uniform, finally. She had read the letter the moment she'd come through the door. And hours later she was still wearing her coat.

Under the blue-tinged whiteness of the fluorescent light, Jodi's hands looked as cold as they felt. She rested her fingers on the keys of the organ, but didn't flick the switch to release the sound. This was the caesura, that moment of stillness at the natural end of a rhythmic line, a pause for breath, where the things that are to follow become possible. Slowly, she let her hands come to life; silently, she felt her way through the music she remembered. She could imagine the music. She touched the keys carefully, shaping the possibility, keeping her hands occupied, until she could stand to imagine herself standing on her mother's doorstep in the morning.

Mara Wild is a forty year old redhead. Raised in Scotland of Jewish\German and Scottish\English parents, she knows her courage, her determination and her fear stem from these roots. She believes in the power of spirit, the wonder of love, the possibility of true healing and the need for honesty with compassion. She is a writer, editor, yoga teacher, adult educator and massage therapist. She now lives in rural northern California where she delights in the women and the land who reflect her joy and passion.

She hopes "The Darkwalkers" will encourage all of us who are learning to validate our deepest and wildest selves in the face of the fear that has kept past generations of women silent.

THE DARKWALKERS

<u>Carole</u>.

Fear dominated her days. It rose with the sun as she pulled herself from the realms of dreams and dragged her body into the grey light.

Fear - it had been the greatest struggle to name it; to see it as separate. A concept that could be named of itself could also be removed; it was not essentially of her, nor of life. Yet for years it was all she had known....before the struggle in her mind .... before the sense of other ....before the dreams.

This morning Carole's smile slowly faded as the dream world slipped away. Before opening her eyes she fought to re-member, to re-call an image, a voice, but they were gone... again. Now a thick mist seemed to fill her mind, shrouding that place beyond day thought. Carole looked out to the ever-clouded sky of the academy's dome. Her mind allowed a brief memory of a childhood scene; the sun breaking through, mist rising from the valleys below her grandmother's cottage.... or was that only image-ation, tricks of the brain they had warned her about at the training academy.

Ten years of acceptance and training, of eradicating own-thought. She thought she had been successful...so did her trainers. Yet now she could no longer sustain what had become automatic. Her nights were out of control. She had failed. Or had she? The will to recall; she struggled to allow it, then she struggled to prevent it.

She looked about, checking she was the first awake, and reached under the bedclothes for her gown. She eased out of bed, taking care not to disturb her room companions, not to alert anyone to the slight change in her routine.

She shuffled to the cook area to heat her measured water - a cupful for drinking, a bowl to wash. She waited, fighting to pull her night world back to her, to perceive this place with a different self... but still it eluded her and she gazed blankly through the thick glass at the high walls of concrete and metal.

"You're up early, Carole. Again." Carole jumped. "You want to watch out or you'll be on extra work schedule." Carole held her breath in an attempt to appear unshaken, and let it out slowly.

"Control. Calm," she told herself. She remained still, silent. She could trust no-one. Sandra appeared harmless enough but you could never tell. Look what had happened to Sal. It would only take slight suspicion to be voiced and the authorities would clamp down on her and have her in for mind drill; maybe worse.

Two months later.

It hadn't always been this way. Carole recalled the years before the constant greyness. She could do this now without effort. Recollection.

Carole's grandmother, Martha, stood before her. Eyes bright and shoulders back, she had always seemed taller than her five foot two. Such a strong presence. "This world values similarity too much, Carole -- we need community but we need diversity. Respect and honor your own way and those of others. Don't be afraid to stand against those who do not show respect. Trust your own discretion." These words came flooding back to Carole and her mind struggled with their meaning yet her heart already seemed to understand, and she noticed her body shift, taking on Martha's stance. How different it felt to push her shoulders back!

Later she realised that this simple change in her posture was one of the signs that had alerted Sandra. It must have been obvious that her fear had shifted.

Martha. Massel. For a moment the two images, the two voices, merged in her consciousness. Her future, her past, her mentors. The wise women who reflected the light she struggled to move towards.

Martha had died during the war, and now, thirteen years later, Carole felt the loss keenly. So many had died, so many had disappeared. At least Carole knew how Martha had died and how she had fought to the last to defend her beliefs. It was years since Carole had thought of these events. She caught herself and came back to the present, to the academy. Such different worlds. In contrast to her memories and the world she visited at nights, the academy was austere, routine and controlled.

After the war there was nothing else. The Wild became quite inaccessible, eventually even in her mind. The past faded into confusion. She did know things had changed for the worse -- after the war, after the fleecing of the Wilds, after the brain-drain machines -- yet somewhere in her remained a flicker of hope for years, a flicker she could never have named until now, until Massel had fanned it into flame again.

Sometimes she wasn't sure if she was remembering or dreaming the sensations, voices and images, light, sunshine, a lightness in her body ---- and women, women dressed in bright colors, women smiling, women at ease. She recalled, she dreamt, she desired.

At first the very fact of dreams that held anything else but routine messages of the academy values, the new order, tasks to be completed, the monotone of the main trainer's voice ringing from day into night, confused and frightened her. At least when her sleep was full of academy images and business, there was a familiar sense to the day.

More recently she woke with a strong sense of having been elsewhere, as if she had travelled to a distant land and found herself returned to the academy each morning in time for the bell. Gradually she came to realise that exactly that was happening, and the confusion and anxiety that had accompanied the memories and the nightly shifts of focus, gave way to determination and hope.

<u>Massel</u>.

A strange force hit Elam. It rose from another sphere, bounced off our pickup shields and hung in the atmosphere. It sent our psychatalents reeling.

At first we thought it some new challenge directed at us by Orros but we soon discovered that it came from further afield. It was not the way of Orros to interrupt our sensitives and new competition was not scheduled by our foreplanners for another ninety cycles as we are now in a time of deepwork that requires no such distraction.

The circles gathered. We found no record of such disturbing force except in the readings a full sixty cycles back when the shields had picked up eruption from a distant galaxy. We thought it their sun. Later we found it was a thing they called war. This recent force gave a similar reading to that cycle, to the time after the explosions of light. Our sensitives reported a steady increase in the readings. They also picked up threads of search. People were trying to connect.

Our policy has never been to intervene in the events of other spheres, we need only to follow to the source, to observe. We absorb the sense of it, then decide on its inclusion or shading from our ways. Eventually our psychatalents isolated the force's essence: an absence of love, "control over" in the place of trust. We certainly opted to screen out this force from Elam; however we felt clearly drawn to reach in return to those who searched for help.

We decided to make the connection with those who were open. Of course we did it in their darkwalking time. Many of their species had closed to even that, for they were so full of the negative charge that all psychatalent had drained from their spirits. We had to choose the strong. We found they were placed in the most restrictive surroundings by those they called the trainers. There were some whose channels allowed us through. After much consultation the circles agreed these would be offered the opportunity to relearn the talent of separating. No-one was to be lifted who could not reach. Few were able to return with us.

The first was Sal in the place called Academy but their "fear" took over and we lost her to the middle realms. Then Ffion from the place called Asylum. She opened as if one of us and within one quarter suncycle Kasse had shown her how to separate over. Our work then became a little easier for through Ffion we were able to understand a little more of the Blue White Water Planet where this force called "fear" had taken hold. She told us of the great war those before her had survived, of the pervasive "fear" that had dominated since those they called the trainers had brought everyone to the academies, asylums and prisons. Some had fled, she explained, some of both the males and females lived in places called Wild but she had heard few stories of their rebellion. She had tried to find out more about them. She was transferred from academy to asylum. Too many questions, they said.

Once we had succeeded with Ffion our circle of thirteen reachers spread out to find the females who searched to us. There were males at risk too - those few who had neither been destroyed nor taken to the all-power ways of the "trainers". Those not in the Wild were kept in prisons. Their channels were not open to us. Their gender had caused such imbalance that even the darkwalking talent had left them.

I returned to the place of Sal for I had picked up another strong darkwalker there. The one called Carole. At first I reached her to open her to memory, then visioning. Gradually she allowed this to stay with her in the grey light they called day. I could see the change was a strain yet her deepest part answered me so I reached further until she recognised my form. The process was slow. I could not risk another splitting. But as her talents increased she was noticed. We had no choice.

Carole, four months later.

It had not been easy, but Massel's patience throughout the constant coaching process was unshakeable. At first Carole had doubted her visions and then her teacher. Was it possible that Elam existed, that she could not only connect with Massel but learn to transcend the present reality and reach Elam --- that Ffion was there now and had not been executed for dissidence as the speaker reports had stated? Had Martha somehow known of Elam? Had the women of her childhood known of this too?

Ffion --- yes, the message Massel relayed could come from no one else, and the words of encouragement strengthened Carole's resolve. To be in a place of freedom, to be with women who held their bodies and hearts bold and open, their minds light, and to be with

Ffion in this place --- the unthinkable moved through the impossible dream to be the desires she dared rekindle.

As Carole re-awakened to her deep sense of self and direction she was astounded and even ashamed at how she had taken given herself to the trainers' programme. Yet it was only the fact of her doing this that had kept her safe. She had become a trusted member of the academy staff ---never a trainer of course for she was not only female but of rebel stock. Yet her grandmother's reputation made it a greater challenge for the trainers, and they were proud of her, or rather of the role model she provided. Carole's perceptive and quick mind had made it appear that she had rapidly given in to their ways, while her true self had in fact remained intact under the layers of conditioning. "You humans have an astounding ability to protect your selves at the core when faced with adversity," Massel told her, "but after so long you need considerable help and support to re-cover the truth of your soul."

"The truth of your soul," thought Carole. What was that? Did Sandra share such a truth and if so, how buried must it be, that she had reported her to Craig. Her cooperative reputation had earned her time but she had been watched and now she was in the asylum for tests. Not mind drill. Unless absolutely necessary they didn't want to lose her, she was too useful in the programme patterning.

But she knew she had overstepped boundaries, trying to reach other "guests" to discover allies in memory or vision dreaming. And the Wild, she wanted to know about the Wild. No one gave anything away. Massel had chastised her: "You have shortened our time with your questions, Carole. You will have to wait for the answers. Perhaps later you will choose to return to the Wild and offer your help. You would have access to that possibility in a way that those of us from Elam do not. In the meantime we must hurry, for they will not tolerate the changes in you any longer."

First the dreams, the new ways of darkwalking, then Martha and Massel, her guides, her inspiration. Later the recognition of her own desires, her own will to continue, to explore the incredible possibility that Massel offered. Incredible, yet familiar, for Carole was certainly familiar with the many layers of mind, and "separating" was really a matter of faith, a matter of remembering who she was and where her spirit belonged. The time she needed was not so much to learn the process but to shed the doubts and fears, to know that the deeper she went, the further from the stagnant ways that had taken hold, the

The Darkwalkers - Mara Wild

clearer the process became. She came to know how to drop in and to visualise letting go completely but she could not do more than this until it was time. Still, her resolve strengthened with her visions.

"By the time they notice it will be too late to bring me back. As long as I can move through without them catching on.... this is the moment I've been practising for.
"Steady. Slow. Breathe evenly. No more agitation than for the usual session. But this is not the usual session. I can tell by who's here. Kraf, he's the top man, looked me over when they first brought me to the academy. Sanec, I know he's in asylum research. Brains behind the control training. Don't like the look of him. And Craig, much more on edge than I've ever seen him. Steady. You know you can do this. Breathe Down... down...don't forget the locks. No point if they can pursue before I'm out of their realm. Release. Let go."

Carole focussed on the verse Massel had taught her by night.

"Illusions shattered
  dreams disturbed
  she flees
  the seething brain mass
  for lower lands of mirth
  warm, pulsating through
  cold stinging night
  deeps are free
  ever shining welcome
  sink
  breathe
  surrounding
  soft
      floating.... "

The brain floated. Cerebral fluids viscous. Not a moment too soon with the skull locks. Bone to bone tightening, closing in around soft tissue. It was no easy task and certainly not one her asylum training had ever encouraged. At first the strange sensations had scared her - a heightened inner awareness, yet her body flat, a cardboard cut-out, stiff and dry. She'd learned to stay with it, finally moving through to approach the deeps.

"Well, my dear, we hear you've been straying into own thought, image-ation and have attempted dialogue with other asylum guests. Preliminary treatments seem to have calmed you, Carole. Today's formula should speed up the corrective process. You'll then be able to return to complex nine."

"Sanec. He's talking to me. Re-connect, just enough to acknowledge. Good, now they're conferring again. Turning on the probe. It won't be long. No time to reconnect again. No. Release the chords. No going back now. I'd rather be lost between realms than face Sanec's treatments."

The thought of what she was leaving pushed Carole onwards.

The descent alarmed her. She had to go too far too fast. Her eyes felt bathed in blood, saw only red; her throat raw, she tasted salt. Suddenly she achieved brain release, without shattering a fragment, and, even more skilful, without alerting the three men.

"Keep the rhythm. Deep and slow." She heard Massel's voice clearly. Carole felt her boundaries merging. She reminded herself of what lay ahead. She would resurface in that place she had come to know as her future. Once again she had connected totally with the rhythm. Slow. Deep. The transition inevitable.

She had named fear and was going beyond.